Excel®
Dashboards &
Reports

FOR

DUMMIES®

A Wiley Brand

2nd Edition

by Michael Alexander

FOR

DUMMIES®

A Wiley Brand

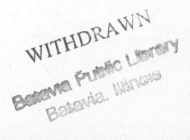

Excel® Dashboards & Reports For Dummies®, 2nd Edition

Published by: **John Wiley & Sons, Inc.**, 111 River Street, Hoboken, NJ 07030-5774, www.wiley.com

Copyright © 2014 by John Wiley & Sons, Inc., Hoboken, New Jersey

Media and software compilation copyright © 2014 by John Wiley & Sons, Inc. All rights reserved.

Published simultaneously in Canada

For general information on our other products and services, please contact our Customer Care Department within the U.S. at 877-762-2974, outside the U.S. at 317-572-3993, or fax 317-572-4002. For technical support, please visit www.wiley.com/techsupport.

Wiley publishes in a variety of print and electronic formats and by print-on-demand. Some material included with standard print versions of this book may not be included in e-books or in print-on-demand. If this book refers to media such as a CD or DVD that is not included in the version you purchased, you may download this material at http://booksupport.wiley.com. For more information about Wiley products, visit www.wiley.com.

Library of Congress Control Number: 2013954103

ISBN 978-1-118-84224-9 (pbk); ISBN 978-1-118-84242-3 (ebk); ISBN 978-1-118-84236-2 (ebk)

Manufactured in the United States of America

10 9 8 7 6 5 4 3 2 1

Table of Contents

Introduction

*T*he term *business intelligence (BI),* coined by Howard Dresner of the Gartner Inc., describes the set of concepts and methods to improve business decision-making by using fact-based support systems. Practically speaking, BI is what you get when you analyze raw data and turn that analysis into knowledge. BI can help an organization identify cost-cutting opportunities, uncover new business opportunities, recognize changing business environments, identify data anomalies, and create widely accessible reports.

Over the last few years, the BI concept has overtaken corporate executives who are eager to turn impossible amounts of data into knowledge. As a result of this trend, whole industries have been created. Software vendors that focus on BI and dashboarding are coming out of the woodwork. New consulting firms touting their BI knowledge are popping up virtually every week. And even the traditional enterprise solution providers like Business Objects and SAP are offering new BI capabilities.

This need for BI has manifested itself in many forms. Most recently, it has come in the form of dashboard fever. *Dashboards* are reporting mechanisms that deliver business intelligence in a graphical form.

Maybe *you've* been hit with dashboard fever. Or maybe your manager is hitting you with dashboard fever. Nevertheless, you're probably holding this book because you're being asked to create BI solutions (that is, dashboards) in Excel.

Although many IT managers would scoff at the thought of using Excel as a BI tool, Excel is inherently part of the enterprise BI tool portfolio. Whether or not IT managers are keen to acknowledge it, most of the data analysis and reporting done in business today is done by using a spreadsheet. There are several significant reasons to use Excel as the platform for your dashboards and reports, including the following:

✔ **Tool familiarity:** If you work in corporate America, you are conversant in the language of Excel. You can send even the most seasoned of senior vice presidents an Excel-based reporting tool and trust he will know what to do with it. With an Excel reporting process, your users spend less time figuring out how to use the tool and more time looking at the data.

✔ **Built-in flexibility:** With most enterprise dashboarding solutions, the capability to perform analyses outside the predefined views is either disabled or unavailable. How many times have you dumped enterprise-level data into Excel so you can analyze it yourself? I know I have. You can bet that if you give users an inflexible reporting mechanism, they'll do what it takes to create their own usable reports. In Excel, features such as pivot tables, autofilters, and Form controls allow you to create mechanisms that don't lock your audience into one view. And because you can have multiple worksheets in one workbook, you can give them space to do their own side analysis as needed.

✔ **Rapid development:** Building your own reporting capabilities in Excel can liberate you from the IT Department's resource and time limitations. With Excel, you can not only develop reporting mechanisms faster, but you also have the flexibility to adapt more quickly to changing requirements.

✔ **Powerful data connectivity and automation capabilities:** Excel is not the toy application some IT managers make it out to be. With its own native programming language and its robust object model, Excel can be used to automate processes and even connect to various data sources. With a few advanced techniques, you can make Excel a hands-off reporting mechanism that practically runs on its own.

✔ **Little to no incremental costs:** Not all of us can work for multibillion dollar companies that can afford enterprise-level reporting solutions. In most companies, funding for new computers and servers is limited, let alone funding for expensive BI reporting packages. For those companies, leveraging Microsoft Office is frankly the most cost-effective way to deliver key business reporting tools without compromising too deeply on usability and functionality.

All that being said, there are so many reporting functions and tools in Excel that it's difficult to know where to start. Enter your humble author, spirited into your hands via this book. Here, I show you how you can turn Excel into your own personal BI tool. With a few fundamentals and some of the new BI functionality Microsoft has included in this latest version of Excel, you can go from reporting data with simple tables to creating meaningful reporting components that are sure to wow management.

About This Book

The goal of this book is to show you how to leverage Excel functionality to build and manage better reporting mechanisms. Each chapter in this book provides a comprehensive review of the technical and analytical concepts that help you create better reporting components — components that can be used for both dashboards and reports. It's important to note that this book is not a guide to visualizations or dashboarding best practices — although those subjects are worthy of their own book. This book is focused on the technical aspects of using Excel's various tools and functionality and applying them to reporting.

The chapters in this book are designed to be stand-alone chapters that you can selectively refer to as needed. As you move through this book, you'll be able to create increasingly sophisticated dashboard and report components. After reading this book, you'll be able to:

- Analyze large amounts of data and report them in a meaningful way
- Get better visibility into data from different perspectives
- Quickly slice data into various views on the fly
- Automate redundant reporting and analyses
- Create interactive reporting processes

Foolish Assumptions

I make three assumptions about you as the reader:

- I assume you've already installed Microsoft Excel.
- I assume you have some familiarity with the basic concepts of data analysis such as working with tables, aggregating data, and performing calculations.
- I assume you have a strong grasp of basic Excel concepts such as managing table structures, creating formulas, referencing cells, filtering, and sorting.

Icons Used In This Book

As you read this book, you'll see icons in the margins that indicate material of interest (or not, as the case may be).This section briefly describes each icon in this book.

Tips are nice because they help you save time or perform some task without a lot of extra work. The tips in this book are time-saving techniques or pointers to resources that you should try to get the maximum benefit from Excel.

Try to avoid doing anything marked with a Warning icon, which (as you might expect) represents a danger of one sort or another.

Whenever you see this icon, think *advanced* tip or technique. You might find these tidbits of useful information just too boring for words, or they could contain the solution you need to get a program running. Skip these bits of information whenever you like.

If you don't get anything else out of a particular chapter or section, remember the material marked by this icon. This text usually contains an essential process or a bit of information you ought to remember.

Beyond the Book

A lot of extra content that you won't find in this book is available at www.dummies.com. Go online to find the following:

✔ **Excel files used in the examples in this book can be found at**

www.dummies.com/extras/exceldashboardsandreports

This book contains a lot of exercises in which you create and modify tables and Excel workbook files. If you want to follow the exercise but don't have time to, say, create your own data table, just download the data from the Dummies.com website at www.dummies.com/extras/exceldashboardsandreports. The files are organized by chapter.

✔ **Online articles covering additional topics at**

www.dummies.com/extras/exceldashboardsandreports

Here you'll find out how to use conditional formatting to build a simple but effective waffle chart, add an extra dynamic layer of analysis to your charts, and create dynamic labels, among other details to aid you in your Excel dashboards journey.

✔ **The Cheat Sheet for this book is at**

www.dummies.com/cheatsheet/exceldashboardsandreports

Here you'll find an extra look at how you can use fancy fonts like Wingdings and Webdings to add visualizations to your dashboards and reports. You'll also find a list of websites you can visit to get ideas and fresh new perspectives on building dashboards.

✔ **Updates to this book, if we have any, are also available at**

www.dummies.com/extras/exceldashboardsandreports

Where to Go from Here

It's time to start your Excel dashboarding adventure! If you're a complete dashboard novice, start with Chapter 1 and progress through the book at a pace that allows you to absorb as much of the material as possible. If you're an Excel whiz, you could possibly skip to Part III, which covers advanced topics.

Part I

Getting Started with Excel Dashboards and Reports

Go to www.dummies.com for great Dummies content online.

In this part . . .

- ✔ Discover how to think about your data in terms of creating effective dashboards and reports.

- ✔ Get a solid understanding of the fundamentals and basic ground rules for creating effective dashboards and reports.

- ✔ Uncover the best practices for setting up the source data for your dashboards and reports.

- ✔ Explore the key Excel functions that help you build effective dashboard models.

Chapter 1

Getting in the Dashboard State of Mind

- -

In This Chapter

▶ Comparing dashboards to reports

▶ Getting started on the right foot

▶ Dashboarding best practices

- -

*I*n his song, "New York State of Mind," Billy Joel laments the differences between California and New York. In this homage to the Big Apple, he implies a mood and a feeling that comes with thinking about New York. I admit it's a stretch, but I'll extend this analogy to Excel — don't laugh.

In Excel, the differences between building a dashboard and creating standard table-driven analyses are as great as the differences between California and New York. To approach a dashboarding project, you truly have to get into the dashboard state of mind. As you'll come to realize in the next few chapters, dashboarding requires far more preparation than standard Excel analyses. It calls for closer communication with business leaders, stricter data modeling techniques, and the following of certain best practices. It's beneficial to have a base familiarity with fundamental dashboarding concepts before venturing off into the mechanics of building a dashboard.

In this chapter, you get a solid understanding of these basic dashboard concepts and design principles as well as what it takes to prepare for a dashboarding project.

Defining Dashboards and Reports

It isn't difficult to use *report* and *dashboard* interchangeably. In fact, the line between reports and dashboards frequently gets muddied. I've seen countless reports referred to as dashboards just because they included a few charts. Likewise, I've seen many examples of what could be considered dashboards but have been called reports.

Now this may all seem like semantics to you, but it's helpful to clear the air a bit and understand the core attributes of what are considered to be reports and dashboards.

Defining reports

Reports are probably the most common application of business intelligence. A *report* can be described as a document that contains data used for reading or viewing. It can be as simple as a data table or as complex as a subtotaled view with interactive drill downs, similar to Excel's Subtotal or pivot table functionality.

The key attribute of a report is that it doesn't lead a reader to a predefined conclusion. Although a report can include analysis, aggregations, and even charts, reports often allow for the end users to apply their own judgment and analysis to the data.

To clarify this concept, Figure 1-1 shows an example of a report. This report shows the National Park overnight visitor statistics by period. Although this data can be useful, it's clear this report isn't steering the reader in any predefined judgment or analysis; it's simply presenting the aggregated data.

	A	B	C	D	E	F
4		Number of Visitors (thousands)				
5		2001	2002	2003	2004	2005
6	Great Smoky Mountains NP	9,198	9,316	9,367	9,167	9,192
7	Grand Canyon NP	4,105	4,002	4,125	4,326	4,402
8	Yosemite NP	3,369	3,362	3,379	3,281	3,304
9	Olympic NP	3,416	3,691	3,225	3,074	3,143
10	Yellowstone NP	2,759	2,974	3,019	2,868	2,836
11	Rocky Mountain NP	3,140	2,988	3,067	2,782	2,798
12	Cuyahoga Valley NP	3,123	3,218	2,880	3,306	2,534
13	Zion NP	2,218	2,593	2,459	2,677	2,587
14	Grand Teton NP	2,535	2,613	2,356	2,360	2,463
15	Acadia NP	2,517	2,559	2,431	2,208	2,051
16	Glacier NP	1,681	1,906	1,664	2,034	1,925
17	Hot Springs NP	1,297	1,440	1,561	1,419	1,340
18	Hawaii Volcanoes NP	1,343	1,111	992	1,307	1,661

Figure 1-1: Reports present data for viewing but don't lead readers to conclusions.

Defining dashboards

A *dashboard* is a visual interface that provides at-a-glance views into key measures relevant to a particular objective or business process. Dashboards have three main attributes:

- Dashboards are typically graphical in nature, providing visualizations that help focus attention on key trends, comparisons, and exceptions.

- Dashboards often display only data that are relevant to the goal of the dashboard.

- Because dashboards are designed with a specific purpose or goal, they inherently contain predefined conclusions that relieve the end user from performing his own analysis.

Figure 1-2 illustrates a dashboard that uses the same data shown in Figure 1-1. This dashboard displays key information about the National Park overnight visitor stats. As you can see, this presentation has all the main attributes that define a dashboard. First, it's a visual display that allows you to quickly recognize the overall trending of the overnight visitor stats. Second, you can see that not all the detailed data is shown here — only the key pieces of information relevant to support the goal of this dashboard. Finally, by virtue of its objective, this dashboard effectively presents you with analysis and conclusions about the trending of overnight visitors.

Figure 1-2:
Dashboards provide at-a-glance views into key measures relevant to a particular objective or business process.

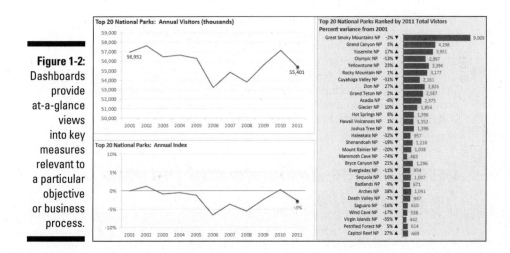

Preparing for Greatness

Imagine your manager asks you to create a dashboard that tells him everything he should know about monthly service subscriptions. Do you jump to action and slap together whatever comes to mind? Do you take a guess at what he wants to see and hope it's useful? These questions sound ridiculous, but such situations happen more than you think. I'm constantly called to create the next great reporting tool but am rarely provided the time to gather the true requirements for it. Between limited information and unrealistic deadlines, the end product often ends up being unused or having little value.

This brings me to one of the key steps in preparing for dashboarding — collecting user requirements.

In the non-IT world of the Excel analyst, user requirements are practically useless because of sudden changes in project scope, constantly changing priorities, and shifting deadlines. The gathering of user requirements is viewed to be a lot of work and a waste of valuable time in the ever-changing business environment. But as I mention at the start of this chapter, it's time to get into the dashboard state of mind.

Consider how many times a manager has asked you for an analysis and then said "No, I meant this." Or, "Now that I see it, I realize I need this." As frustrating as this can be for a single analysis, imagine running into it again and again during the creation of a complex dashboard with several data integration processes. The question is, would you rather spend your time on the front end gathering user requirements or spend time painstakingly redesigning the dashboard you'll surely come to hate?

The process of gathering user requirements doesn't have to be an overly complicated or formal one. Here are some simple things you can do to ensure you have a solid idea of the purpose of the dashboard.

Establish the audience and purpose for the dashboard

Chances are your manager has been asked to create the reporting mechanism, and he has passed the task to you. Don't be afraid to ask about the source of the initial request. Talk to the requestors about what they're really asking for. Discuss the purpose of the dashboard and the triggers that caused them to ask for a dashboard in the first place. You may find, after discussing the matter, that a simple Excel report meets their needs, foregoing the need for a full-on dashboard.

If a dashboard is indeed warranted, talk about who the end users are. Take some time to meet with a few of the end users to talk about how they'd use the dashboard. Will the dashboard be used as a performance tool for regional managers? Will the dashboard be used to share data with external customers? Talking through these fundamentals with the right people helps align your thoughts and avoids the creation of a dashboard that doesn't fulfill the necessary requirements.

Delineate the measures for the dashboard

Most dashboards are designed around a set of measures, or *key performance indicators (KPIs)*. A KPI is an indicator of the performance of a task deemed to be essential to daily operations or processes. The idea is that a KPI reveals performance that is outside the normal range for a particular measure, so it therefore often signals the need for attention and intervention. Although the measures you place into your dashboards may not officially be called KPIs, they undoubtedly serve the same purpose — to draw attention to problem areas.

The topic of creating effective KPIs for your organization is a subject worthy of its own book and is out of the scope of this endeavor. For a detailed guide on KPI development strategies, pick up David Parmenter's *Key Performance Indicators: Developing, Implementing, and Using Winning KPIs* (John Wiley & Sons, Inc.). This book provides an excellent step-by-step approach to developing and implementing KPIs.

The measures used on a dashboard should absolutely support the initial purpose of that dashboard. For example, if you're creating a dashboard focused on supply chain processes, it may not make sense to have human resources headcount data incorporated. It's generally good practice to avoid nice-to-know data in your dashboards simply to fill white space or because the data is available. If the data doesn't support the core purpose of the dashboard, leave it out.

Here's another tip: When gathering the measures required for the dashboard, I find that it often helps to write a sentence to describe the measure needed. For example, instead of simply adding the word *Revenue* into my user requirements, I write what I call a *component question,* such as, "What is the overall revenue trend for the last two years?" I call it a *component question* because I intend to create a single component, such as a chart or a table, to answer the question. For instance, if the component question is, "What is the overall revenue trend for the last two years?" you can imagine a chart component answering that question by showing the two-year revenue trend.

I sometimes take this a step further and actually incorporate the component questions into a mock layout of the dashboard to get a high-level sense of the data the dashboard will require. Figure 1-3 illustrates an example.

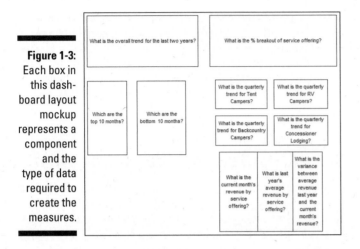

Figure 1-3:
Each box in this dash-board layout mockup represents a component and the type of data required to create the measures.

Each box in this dashboard layout mockup represents a component on the dashboard and its approximate position. The questions within each box provide a sense of the types of data required to create the measures for the dashboard.

Catalog the required data sources

When you have the list of measures that need to be included on the dashboard, it's important to take a tally of the available systems to determine if the data required to produce those measures are available. Ask yourself the following questions:

- ✔ Do you have access to the data sources necessary?
- ✔ How often are those data sources refreshed?
- ✔ Who owns and maintains those data sources?
- ✔ What are the processes to get the data from those resources?
- ✔ Does the data even exist?

These are all questions you need answered when negotiating dashboard development time, data refresh intervals, and change management.

Conventional wisdom says that the measures on your dashboard shouldn't be governed by the availability of data. Instead, you should let dashboard KPIs and measures govern the data sources in your organization. Although I agree with the spirit of that statement, I've been involved in too many dashboard projects that have fallen apart because of lack of data. Real-world experience has taught me the difference between the *ideal* and the *ordeal*.

If your organizational strategy requires that you collect and measure data that is nonexistent or not available, press pause on the dashboard project and turn your attention to creating a data collection mechanism that will get the data you need.

Define the dimensions and filters for the dashboard

In the context of reporting, a *dimension* is a data category used to organize business data. Examples of dimensions are Region, Market, Branch, Manager, or Employee. When you define a dimension in the user requirements stage of development, you're determining how the measures should be grouped or distributed. For example, if your dashboard should report data by employee, you need to ensure that your data collection and aggregation processes include employee detail. As you can imagine, adding a new dimension after the dashboard is built can get complicated, especially when your processes require many aggregations across multiple data sources. The bottom line is that locking down the dimensions for a dashboard early in the process definitely saves you headaches.

Along those same lines, you want to get a clear sense of the types of filters that are required. In the context of dashboards, *filters* are mechanisms that allow you to narrow the scope of the data to a single dimension. For example, you can filter on Year, Employee, or Region. Again, if you don't account for a particular filter while building your dashboarding process, you'll likely be forced into an unpleasant redesign of both your data collection processes and your dashboard.

If you're confused by the difference between dimensions and filters, think about a simple Excel table. A dimension is like a column of data (such as a column containing employee names) in an Excel table. A filter, then, is the mechanism that allows you to narrow your table to show only the data for a particular employee. For example, if you apply Excel's AutoFilter to the employee column, you are building a filter mechanism into your table.

Determine the need for drill-down features

Many dashboards provide *drill-down features* that allow users to "drill" into the details of a specific measure. You want to get a clear understanding of the types of drill-downs your users have in mind.

To most users, *drill-down feature* means the ability to get a raw data table supporting the measures shown on the dashboard. Although getting raw data isn't always practical or possible, discussing these requests will at a minimum allow you to talk to your users about additional reporting, links to other data sources, and other solutions that may help them get the data they need.

Establish the refresh schedule

A *refresh schedule* refers to the schedule by which a dashboard is updated to show the latest information available. Because you're the one responsible for building and maintaining the dashboard, you should have a say in the refresh schedules — your manager may not know what it takes to refresh the dashboard in question.

While you're determining the refresh schedule, keep in mind the refresh rates of the different data sources whose measures you need to get. You can't refresh your dashboard any faster than your data sources. Also, negotiate enough development time to build macros that aid in automation of redundant and time-consuming refresh tasks.

A Quick Look at Dashboard Design Principles

When collecting user requirements for your dashboarding project, there's a heavy focus on the data aspects of the dashboard: The types of data needed, the dimensions of data required, the data sources to be used, and so on. This is a good thing — without solid data processes, your dashboards won't be effective or maintainable. That being said, here's another aspect to your dashboarding project that calls for the same fervor in preparation: the *design aspect*.

Excel users live in a world of numbers and tables, not visualization and design. Your typical Excel analysts have no background in visual design and are often left to rely on their own visual instincts to design their dashboards. As a result, most Excel-based dashboards have little thought given to effective visual design, often resulting in overly cluttered and ineffective user interfaces.

The good news is that dashboarding has been around for such a long time that there's a vast knowledge base of prescribed visualization and dashboard design principles. Many of these principles seem like common sense; even so, these are concepts that Excel users don't often find themselves thinking about. Because this chapter is about getting into the dashboard state of mind, I break that trend and review a few dashboard design principles that improve the look and feel of your Excel dashboards.

Many of the concepts in this section come from the work of Stephen Few, visualization expert and author of several books and articles on dashboard design principles. This book is primarily focused on the technical aspects of building reporting components in Excel, but this section offers a high-level look at dashboard design. If you find that you're captivated by the subject, feel free to visit Stephen Few's website at www.perceptualedge.com.

Rule number 1: Keep it simple

Dashboard design expert, Stephen Few, has the mantra, "Simplify, Simplify, Simplify." The basic idea is that dashboards cluttered with too many measures or too much eye candy can dilute the significant information you're trying to present. How many times has someone told you that your reports look "busy"? In essence, this complaint means that too much is going on in the page or screen, making it hard to see the actual data.

Here are a few actions you can take to ensure simpler and more effective dashboard designs.

Don't turn your dashboard into a data repository

Admit it. You include as much information onto a report as possible, primarily to avoid being asked for additional information. We all do it. But in the dashboard state of mind, you have to fight the urge to force every piece of data available onto your dashboards.

Overwhelming users with too much data can cause them to lose sight of the primary goal of the dashboard and focus on inconsequential data. The measures used on a dashboard should support the initial purpose of that dashboard. Avoid the urge to fill white space for the sake of symmetry and appearances. Don't include nice-to-know data just because the data is available. If the data doesn't support the core purpose of the dashboard, leave it out.

Avoid the fancy formatting

The key to communicating effectively with your dashboards is to present your data as simply as possible. There's no need to wrap it in eye candy to make it more interesting. It's okay to have a dashboard with little to no color or formatting. You'll find that the lack of fancy formatting only serves to call attention to the actual data. Focus on the data and not the shiny happy graphics. Here are a few guidelines:

- ✔ **Avoid using colors or background fills to partition your dashboards.** Colors, in general, should be used sparingly, reserved for providing information about key data points. For example, assigning the colors red, yellow, and green to measures traditionally indicates performance level. Adding these colors to other sections of your dashboard only serves to distract your audience.

- ✔ **De-emphasize borders, backgrounds, and other elements that define dashboard areas.** Try to use the natural white space between your components to partition your dashboard. If borders are necessary, format them to hues lighter than the ones you've used for your data. Light grays are typically ideal for borders. The idea is to indicate sections without distracting from the information displayed.

✔ **Avoid applying fancy effects such as gradients, pattern fills, shadows, glows, soft edges, and other formatting.** Excel 2007 makes it easy to apply effects that make everything look shiny, glittery, and generally happy. Although these formatting features make for great marketing tools, they don't do your reporting mechanisms any favors.

✔ **Don't try to enhance your dashboards with clip art or pictures.** Not only do they do nothing to further data presentation, they often just look tacky.

Limit each dashboard to one printable page

Dashboards, in general, should provide at-a-glance views into key measures relevant to particular objectives or business processes. This implies that all the data is immediately viewable on the one page. Although including all your data on one page isn't always the easiest thing to do, there's much benefit to being able to see everything on one page or screen. You can compare sections more easily, you can process cause and effect relationships more effectively, and you rely less on short-term memory. When a user has to scroll left, right, or down, these benefits are diminished. Furthermore, users tend to believe that when information is placed out of normal view (areas that require scrolling), it's somehow less important.

But what if you can't fit all the data on one sheet? First, review the measures on your dashboard and determine if they really need to be there. Next, format your dashboard to use less space (format fonts, reduce white space, and adjust column and row widths). Finally, try adding interactivity to your dashboard, allowing users to dynamically change views to show only those measures that are relevant to them.

Use layout and placement to draw focus

As I discuss earlier in this chapter, only measures that support the dashboard's utility and purpose should be included on the dashboard. However, it should be said that just because all measures on your dashboard are significant, they may not always have the same level of importance. In other words, you'll frequently want one component of your dashboard to stand out from the others.

Instead of using bright colors or exaggerated sizing differences, you can leverage location and placement to draw focus to the most important components on your dashboard.

Various studies have shown that readers have a natural tendency to focus on particular regions of a document. For example, researchers at the Poynter Institute's Eyetrack III project have found that readers view various regions on a screen in a certain order, paying particular attention to specific regions onscreen. They use the diagram in Figure 1-4 to illustrate what they call *priority zones.* Regions with the number 1 in the diagram seem to have high prominence, attracting the most attention for longer periods of time. Meanwhile, number 3 regions seem to have low prominence.

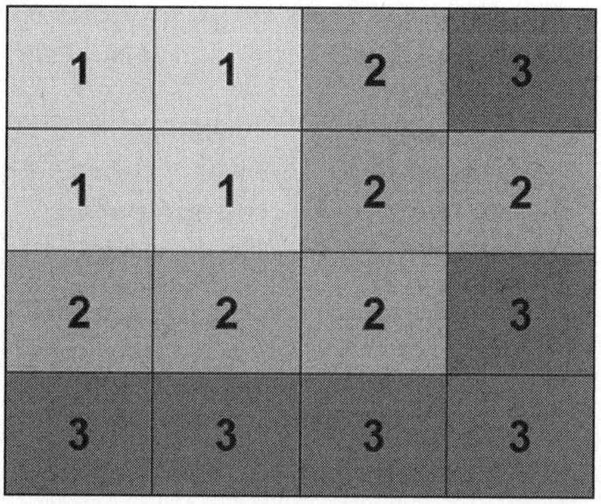

Figure 1-4:
Studies
show that
users pay
particular
attention to
the upper-
left and mid-
dle-left of a
document.

1	1	2	3
1	1	2	2
2	2	2	3
3	3	3	3

You can leverage these priority zones to promote or demote certain components based on significance. If one of the charts on your dashboard warrants special focus, you can simply place that chart in a region of prominence.

Note that surrounding colors, borders, fonts, and other formatting can affect the viewing patterns of your readers, de-emphasizing a previously high prominence region.

Format numbers effectively

There will undoubtedly be lots of numbers on your dashboards. Some of them will be in charts, and others will be in tables. Remember that every piece of information on your dashboard should have a reason for being there. It's important that you format your numbers effectively to allow your users to understand the information they represent without confusion or hindrance. Here are some guidelines to keep in mind when formatting the numbers on your dashboards and reports:

- **Always use commas to make numbers easier to read.** For example, instead of 2345, show 2,345.

- **Only use decimal places if that level of precision is required.** For instance, there's rarely a benefit for showing the decimal places in a dollar amount, such as $123.45. In most cases, the $123 will suffice. Likewise in percentages, use only the minimum number of decimals required to represent the data effectively. For example instead of 43.21%, you may be able to get away with 43%.

✔ **Only use the dollar symbol when you need to clarify that you're referring to monetary values.** If you have a chart or table that contains all revenue values, and there's a label clearly stating this, you can save room and pixels by leaving out the dollar symbol.

✔ **Format very large numbers to the thousands or millions place.** For instance, instead of displaying 16,906,714, you can format the number to read 17M.

In Chapter 3 of this book, you explore how to leverage number formatting tricks to enhance the readability of your dashboards and reports.

Use titles and labels effectively

It's common sense, but many people often fail to label items on dashboards effectively. If your manager looks at your dashboard and asks you, "What is this telling me?" you likely have labeling issues. Here are a few guidelines for effective labeling on your dashboards and reports:

✔ **Always include a timestamp on your reporting mechanisms.** This minimizes confusion when distributing the same dashboard or report in monthly or weekly installments.

✔ **Always include some text indicating when the data for the measures was retrieved.** In many cases, the timing of the data is a critical piece of information when analyzing a measure.

✔ **Use descriptive titles for each component on your dashboard.** This allows users to clearly identify what they're looking at. Be sure to avoid cryptic titles with lots of acronyms and symbols.

✔ **Although it may seem counterintuitive, it's generally good practice to de-emphasize labels by formatting them to hues lighter than the ones used for your data.** Lightly colored labels give your users the information they need without distracting them from the information displayed. Ideal colors for labels are colors commonly found in nature: soft grays, browns, blues, and greens.

Chapter 2

Building a Super Model

*O*ne of Excel's most attractive features is its flexibility. You can create an intricate system of interlocking calculations, linked cells, and formatted summaries that work together to create a final analysis. However, years of experience has brought me face to face with an ugly truth: Excel is like the cool gym teacher that lets you do anything you want — the freedom can be fun, but a lack of structure in your data models can lead to some serious headaches in the long run.

What's a data model? A *data model* provides the foundation upon which your reporting mechanism is built. When you build a spreadsheet that imports, aggregates, and shapes data, you're essentially building a data model that feeds your dashboards and reports.

Creating a poorly designed data model can mean hours of manual labor maintaining and refreshing your reporting mechanisms. On the other hand, creating an effective model allows you to easily repeat monthly reporting processes without damaging your reports or your sanity.

The goal of this chapter is to show you the concepts and techniques that help you build effective data models. In this chapter, you discover that creating a successful reporting mechanism requires more than slapping data onto a spreadsheet. Although you see how to build cool dashboard components in later chapters, those components won't do you any good if you can't effectively manage your data models. On that note, let's get started.

Data Modeling Best Practices

Building an effective model isn't as complicated as you may think. It's primarily a matter of thinking about your reporting processes differently. Most people spend very little time thinking about the supporting data model behind a reporting process. If they think about it at all, they usually start by imagining a mockup of the finished dashboard and work backward from there.

Instead of seeing just the finished dashboard in your head, try to think of the end-to-end process. Where will you get the data? How should the data be structured? What analysis will need to be performed? How will the data be fed to the dashboard? How will the dashboard be refreshed?

Obviously the answers to these questions are highly situation specific. However, some data modeling best practices will guide you to a new way of thinking about your reporting process. These are discussed in the next few sections.

Separating data, analysis, and presentation

One of the most important concepts in a data model is the separation of data, analysis, and presentation. The fundamental idea is that you don't want your data to become too tied into any one particular way of presenting that data.

To get your mind around this concept, think about an invoice. When you receive an invoice, you don't assume the financial data on that invoice is the true source of your data. It's merely a presentation of data that's actually stored in some database. That data can be analyzed and presented to you in many other manners: in charts, in tables, or even on websites. This sounds obvious, but Excel users often fuse data, analysis, and presentation together.

For instance, I've seen Excel workbooks that contain 12 tabs, each representing a month. On each tab, data for that month is listed along with formulas, pivot tables, and summaries. Now what happens when you're asked to provide summary by quarter? Do you add more formulas and tabs to consolidate the data on each of the month tabs? The fundamental problem in this scenario is that the tabs actually represent data values that are fused into the presentation of your analysis.

For an example more in-line with reporting, take a look at Figure 2-1. Hardcoded tables like this are common. This table is an amalgamation of data, analysis, and presentation. Not only does this table tie you to a specific analysis, but there's little to no transparency into what the analysis exactly consists of. Also, what happens when you need to report by quarters or when another dimension of analysis is needed? Do you import a table that consists of more columns and rows? How does that affect your model?

Figure 2-1:
Avoid using
hard-coded
tables that
fuse data,
analysis, and
presentation.

	Jan	Feb	Mar	Apr	May	Jun	Jul
Sales	3.69 M	6.99 M	5.77 M	4.96 M	8.48 M	4.71 M	7.48 M
% Distribution	5%	9%	7%	6%	10%	6%	9%

The alternative is to create three layers in your data model: a data layer, an analysis layer, and a presentation layer. You can think of these layers as three different spreadsheets in an Excel workbook. One sheet to hold the raw data that feeds your report, one sheet to serve as a staging area where the data is analyzed and shaped, and one to serve as the presentation layer. Figure 2-2 illustrates the three layers of an effective data model.

As you can see in Figure 2-2, the raw dataset is located on its own sheet. Although the dataset has some level of aggregation applied to keep it manageably small, no further analysis is done on the data sheet.

The analysis layer consists primarily of formulas that analyze and pull data from the data layer into formatted tables commonly referred to as *staging tables*. These staging tables ultimately feed the reporting components in your presentation layer. In short, the sheet that contains the analysis layer becomes the staging area where data is summarized and shaped to feed the reporting components. Notice in the analysis tab in Figure 2-2, the formula bar illustrates that the table consists of formulas that reference the data tab.

There are a couple of benefits to this setup. First, the entire reporting model can be refreshed easily by simply replacing the raw data with an updated dataset. The formulas in the analysis tab continue to work with the latest data. Second, any additional analysis can easily be created by using different combinations of formulas on the analysis tab. If you need data that doesn't exist in the data sheet, you can easily append a column to the end of the raw dataset without disturbing the analysis or presentation sheets.

Note that you don't necessarily have to place your data, analysis, and presentation layers on different spreadsheets. In small data models, you may find it easier to place your data in one area of a spreadsheet while building your staging tables in another area of the same spreadsheet.

Along those same lines, remember that you're not limited to just three spreadsheets either. That is to say, you can have several sheets that provide the raw data, several sheets that analyze, and several that serve as the presentation layer.

DATA

ANALYSIS

PRESENTATION

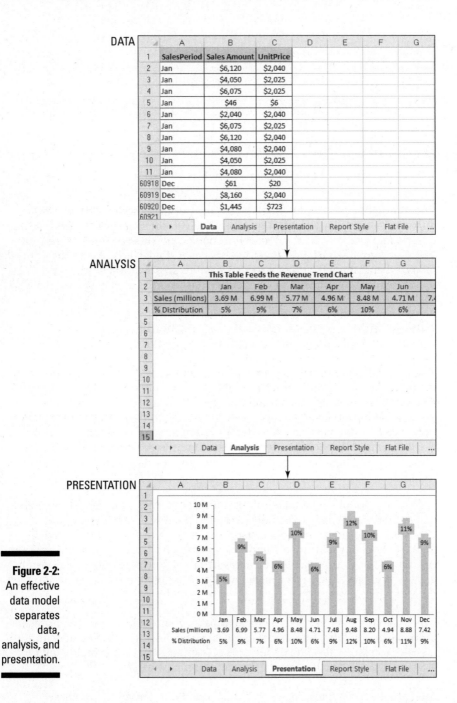

Figure 2-2:
An effective
data model
separates
data,
analysis, and
presentation.

Wherever you choose to place the different layers, keep in mind that the idea remains the same. The analysis layer should primarily consist of formulas that pull data from the data sheets into staging tables used to feed your presentation. Later in this chapter, you explore some of the formulas that can be used in your analysis sheets.

Starting with appropriately structured data

Not all datasets are created equal. Although some datasets work in a standard Excel environment, they may not work for data modeling purposes. Before building your data model, ensure your source data is appropriately structured for dashboarding purposes.

At the risk of oversimplification, I assert that datasets typically used in Excel come in three fundamental forms:

✔ **The spreadsheet report**

✔ **The flat data file**

✔ **The tabular dataset**

The punch line is that only flat data files and tabular datasets make for effective data models. I review and discuss each of these different forms in the next few sections.

Spreadsheet reports make for ineffective data models

Spreadsheet reports display highly formatted, summarized data and are often designed as presentation tools for management or executive users. A typical spreadsheet report makes judicious use of empty space for formatting, repeats data for aesthetic purposes, and presents only high-level analysis. Figure 2-3 illustrates a spreadsheet report.

Although a spreadsheet report may look nice, it doesn't make for an effective data model. Why? The primary reason is that these reports offer you no separation of data, analysis, and presentation. You're essentially locked into one analysis.

Although you could make charts from the report shown in Figure 2-3, it'd be impractical to apply any analysis outside what's already there. For instance, how would you calculate and present the average of all bike sales? How would you calculate a list of the top ten best performing markets?

	A	B	C	D	E	F	G
1							
2		Europe				North America	
3	France				Canada		
4	Segment	Sales Amount	Unit Price		Segment	Sales Amount	Unit Price
5	Accessories	$48,942	$7,045		Accessories	$119,303	$22,381
6	Bikes	$3,597,879	$991,098		Bikes	$11,714,700	$3,908,691
7	Clothing	$129,508	$23,912		Clothing	$383,022	$72,524
8	Components	$871,125	$293,854		Components	$2,246,255	$865,410
9							
10	Germany				Northeast		
11	Segment	Sales Amount	Unit Price		Segment	Sales Amount	Unit Price
12	Accessories	$35,681	$5,798		Accessories	$51,246	$9,666
13	Bikes	$1,602,487	$545,175		Bikes	$5,690,285	$1,992,517
14	Clothing	$75,593	$12,474		Clothing	$163,442	$30,969
15	Components	$337,787	$138,513		Components	$1,051,702	$442,598
16							
17	United Kingdom				Northwest		
18	Segment	Sales Amount	Unit Price		Segment	Sales Amount	Unit Price
19	Accessories	$43,180	$7,419		Accessories	$53,308	$11,417
20	Bikes	$3,435,134	$1,094,354		Bikes	$10,484,495	$3,182,041
21	Clothing	$120,225	$21,981		Clothing	$201,052	$40,055
22	Components	$712,588	$253,458		Components	$1,784,207	$695,876

Figure 2-3: A spreadsheet report.

With this setup, you're forced into very manual processes that are difficult to maintain month after month. Any analysis outside the high-level ones already in the report is basic at best — even with fancy formulas. Furthermore, what happens when you're required to show bike sales by month? When your data model requires analysis with data that isn't in the spreadsheet report, you're forced to search for another dataset.

Flat data files lend themselves nicely to data models

The next type of file format is a flat file. *Flat files* are data repositories organized by row and column. Each row corresponds to a set of data elements, or a *record.* Each column is a *field.* A field corresponds to a unique data element in a record. Figure 2-4 contains the same data as the report in Figure 2-3 but expressed in a flat data file format.

Notice that every data field has a column, and every column corresponds to one data element. Furthermore, there's no extra spacing, and each row (or record) corresponds to a unique set of information. But the key attribute that makes this a flat file is that no single field uniquely identifies a record. In fact, you'd have to specify four separate fields (Region, Market, Business Segment, and a month's sales amount) before you could uniquely identify the record.

Flat files lend themselves nicely to data modeling in Excel because they can be detailed enough to hold the data you need and still be conducive to a wide array of analysis with simple formulas — `SUM`, `AVERAGE`, `VLOOKUP`, and `SUMIF`, just to name a few. Later in this chapter, you explore formulas that come in handy in a reporting data model.

⬛	A	B	C	D	E	F
				Jan Sales	Feb Sales	Mar Sales
1	Region	Market	Business Segment	Amount	Amount	Amount
2	Europe	France	Accessories	2,628	8,015	3,895
3	Europe	France	Bikes	26,588	524,445	136,773
4	Europe	France	Clothing	6,075	17,172	6,043
5	Europe	France	Components	20,485	179,279	54,262
6	Europe	Germany	Accessories	2,769	6,638	2,615
7	Europe	Germany	Bikes	136,161	196,125	94,840
8	Europe	Germany	Clothing	7,150	12,374	7,159
9	Europe	Germany	Components	46,885	56,611	29,216
10	Europe	United Kingdom	Accessories	4,205	2,579	5,745
11	Europe	United Kingdom	Bikes	111,830	175,522	364,844
12	Europe	United Kingdom	Clothing	7,888	6,763	12,884
13	Europe	United Kingdom	Components	31,331	39,005	124,030
14	North America	Canada	Accessories	3,500	12,350	9,768

Figure 2-4:
A flat data
file.

Tabular datasets are perfect for pivot table–driven data models

Many effective data models are driven primarily by pivot tables. Pivot tables (which I cover in Chapter 3) are Excel's premier analysis tools. For those of you who have used pivot tables before, you know they offer an excellent way to summarize and shape data for use by reporting components, such as charts and tables.

Tabular datasets are ideal for pivot table–driven data models. Figure 2-5 illustrates a tabular dataset. Note that the primary difference between a tabular dataset, as shown in Figure 2-5, and a flat data file is that in tabular datasets the column labels don't double as actual data. For instance, in Figure 2-4, the month identifiers are integrated into the column labels. In Figure 2-5, the Sales Period column contains the month identifier. This subtle difference in structure is what makes tabular datasets optimal data sources for pivot tables. This structure ensures that key pivot table functions, such as sorting and grouping, work the way they should.

The attributes of a tabular dataset are as follows:

- ✔ The first row of the dataset contains field labels that describe the information in each column.

- ✔ The column labels don't pull double-duty as data items that can be used as filters or query criterion (such as months, dates, years, regions, markets, and so on).

- ✔ There are no blank rows or columns — every column has a heading, and a value is in every row.

- ✔ Each column represents a unique category of data.

- ✔ Each row represents individual items in each column.

	A	B	C	D	E
1	Region	Market	Business Segment	Sales Period	Sales Amount
2	Europe	France	Accessories	Jan	1,706
3	Europe	France	Accessories	Feb	3,767
4	Europe	France	Accessories	Mar	1,219
5	Europe	France	Accessories	Apr	3,091
6	Europe	France	Accessories	May	7,057
7	Europe	France	Accessories	Jul	5,930
8	Europe	France	Accessories	Aug	9,628
9	Europe	France	Accessories	Sep	4,279
10	Europe	France	Accessories	Oct	2,504
11	Europe	France	Accessories	Nov	7,493
12	Europe	France	Accessories	Dec	2,268
13	Europe	France	Bikes	Jan	64,895
14	Europe	France	Bikes	Feb	510,102
15	Europe	France	Bikes	Mar	128,806
16	Europe	France	Bikes	Apr	81,301
17	Europe	France	Bikes	May	610,594

Figure 2-5:
A tabular
dataset.

Avoiding turning your data model into a database

In Chapter 1, you might have read that measures used on a dashboard should absolutely support the initial purpose of that dashboard. The same concept applies to the back-end data model. You should only import data that's necessary to fulfill the purpose of your dashboard or report.

In an effort to have as much data as possible at their fingertips, many Excel users bring into their spreadsheets every piece of data they can get their hands on. You can spot these people by the 40 megabyte files they send through e-mail. You've seen these spreadsheets — two tabs that contain presentation and then six hidden tabs that contain thousands of lines of data (most of which isn't used). They essentially build a database in their spreadsheet.

What's wrong with utilizing as much data as possible? Well, here are a few issues:

- **Aggregating data within Excel increases the number of formulas.** If you're bringing in all raw data, you have to aggregate that data in Excel. This inevitably causes you to exponentially increase the number of formulas you have to employ and maintain. Remember that your data model is a vehicle for presenting analyses, not processing raw data. The data that works best in reporting mechanisms is what's already been aggregated and summarized into useful views that can be navigated and fed to dashboard components. Importing data that's already been aggregated as much as possible is far better. For example, if you need to report on Revenue by Region and Month, there's no need to import sales trans-actions into your data model. Instead, use an aggregated table consisting of Region, Month, and Sum of Revenue.

✔ **Your data model will be distributed with your dashboard.** In other words, because your dashboard is fed by your data model, you need to maintain the model behind the scenes (likely in hidden tabs) when distributing the dashboard. Besides the fact that it causes the file size to be unwieldy, including too much data in your data model can actually degrade the performance of your dashboard. Why? When you open an Excel file, the entire file is loaded into memory or *RAM* to ensure quick data processing and access. The drawback to this behavior is that Excel requires a great deal of RAM to process even the smallest change in your spreadsheet. You may have noticed that when you try to perform an action on a large formula-intensive dataset, Excel is slow to respond, giving you a Calculating indicator in the status bar. The larger your data-set is, the less efficient the data crunching in Excel is.

✔ **Large datasets can cause difficulty in scalability.** Imagine that you're working in a small company and you're using monthly transactions in your data model. Each month holds 80,000 lines of data. As time goes on, you build a robust process complete with all the formulas, pivot tables, and macros you need to analyze the data that's stored in your neatly maintained tab. Now what happens after one year? Do you start a new tab? How do you analyze two datasets on two different tabs as one entity? Are your formulas still good? Do you have to write new macros?

These are all issues that can be avoided by importing only aggregated and summarized data that's useful to the core purpose of your reporting needs.

Using tabs to document and organize your data model

Wanting to keep your data model limited to one worksheet tab is natural. In my mind, keeping track of one tab is much simpler than using different tabs. However, limiting your data model to one tab has its drawbacks, including the following:

✔ **Using one tab typically places limits on your analysis.** Because only so many datasets can fit on a tab, using one tab limits the number of analyses that can be represented in your data model. This in turn limits the analysis your dashboard can offer. Consider adding tabs to your data model to provide additional data and analysis that may not fit on just one tab.

✔ **Too much on one tab makes for a confusing data model.** When working with large datasets, you need plenty of staging tables to aggregate and shape the raw data so that it can be fed to your reporting components. If you use only one tab, you're forced to position these staging tables below or to the right of your datasets. Although this may provide all the elements needed to feed your presentation layer, a good deal of scrolling is necessary to view all the elements positioned in a wide range of areas. This makes the data model difficult to understand and maintain. Use separate tabs to hold your analysis and staging tables, particularly in data models that contain large datasets occupying a lot of real estate.

✔ **Using one tab limits the amount of documentation you can include.** You'll find that your data models easily become a complex system of intertwining links among components, input ranges, output ranges, and formulas. Sure, it all makes sense while you're building your data model, but try coming back to it after a few months. You'll find you've forgotten what each data range does and how each range interacts with the final presentation layer. To avoid this problem, consider adding a model map tab to your data model. The *model map* tab essentially summarizes the key ranges in the data model and allows you to document how each range interacts with the reporting components in the final presentation layer. As you can see in Figure 2-6 the model map is nothing fancy, just a table that lists some key information about each range in the model.

You can include any information you think appropriate in your model map. The idea is to give yourself a handy reference that guides you through the elements in your data model.

Figure 2-6: A model map allows you to document how each range interacts with your data model.

Tab	Range	Purpose	Linked Component/s
Analysis 1	A2:A11	Provides the data source for the trend graph component.	United States trend 1
Analysis 2	A3:A11	Data source for the List Box component.	List Box 1
Analysis 2	C1	Output range for the selected item in the List Box component.	Conditional trend icon
Analysis 2	D1:R1	Vlookup formulas that reference cell C1. This range also serves as the source data for the Combination Chart component.	Combination Chart 1
Data	C4:R48	Main data set for this data model.	

Speaking of documenting your data model . . .

Another way to document the logic in your data model is to use comments and labels liberally. It's amazing how a few explanatory comments and labels can help clarify your spreadsheets. The general idea here is that the logic in your model should be clear to you even after you've been away from your data model for a long time.

Also, consider using colors to identify the ranges in your data model. Using colors in your data model enables you to quickly look at a range of cells and get a basic indication of what that range does. The general concept behind this best practice is that each color represents a range type. For example, you could use yellow to represent staging tables used to feed the charts and the tables in your presentation layer. You could use gray to represent formulas that aren't to be altered or touched, or purple to represent reference tables used for lookups and drop-down lists.

You can use any color you want; it's up to you to give these colors meaning. The important thing is that you have a visual distinction between the various ranges being used in your data model.

Testing your data model before building reporting components on top of it

This best practice is simple. Make sure your data model does what it's supposed to do before building dashboard components on top of it. In that vein, here are a few things to watch for:

- ✔ **Test your formulas to ensure they're working properly:** Make sure your formulas don't produce errors and that each formula outputs expected results.

- ✔ **Double-check your main dataset to ensure it's complete:** Check that your data table has not truncated when transferring to Excel. Also, be sure that each column of data is present with appropriate data labels.

- ✔ **Make sure all numeric formatting is appropriate:** Be sure that the formatting of your data is appropriate for the field. For example, check to see that dates are formatted as dates, currency values are formatted properly, and that the correct number of decimal places is displayed where needed.

The obvious goal here is to eliminate easily avoidable errors that may cause complications later.

Excel Functions That Really Deliver

As you discover in this chapter, the optimal data model for any reporting mechanism is one in which data, analysis, and presentation are separated into three layers. Although all three layers are important, the analysis layer is where the real art comes into play. The fundamental task of the analysis layer is to pull information from the data layer and then create staging tables that feed your charts, tables, and other reporting components. To do this effectively, you need to employ formulas that serve as data delivery mechanisms — formulas that deliver data to a destination range.

You see, the information you need lives in your data layer (typically a table containing aggregated data). *Data delivery formulas* are designed to get that data and deliver it to the analysis layer so it can be analyzed and shaped. The cool thing is that after you've set up you data delivery formulas, your analysis layer automatically updates each time your data layer is refreshed.

Confused? Don't worry — in this section, I show you a few Excel functions that work particularly well in data delivery formulas. As you go through the examples here, you'll start to see how these concepts come together.

The VLOOKUP function

The VLOOKUP function is the king of all lookup functions in Excel. I'd be willing to bet you've at least heard of VLOOKUP, if not used it a few times yourself. The purpose of VLOOKUP is to find a specific value from a column of data where the leftmost row value matches a given criterion.

VLOOKUP basics

Take a look at Figure 2-7 to get the general idea. The table on the left shows sales by month and product number. The bottom table translates those product numbers to actual product names. The VLOOKUP function can help in associating the appropriate name to each respective product number.

To understand how VLOOKUP formulas work, take a moment to review the basic syntax. A VLOOKUP formula requires four arguments:

```
VLOOKUP(Lookup_value, Table_array, Col_index_num, Range_lookup)
```

> **Lookup_value:** The `Lookup_value` argument identifies the value being looked up. This is the value that needs to be matched to the lookup table. In the example in Figure 2-7, the `Lookup_value` is the product number. Therefore the first argument for all the formulas shown in Figure 2-7 references column C (the column that contains the product number).

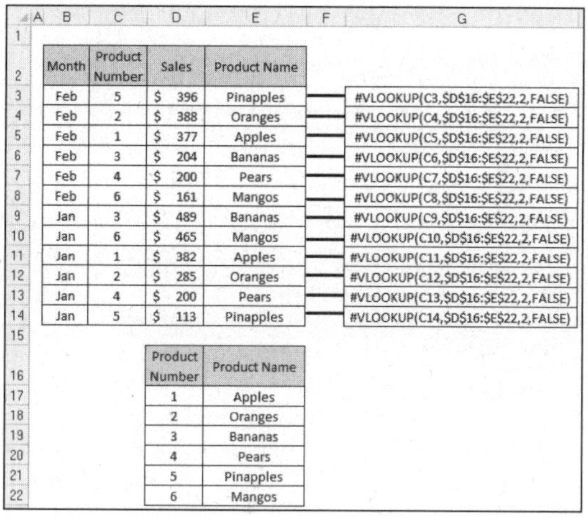

Month	Product Number	Sales	Product Name	
Feb	5	$ 396	Pinapples	#VLOOKUP(C3,$D$16:$E$22,2,FALSE)
Feb	2	$ 388	Oranges	#VLOOKUP(C4,$D$16:$E$22,2,FALSE)
Feb	1	$ 377	Apples	#VLOOKUP(C5,$D$16:$E$22,2,FALSE)
Feb	3	$ 204	Bananas	#VLOOKUP(C6,$D$16:$E$22,2,FALSE)
Feb	4	$ 200	Pears	#VLOOKUP(C7,$D$16:$E$22,2,FALSE)
Feb	6	$ 161	Mangos	#VLOOKUP(C8,$D$16:$E$22,2,FALSE)
Jan	3	$ 489	Bananas	#VLOOKUP(C9,$D$16:$E$22,2,FALSE)
Jan	6	$ 465	Mangos	#VLOOKUP(C10,$D$16:$E$22,2,FALSE)
Jan	1	$ 382	Apples	#VLOOKUP(C11,$D$16:$E$22,2,FALSE)
Jan	2	$ 285	Oranges	#VLOOKUP(C12,$D$16:$E$22,2,FALSE)
Jan	4	$ 200	Pears	#VLOOKUP(C13,$D$16:$E$22,2,FALSE)
Jan	5	$ 113	Pinapples	#VLOOKUP(C14,$D$16:$E$22,2,FALSE)

Product Number	Product Name
1	Apples
2	Oranges
3	Bananas
4	Pears
5	Pinapples
6	Mangos

Figure 2-7: In this example, the VLOOKUP function helps to look up the appropriate product names for each prodct number.

`Table_array`: The `Table_array` argument specifies the range that contains the lookup values. In Figure 2-7, that range is D16:E22. Here are a couple points to keep in mind with this argument. First, for a VLOOKUP to work, the leftmost column of the table must be the matching value. For instance, if you're trying to match product numbers, the leftmost column of the lookup table must contain product numbers. Second, notice that the reference used for this argument is an absolute reference. This means the column and row references are prefixed with dollar ($) signs — as in $D$16:$E$22. This ensures that the references don't shift while you copy the formulas down or across.

`Col_index_num`: The `Col_index_num` argument identifies the column number in the lookup table that contains the value to be returned. In the example in Figure 2-7, the second column contains the product name (the value being looked up), so the formula uses the number 2. If the product name column was the fourth column in the lookup table, the number 4 would be used.

`Range_lookup`: The `Range_lookup` argument specifies whether you're looking for an exact match or an approximate match. If an exact match is needed, you'd enter FALSE for this argument. If the closest match will do, you'd enter TRUE or leave the argument blank.

Applying VLOOKUP formulas in a data model

As you can imagine, there are countless ways to apply a VLOOKUP formula in your data model. No reason to start bland though. One of the more intriguing ways is to implement VLOOKUPs.

With a few VLOOKUP formulas and a simple drop-down list, you can create a data model that not only delivers data to the appropriate staging table, but allows you to dynamically change data views based on a selection you make. Figure 2-8 illustrates the setup.

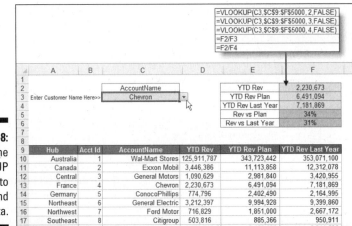

Figure 2-8:
Using the
VLOOKUP
function to
extract and
shape data.

To see this effect in action, get the `Chapter 2 Samples.xlsx` workbook from this book's companion website. Open that workbook to see a `VLOOKUP1` tab.

The data layer in the model shown in Figure 2-8 resides in the range `A9:F209`. The analysis layer is held in range `E2:F6`. The data layer consists of all formulas that extract and shape the data as needed. As you can see, the `VLOOKUP` formulas use the Customer Name value in cell C3 to look up the appropriate data from the data layer. So, if you entered **Chevron** in cell C3, the `VLOOKUP` formulas would extract the data for Chevron.

You may have noticed that the `VLOOKUP` formulas in Figure 2-8 specify a `Table_array` argument of `$C$9:$F$5000`. This means that the lookup table they're pointing to stretches from C9 to F5000. That seems strange because the table ends at F209. Why would you force your `VLOOKUP` formulas to look at a range far past the end of the data table?

Well, remember the idea behind separating the data layer and the analysis layer is so that your analysis layer can be automatically updated when your data is refreshed. When you get new data next month, you should be able to simply replace the data layer in the model without having to rework your analysis layer. Allowing for more rows than necessary in your `VLOOKUP` formulas ensures that if your data layer grows, records won't fall outside the lookup range of the formulas.

Later in this chapter, I show you how to automatically keep up with growing data tables by using smart tables.

Using data validation drop-down lists in your data model

In the example illustrated in Figure 2-8, the data model allows you to select customer names from a drop-down list when you click cell C3. The customer name serves as the lookup value for the VLOOKUP formulas. Changing the customer name extracts a new set of data from the data layer. This allows you to quickly switch from one customer to another without having to remember and type the customer name.

Now, as cool as this seems, the reasons for this setup aren't all cosmetic. There are practical reasons for adding drop-down lists to your data models.

Many of your models consist of multiple analytical layers in which each shows a different set of analyses. Although each analysis layer is different, they often need to revolve around a shared dimension, such as the same customer name, the same market, or the same region. For instance, when you have a data model that reports on Financials, Labor Statistics, and Operational Volumes, you want to make certain that when the model is reporting financials for the South region, the Labor Statistics are for the South region as well.

An effective way to ensure this happens is to force your formulas to use the same dimension references. If cell C3 is where you switch customers, every analysis that is customer-dependent should reference cell C3. Drop-down lists allow you to have a predefined list of valid variables located in a single cell. With a drop-down list, you can easily switch dimensions while building and testing multiple analysis layers.

Adding a drop-down list is relatively easy with Excel's Data Validation functionality. To add a drop-down list, follow these steps:

1. **Select the Data tab on the Ribbon.**

2. **Click the Data Validation button.**

3. **Select the Settings tab in the newly activated Data Validation dialog box; see Figure 2-9.**

4. **In the Allow drop-down list, choose List.**

5. **In the Source input box, reference the range of cells that contain your predefined selection list.**

6. **Click OK.**

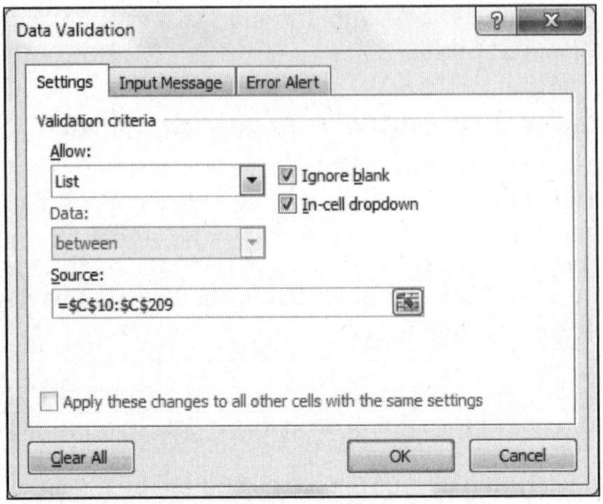

Figure 2-9: You can use data validation to create a predefined list of valid variables for your data model.

The HLookup function

The HLOOKUP function is the less popular cousin of the VLOOKUP function. The *H* in HLOOKUP stands for *horizontal*. Because Excel data is typically vertically oriented, most situations require a vertical lookup, or VLOOKUP. However, some data structures are horizontally oriented, requiring a horizontal lookup; thus the HLOOKUP function comes in handy. The HLOOKUP searches a lookup table to find a single value from a row of data where the column label matches a given criterion.

HLOOKUP basics

Figure 2-10 demonstrates a typical scenario in which HLOOKUP formulas are used. The table in C5 requires quarter-end numbers (March and June) for 2011. The HLOOKUP formulas use the column labels to find the correct month columns and then locate the 2011 data by moving down the appropriate number of rows. In this case, 2011 data is in row 4, so the number 4 is used in the formulas.

To get your mind around how this works, take a look at the basic syntax of the HLOOKUP function.

```
HLOOKUP(Lookup_value, Table_array, Row_index_num, Range_lookup)
```

> ***Lookup_value:*** The *Lookup_value* argument identifies the value being looked up. In most cases, these values are column names. In the example in Figure 2-10, the column labels are being referenced for the *Lookup_value*. This points the HLOOKUP function to the appropriate column in the lookup table.

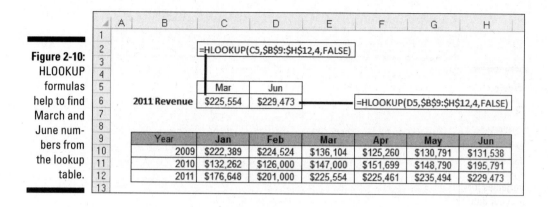

Figure 2-10:
HLOOKUP
formulas
help to find
March and
June num-
bers from
the lookup
table.

Table_array: The *Table_array* argument identifies the range that contains the lookup table. In Figure 2-10, that range is B9:H12. Like the VLOOKUP examples earlier in this chapter, notice that the references used for this argument are absolute. This means the column and row references are prefixed with dollar ($) signs — as in $B$9:$H$12. This ensures that the reference doesn't shift while you copy the formula down or across.

Row_index_num: The *Row_index_num* argument identifies the row number that contains the value you're looking for. In the example in Figure 2-10, the 2011 data is located in row 4 of the lookup table. Therefore, the formulas use the number 4.

Range_lookup: The *Range_lookup* argument specifies whether you're looking for an exact match or an approximate match. If an exact match is needed, you'd enter FALSE for this argument. If the closest match will do, you'd enter TRUE or leave the argument blank.

Applying HLOOKUP formulas in a data model

HLOOKUPs are especially handy for shaping data into structures appropriate for charting or other types of reporting. A simple example is demonstrated in Figure 2-11. With HLOOKUPs, the data shown in the raw data table at the bottom of the figure is reoriented in a staging table at the top. When the raw data is changed or refreshed, the staging table captures the changes.

The Sumproduct function

The SUMPRODUCT function is actually listed under the math and trigonometry category of Excel functions. Because the primary purpose of SUMPRODUCT is to calculate the sum product, most people don't know you can actually use it to look up values. In fact, you can use this versatile function quite effectively in most data models.

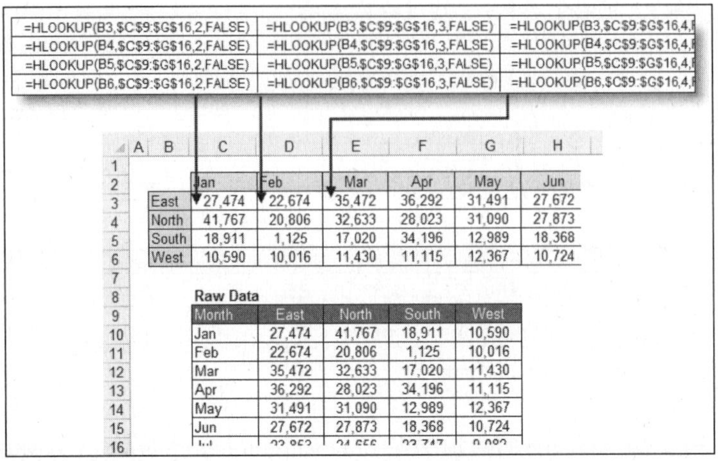

=HLOOKUP(B3,$C$9:$G$16,2,FALSE)	=HLOOKUP(B3,$C$9:$G$16,3,FALSE)	=HLOOKUP(B3,$C$9:$G$16,4,[
=HLOOKUP(B4,$C$9:$G$16,2,FALSE)	=HLOOKUP(B4,$C$9:$G$16,3,FALSE)	=HLOOKUP(B4,$C$9:$G$16,4,[
=HLOOKUP(B5,$C$9:$G$16,2,FALSE)	=HLOOKUP(B5,$C$9:$G$16,3,FALSE)	=HLOOKUP(B5,$C$9:$G$16,4,[
=HLOOKUP(B6,$C$9:$G$16,2,FALSE)	=HLOOKUP(B6,$C$9:$G$16,3,FALSE)	=HLOOKUP(B6,$C$9:$G$16,4,[

Figure 2-11:
In this example, HLOOKUP formulas pull and reshape data without disturbing the raw data table.

	A	B	C	D	E	F	G	H
1								
2			Jan	Feb	Mar	Apr	May	Jun
3		East	27,474	22,674	35,472	36,292	31,491	27,672
4		North	41,767	20,806	32,633	28,023	31,090	27,873
5		South	18,911	1,125	17,020	34,196	12,989	18,368
6		West	10,590	10,016	11,430	11,115	12,367	10,724
7								
8		Raw Data						
9		Month	East	North	South	West		
10		Jan	27,474	41,767	18,911	10,590		
11		Feb	22,674	20,806	1,125	10,016		
12		Mar	35,472	32,633	17,020	11,430		
13		Apr	36,292	28,023	34,196	11,115		
14		May	31,491	31,090	12,989	12,367		
15		Jun	27,672	27,873	18,368	10,724		
16		...	22,852	24,555	22,747	9,092		

SUMPRODUCT basics

The SUMPRODUCT function is designed to multiply values from two or more ranges of data and then add the results together to return the sum of the products. Take a look at Figure 2-12 to see a typical scenario in which the SUMPRODUCT is useful.

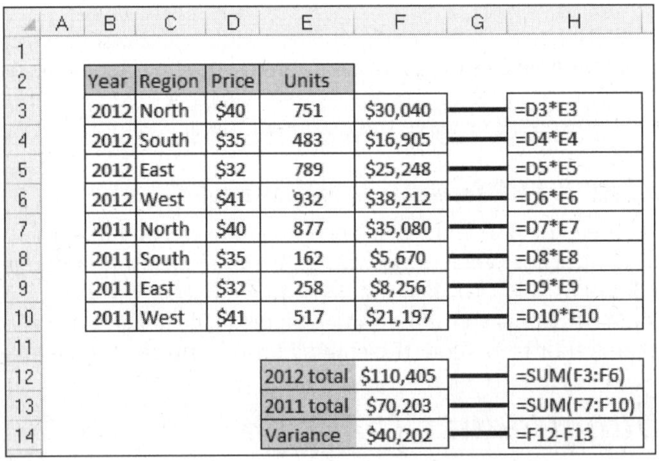

Figure 2-12:
Without the SUM-PRODUCT, getting the total sales for each year involves a two-step process: first multiply price and units and then sum the results.

	A	B	C	D	E	F	G	H
1								
2		Year	Region	Price	Units			
3		2012	North	$40	751	$30,040		=D3*E3
4		2012	South	$35	483	$16,905		=D4*E4
5		2012	East	$32	789	$25,248		=D5*E5
6		2012	West	$41	932	$38,212		=D6*E6
7		2011	North	$40	877	$35,080		=D7*E7
8		2011	South	$35	162	$5,670		=D8*E8
9		2011	East	$32	258	$8,256		=D9*E9
10		2011	West	$41	517	$21,197		=D10*E10
11								
12					2012 total	$110,405		=SUM(F3:F6)
13					2011 total	$70,203		=SUM(F7:F10)
14					Variance	$40,202		=F12-F13

In Figure 2-12, you see a common analysis in which you need the total sales for the years 2011 and 2012. As you can see, to get the total sales for each year, you first have to multiply Price by the number of Units to get the total for each Region. Then you have to sum those results to get the total sales for each year.

With the SUMPRODUCT function, you can perform the two-step analysis with just one formula. Figure 2-13 shows the same analysis with SUMPRODUCT formulas. Instead of using 11 formulas, you can accomplish the same analysis with just 3!

The syntax of the SUMPRODUCT function is fairly simple:

```
SUMPRODUCT(Array1, Array2, . . .)
```

> **Array:** *Array* represents a range of data. You can use anywhere from 2 to 255 arrays in a SUMPRODUCT formula. The arrays get multiplied together and then added. The only hard and fast rule you have to remember is that all the arrays must have the same number of values. That is to say, you can't use the SUMPRODUCT if range X has 10 values and range Y has 11 values. Otherwise, you get the #VALUE! error.

A twist on the SUMPRODUCT function

The interesting thing about the SUMPRODUCT function is that it can be used to filter out values. Take a look at Figure 2-14 to see what I mean.

Figure 2-13: The SUM-PRODUCT function allows you to perform the same analysis with just 3 formulas instead of 11.

	A	B	C	D	E	F	G
1							
2		Year	Region	Price	Units		
3		2012	North	$40	751		
4		2012	South	$35	483		
5		2012	East	$32	789		
6		2012	West	$41	932		
7		2011	North	$40	877		
8		2011	South	$35	162		
9		2011	East	$32	258		
10		2011	West	$41	517		
11							
12			2012 total	$110,405			=SUMPRODUCT(D3:D6,E3:E6)
13			2011 total	$70,203			=SUMPRODUCT(D7:D10, E7:E10)
14			Variance	$40,202			=E12-E13
15							

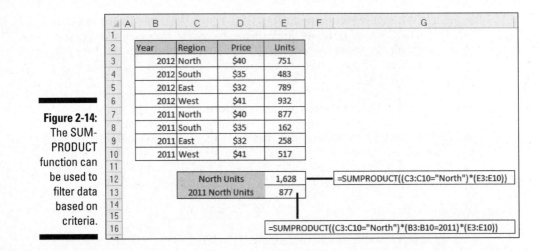

Figure 2-14:
The SUM-
PRODUCT
function can
be used to
filter data
based on
criteria.

The formula in cell E12 is pulling the sum of total units for just the North region. Meanwhile, cell E13 is pulling the units logged for the North region in the year 2011.

To understand how this works, take a look at the formula in cell E12 shown in Figure 2-14. That formula reads SUMPRODUCT((C3:C10="North")* (E3:E10)).

In Excel, TRUE evaluates to 1 and FALSE evaluates to 0. Every value in column C that equals North evaluates to TRUE or 1. Where the value is not North, it evaluates to FALSE or 0.The part of the formula that reads (C3:C10="North") enumerates through each value in the range C3:C10, assigning a 1 or 0 to each value. Then internally, the SUMPRODUCT formula translates to

```
(1*E3)+(0*E4)+(0*E5)+(0*E6)+(1*E7)+(0*E8)+(0*E9)+(0*E10).
```

This gives you the answer of 1628 because

```
(1*751)+(0*483)+(0*789)+(0*932)+(1*877)+(0*162)+(0*258)+(0*517)
```

equals 1628.

Applying SUMPRODUCT formulas in a data model

As always in Excel, you don't have to hard-code the criteria in your formulas. Instead of explicitly using "North" in the SUMPRODUCT formula, you could reference a cell that contains the filter value. You can imagine that cell A3 contains the word `North`, in which case you can use (`C3:C10=A3`) instead of (`C3:C10="North"`). This way, you can dynamically change your filter criteria, and your formula keeps up.

Figure 2-15 demonstrates how you can use this concept to pull data into a staging table based on multiple criteria. Note that each of the `SUMPRODUCT` formulas shown here reference cells B3 and C3 to filter on Account and Product Line. Again, you can add data validation drop-down lists to cells B3 and C3, allowing you to easily change criteria.

Figure 2-15:
The SUM-PRODUCT function can be used to pull summarized numbers from the data layer into staging tables.

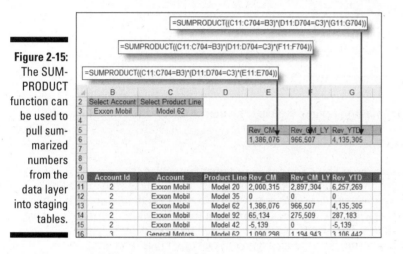

The Choose function

The `CHOOSE` function returns a value from a specified list of values based on a specified position number. For instance, if you enter the formulas `CHOOSE(3, "Red", "Yellow", "Green", "Blue")` into a cell, Excel returns `Green` because Green is the third item in the list of values. The formula `CHOOSE(1, "Red", "Yellow", "Green", "Blue")` would return `Red`. Although this may not look useful on the surface, the `CHOOSE` function can dramatically enhance your data models.

CHOOSE basics

Figure 2-16 illustrates how `CHOOSE` formulas can help pinpoint and extract numbers from a range of cells. Note that instead of using hard-coded values, like `Red`, `Green`, and so on, you can use cell references to list the choices.

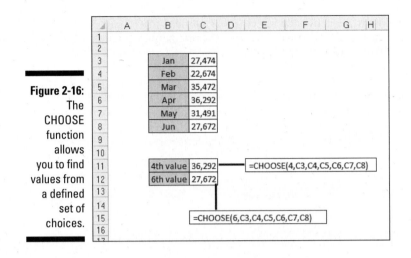

Take a moment to review the basic syntax of the CHOOSE function:

```
CHOOSE(Index_num, Value1, Value2, . . .)
```

Index_num: The *Index_num* argument specifies the position number of the chosen value in the list of values. If the third value in the list is needed, the *Index_num* is 3. The *Index_num* argument must be an integer between one and the maximum number of values in the defined list of values. That is to say, if there are ten choices defined in the CHOOSE formula, the *Index_num* argument can't be more than ten.

Value: Each *Value* argument represents a choice in the defined list of choices for that CHOOSE formula. The *Value>* arguments can be hard-coded values, cell references, defined names, formulas, or functions. You can have up to 255 choices listed in your CHOOSE formulas.

Applying CHOOSE formulas in a data model

The CHOOSE function is especially valuable in data models in which there are multiple layers of data that need to be brought together. Figure 2-17 illustrates an example in which CHOOSE formulas help pull data together.

In this example, you have two data tables: one for Revenues and one for Net Income. Each contains numbers for separate regions. The idea is to create a staging table that pulls data from both tables so that the data corresponds to a selected region.

To understand what's going on, focus on the formula in cell F3, shown in Figure 2-17. The formula is CHOOSE($C$2,F7,F8,F9,F10). The *Index_num* argument is actually a cell reference that looks at the value in cell C2, which happens to be the number 2. As you can see, cell C2 is actually a VLOOKUP formula that pulls the appropriate index number for the selected region.

The list of defined choices in the CHOOSE formula is essentially the cell references that make up the revenue values for each region: F7, F8, F9, and F10. So the formula in cell F3 translates to CHOOSE(2, 27474, 41767, 18911, 10590). The answer is 41,767.

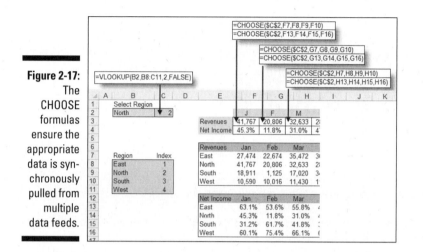

Figure 2-17:
The CHOOSE formulas ensure the appropriate data is synchronously pulled from multiple data feeds.

Using Smart Tables That Expand with Data

One of the challenges you can encounter when building data models is a data table that expands over time. That is to say, the table grows in the number of records it holds due to new data being added. To get a basic understanding of this challenge, take a look at Figure 2-18. In this figure, you see a simple table that serves as the source for the chart. Notice that the table lists data for January through June.

Imagine that next month, this table expands to include July data. You'll have to manually update your chart to include July data. Now imagine you had this same issue across your data model, with multiple data tables that link to multiple staging tables and dashboard components. You can imagine it'd be an extremely painful task to keep up with changes each month.

To solve this issue, you can use Excel's Table feature (you can tell they spent all night coming up with that name). The *Table feature* allows you to convert a range of data into a defined table that's treated independently of other rows and columns on the worksheet. After a range is converted to a table, Excel views the individual cells in the table as a single object with functionality that a typical data range doesn't have.

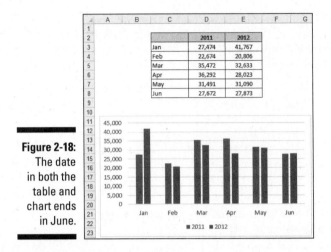

Figure 2-18:
The date
in both the
table and
chart ends
in June.

For instance, Excel tables offer the following features:

- They're automatically enabled with autofilter drop-down headers so that you can filter and sort easily.

- They come with the ability to quickly add a Total row with various aggregate functions.

- You can apply special formatting to Excel tables independent of the rest of the spreadsheet.

- Most importantly for data modeling purposes, they automatically expand to allow for new data.

The Table feature exists in Excel 2003 under a different name: the List feature (found in Excel's Data menu). The benefit of this fact is that Excel Tables are fully compatible with Excel 2003 Lists.

Converting a range to an Excel table

To convert a range of data to an Excel table, follow these steps:

1. **Highlight the range of cells that contain the data you want included in your Excel table.**

2. **On the Insert tab of the Ribbon, click the Table button.**

    This opens the Create Table dialog box, as shown in Figure 2-19.

3. **In the Create Table dialog box, verify the range for the table and specify whether the first row of the selected range is a header row.**

4. **Click OK to apply the changes.**

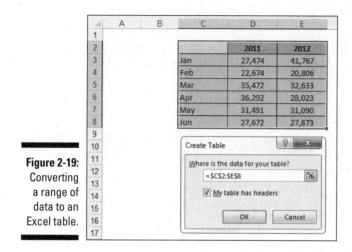

Figure 2-19:
Converting
a range of
data to an
Excel table.

After the conversion takes place, notice a few small changes. Excel put autofilter drop-downs on your header rows, the rows in your table now have alternate shading, and any header that didn't have a value has been named by Excel.

You can use Excel tables as the source for charts, pivot tables, list boxes, or anything else for which you'd typically use a data range. In Figure 2-20, a chart has been linked to the Excel table.

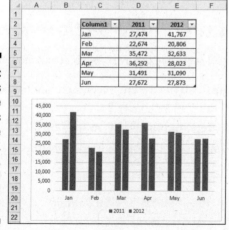

Figure 2-20:
Excel tables
can be
used as
the source
for charts,
pivot tables,
named
ranges, and
so on.

Here's the impressive bit. When data is added to the table, Excel automatically expands the range of the table and incorporates the new range into any linked object. That's just a fancy way of saying that any chart or pivot table tied to an Excel table automatically captures new data without manual intervention.

For example, if I add July and August data to the end of the Excel table, the chart automatically updates to capture the new data. In Figure 2-21, I added July with no data and August with data to show you that the chart captures any new records and automatically plots the data given.

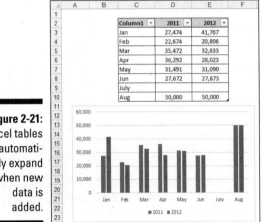

Figure 2-21: Excel tables automatically expand when new data is added.

Take a moment to think about what Excel tables mean to a data model. They mean pivot tables that never have to be reconfigured, charts that automatically capture new data, and ranges that automatically keep up with changes.

Converting an Excel table back to a range

If you want to convert an Excel table back to a range, you can follow these steps:

1. **Place your cursor in any cell inside the Excel table and select the Table Tools' Design subtab on the Ribbon.**

2. **Click the Convert to Range button, as shown in Figure 2-22.**

3. **When asked if you're sure (via a message box), click the Yes button.**

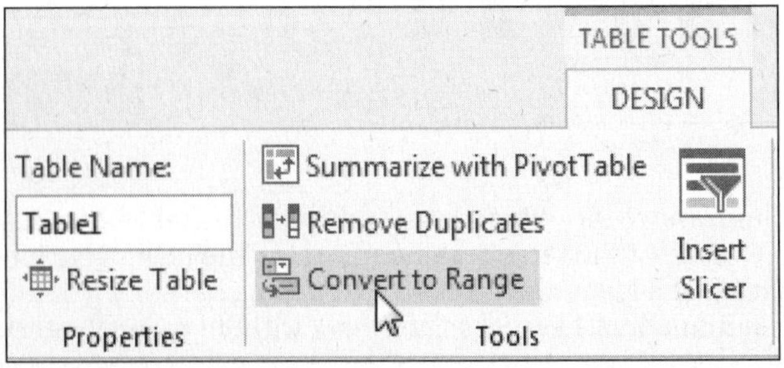

Figure 2-22: To remove Excel table functionality, convert the table back to a range.

TABLE TOOLS

DESIGN

Table Name:

Table1

Resize Table

Properties

Summarize with PivotTable

Remove Duplicates

Convert to Range

Tools

Insert Slicer

Part II
Building Basic Dashboard Components

◢	A	B	C	D	E	F	G	H	I
1		Western	Eastern						
2	Jan	76	76		**WESTERN REGION:** Following a slow start, sales in the 2nd half picked up considerably, and exceeded expectations.				
3	Feb	67	84						
4	Mar	69	79						
5	Apr	71	89						
6	May	87	98						
7	Jun	99	86						
8	Jul	109	83						
9	Aug	143	82		**EASTERN REGION:** Sales were steady throughout the year, significantly below the levels in the Western Region.				
10	Sep	156	87						
11	Oct	178	85						
12	Nov	198	89						
13	Dec	185	81						
14									

In this part . . .

- Uncover the best practices for designing effective data tables.

- See how you can leverage the Sparkline functionality found in Excel 2013.

- Look at the various techniques you can use to visualize data without the use of charts or graphs.

- Explore how pivot tables can enhance your analytical and reporting capabilities, as well as your dashboards.

Chapter 3

Dressing Up Your Data Tables

· ·

· ·

*T*he Excel table is the perfect way to consolidate and relay information. Data tables are very common — you'll find one in any Excel report. And yet, the concept of making tables easier to read and more visually appealing escapes most of us.

Maybe it's because the nicely structured rows and columns of a table lull us into believing that the data is already presented in the best way possible. Maybe the options of adding color and borders make the table seem nicely packaged. Excel makes table creation easy, but even so, you can use several design principles to make your Excel table a more effective platform for conveying your data.

In this chapter, you explore how easy it is to apply a handful of table design best practices. The tips found here ultimately help you create visually appealing tables that make the data within them easier to consume and comprehend.

Table Design Principles

Table design is one of the most underestimated endeavors in Excel reporting. How a table is designed has a direct effect on how well an audience absorbs and interprets the data in that table. Unfortunately, putting together a data table with an eye for economy and ease of consumption is an uncommon skill.

Take for example the table shown in Figure 3-1. This table is similar to many found in Excel reports. The thick borders, the variety of colors, and the poorly formatted numbers are all unfortunate trademarks of tables that come from the average Excel analyst.

Top 10 Domestic Routes by Revenue		Revenue		Margin		Per Passenger	
		Revenue Dollars	Revenue Percent	Margin Dollars	Margin Percent	Revenue per Passenger	Margin per Passenger
From	To						
Atlanta	New York	$3,602,000	8.09%	$955,000	9%	245	65
Chicago	New York	$4,674,000	10.50%	$336,000	3%	222	16
Columbus (Ohio)	New York	$2,483,000	5.58%	$1,536,000	14%	202	125
New York	Detroit	$12,180,000	27.35%	$2,408,000	23%	177	35
New York	Washington	$6,355,000	14.27%	$1,230,000	12%	186	36
New York	Philadelphia	$3,582,000	8.04%	-$716,000	-7%	125	-25
New York	San Francisco	$3,221,000	7.23%	$1,856,000	18%	590	340
New York	Phoenix	$2,846,000	6.39%	$1,436,000	14%	555	280
New York	Toronto	$2,799,000	6.29%	$1,088,000	10%	450	175
New York	Seattle	$2,792,000	6.27%	$467,000	4%	448	75
Total Domestic routes		$44,534,000		$10,596,000		272	53

Figure 3-1:
A poorly designed table.

Throughout this chapter, you improve upon this table by applying these four basic design principles:

- ✔ **Use colors sparingly,** reserving them only for information about key data points.

- ✔ **De-emphasize borders,** using the natural white space between your components to partition your dashboard.

- ✔ **Use effective number formatting** to avoid inundating your table with too much ink.

- ✔ **Subdue your labels and headers.**

Use colors sparingly

Color is most often used to separate the various sections of a table. The basic idea is that the colors applied to a table suggest the relationship between the rows and columns. The problem is that colors often distract and draw attention away from the important data. In addition, printed tables with dark-colored cells are notoriously difficult to read (especially on black-and-white printers). They are also hard on the toner budget, if that holds any importance to you.

Colors in general should be used sparingly, reserved for providing information about key data points. The headers, labels, and natural structure of your table are more than enough to guide your audience. There is no real need to add a layer of color as demarcation for your rows and columns.

Figure 3-2 shows the table from Figure 3-1 with the colors removed. As you can see, it's already easier to read.

Top 10 Domestic Routes by Revenue

| From | To | Revenue | | Margin | | Per Passenger | |
		Revenue Dollars	Revenue Percent	Margin Dollars	Margin Percent	Revenue per Passenger	Margin per Passenger
Atlanta	New York	$3,602,000	8.09%	$955,000	9%	245	65
Chicago	New York	$4,674,000	10.50%	$336,000	3%	222	16
Columbus (Ohio)	New York	$2,483,000	5.58%	$1,536,000	14%	202	125
New York	Detroit	$12,180,000	27.35%	$2,408,000	23%	177	35
New York	Washington	$6,355,000	14.27%	$1,230,000	12%	186	36
New York	Philadelphia	$3,582,000	8.04%	-$716,000	-7%	125	-25
New York	San Francisco	$3,221,000	7.23%	$1,856,000	18%	590	340
New York	Phoenix	$2,846,000	6.39%	$1,436,000	14%	555	280
New York	Toronto	$2,799,000	6.29%	$1,088,000	10%	450	175
New York	Seattle	$2,792,000	6.27%	$467,000	4%	448	75
Total Domestic routes		**$44,534,000**		**$10,596,000**		**272**	**53**

Figure 3-2: Remove unnecessary cell coloring.

If you're working with a table that contains colored cells, you can quickly remove the color by highlighting the cells and choosing the No Fill option under the Theme Colors drop-down on the Home tab. See Figure 3-3.

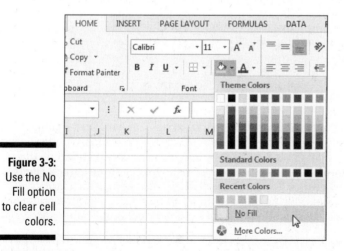

Figure 3-3: Use the No Fill option to clear cell colors.

De-emphasize borders

Believe it or not, borders get in the way of quickly reading the data in a table. Because borders help separate data in nicely partitioned sections, this may seem counterintuitive, but the reality is that a table's borders are the first thing your eyes see when you look at a table. Don't believe it? Stand back a bit from an Excel table and squint. The borders will come popping out at you.

You should always endeavor to de-emphasize borders and gridlines wherever you can. Try to use the natural white space between the columns to partition sections. If borders are necessary, format them to lighter hues than your data; light grays are typically ideal. The idea is to indicate sections without distracting from the information displayed.

Figure 3-4 demonstrates these concepts with the table from Figure 3-1. Notice how the numbers are no longer caged in gridlines and that headings now jump out at you with the addition of Single Accounting underlines.

Top 10 Domestic Routes by Revenue

From	To	Revenue		Margin		Per Passenger	
		Revenue Dollars	Revenue Percent	Margin Dollars	Margin Percent	Revenue per Passenger	Margin per Passenger
Atlanta	New York	$3,602,000	8.09%	$955,000	9%	245	65
Chicago	New York	$4,674,000	10.50%	$336,000	3%	222	16
Columbus (Ohio)	New York	$2,483,000	5.58%	$1,536,000	14%	202	125
New York	Detroit	$12,180,000	27.35%	$2,408,000	23%	177	35
New York	Washington	$6,355,000	14.27%	$1,230,000	12%	186	36
New York	Philadelphia	$3,582,000	8.04%	-$716,000	-7%	125	-25
New York	San Francisco	$3,221,000	7.23%	$1,856,000	18%	590	340
New York	Phoenix	$2,846,000	6.39%	$1,436,000	14%	555	280
New York	Toronto	$2,799,000	6.29%	$1,088,000	10%	450	175
New York	Seattle	$2,792,000	6.27%	$467,000	4%	448	75
Total Domestic routes		**$44,534,000**		**$10,596,000**		272	53

Figure 3-4: Minimize the use of borders and use the single accounting underlines to accent the column headers.

Single accounting underlines are different from the standard underlining you typically apply by pressing Ctrl+U on the keyboard. Standard underlines draw a line only as far as the text goes — that is to say, if you underline the word YES, standard underlines give you a line under the three letters. Single accounting underlines, on the other hand, draw a line across the entire column, regardless of how big or small the word is. This makes for a minimal, but apparent visual demarcation that calls out your column headers nicely.

To format your borders, highlight the cells you are working with, right-click, and select Format Cells. On the Border tab of the Format Cells dialog box, take the following steps as shown in Figure 3-5:

1. **Select an appropriate line thickness.**

   Typically, this means you should select the line with the lightest weight.

2. **Select an appropriate color.**

   Again, lighter hues are the best option.

3. **Use the border buttons to control where your borders are placed.**

Figure 3-5:
Use the Border tab of the Format Cells dialog box to customize your borders.

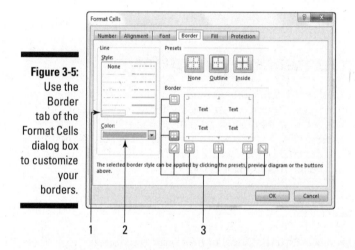

To apply the single accounting underline, right-click the column headings and select Format Cells. Click the Font tab of the Format Cells dialog box and in the Underline drop-down menu, choose the Single Accounting option as demonstrated in Figure 3-6.

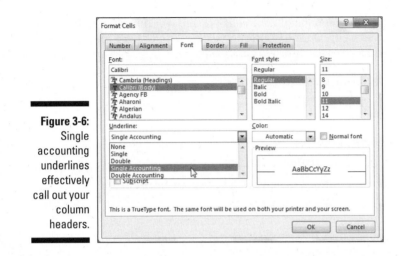

Figure 3-6:
Single accounting underlines effectively call out your column headers.

Use effective number formatting

Every piece of information in your table should have a reason for being there. In an effort to clarify, tables often inundate the audience with superfluous ink that doesn't add value to the information. For example, you'll often see tables that show a number like $145.57 when a simple 145 would be just fine. Why include the extra decimal places, which serve only to add to the mass of numbers that your audience has to plow through?

Here are some guidelines to keep in mind when applying formats to the numbers in your table:

✔ Use decimal places only if that level of precision is required.

✔ In percentages, use only the minimum number of decimals required to represent the data effectively.

✔ Instead of using currency symbols (like $ or £), let your labels clarify that you are referring to monetary values.

✔ Format very large numbers to the thousands or millions place.

✔ Right-align numbers so that they are easier to read and compare.

Figure 3-7 shows the table from Figure 3-1 with appropriate number formatting applied. Notice that the large revenue and margin dollar amounts have been converted to the thousands place. In addition, the labels above the numbers now clearly indicate as such.

Top 10 Domestic Routes by Revenue		Revenue		Margin		Per Passenger	
		Revenue	Revenue	Margin	Margin	$ per	Margin $per
From	To	$ (000's)	%	$ (000's)	%	Passenger	Passenger
Atlanta	New York	3,602	8%	955	9%	245	65
Chicago	New York	4,674	10%	336	3%	222	16
Columbus (Ohio)	New York	2,483	6%	1,536	14%	202	125
New York	Detroit	12,180	27%	2,408	23%	177	35
New York	Washington	6,355	14%	1,230	12%	186	36
New York	Philadelphia	3,582	8%	-716	- 7%	125	-25
New York	San Francisco	3,221	7%	1,856	18%	590	340
New York	Phoenix	2,846	6%	1,436	14%	555	280
New York	Toronto	2,799	6%	1,088	10%	450	175
New York	Seattle	2,792	6%	467	4%	448	75
Total Domestic routes		**44,534**		**10,596**		**272**	**53**

Figure 3-7: Use number formatting to eliminate clutter in your table and draw attention to key metrics.

The percentages have been truncated to show no decimal places. Also, the color coding draws attention to the Margin % column, the key metric in this table.

Amazingly, all of these improvements have been made simply with number formatting. That's right; no formulas were used to convert large numbers to the thousands place, no conditional formatting was used to color code the Margin % field, and there were no other peripheral tricks of any kind.

Subdue your labels and headers

No one would argue that the labels and headers of a table aren't important. On the contrary, they provide your audience with the guidance and structure needed to make sense of the data within. However, many of us have a habit of overemphasizing labels and headers to the point that they overshadow the data within the table. How many times have you seen bold or oversized font applied to headers? The reality is that your audience will benefit more with subdued labels.

De-emphasizing labels by formatting them to lighter hues actually makes the table easier to read and draws more attention to the data within the table. Lightly colored labels give your users the information they need without distracting them from the information being presented. Ideal colors to use for labels are soft grays, light browns, soft blues, and greens.

Font size and alignment also factor in the effective display of tables. Aligning column headers to the same alignment as the numbers beneath them helps reinforce the column structures in your table. Keeping the font size of your labels close to that of the data within the table helps keep your eyes focused on the data — not the labels.

Figure 3-8 illustrates how the original table from Figure 3-1 looks with subdued headers and labels. Note how the data now becomes the focus, while the muted labels work in the background.

Figure 3-8:
Send your
labels and
headers to
the back-
ground by
subduing
their colors
and keeping
their font
sizes in line
with the
data.

Top 10 Domestic Routes by Revenue

		Revenue		Margin		Per Passenger	
		Revenue	Revenue	Margin	Margin	$ per	Margin $
From	To	$ (000's)	%	$ (000's)	%	Passenger	per Passenger
New York	Detroit	12,180	27%	2,408	23%	177	35
New York	Washington	6,355	14%	1,230	12%	186	36
Chicago	New York	4,674	10%	336	3%	222	16
Atlanta	New York	3,602	8%	955	9%	245	65
New York	Philadelphia	3,582	8%	-716	- 7%	125	-25
New York	San Francisco	3,221	7%	1,856	18%	590	340
New York	Phoenix	2,846	6%	1,436	14%	555	280
New York	Toronto	2,799	6%	1,088	10%	450	175
New York	Seattle	2,792	6%	467	4%	448	75
Columbus (Ohio)	New York	2,483	6%	1,536	14%	202	125
Total Domestic routes		**44,534**		**10,596**		**272**	**53**

Sorting is another key factor in the readability of your data. Many tables sort based on labels (alphabetical by route for example). Sorting the table based on a key data point within the data helps establish a pattern your audience can use to quickly analyze the top and bottom values. Note in Figure 3-8 that the data has been sorted by the Revenue dollars. This again adds a layer of analysis, providing a quick look at the top and bottom generating routes.

After making all these improvements, you can see the before and after for the table in Figure 3-9. It's difficult not to see how a few table design principles can greatly enhance your ability to present table driven data.

Top 10 Domestic Routes by Revenue

		Revenue		Margin		Per Passenger	
		Revenue	Revenue	Margin	Margin	Revenue per	Margin per
From	To	Dollars	Percent	Dollars	Percent	Passenger	Passenger
Atlanta	New York	$3,602,000	8.09%	$955,000	9%	245	65
Chicago	New York	$4,674,000	10.50%	$336,000	3%	222	16
Columbus (Ohio)	New York	$2,483,000	5.58%	$1,536,000	14%	202	125
New York	Detroit	$12,180,000	27.35%	$2,408,000	23%	177	35
New York	Washington	$6,355,000	14.27%	$1,230,000	12%	186	36
New York	Philadelphia	$3,582,000	8.04%	-$716,000	-7%	125	-25
New York	San Francisco	$3,221,000	7.23%	$1,856,000	18%	590	340
New York	Phoenix	$2,846,000	6.39%	$1,436,000	14%	555	280
New York	Toronto	$2,799,000	6.29%	$1,088,000	10%	450	175
New York	Seattle	$2,792,000	6.27%	$467,000	4%	448	75
Total Domestic routes		**$44,534,000**		**$10,596,000**		**272**	**58**

Top 10 Domestic Routes by Revenue

		Revenue		Margin		Per Passenger	
		Revenue	Revenue	Margin	Margin	$ per	Margin $
From	To	$ (000's)	%	$ (000's)	%	Passenger	per Passenger
New York	Detroit	12,180	27%	2,408	23%	177	35
New York	Washington	6,355	14%	1,230	12%	186	36
Chicago	New York	4,674	10%	336	3%	222	16
Atlanta	New York	3,602	8%	955	9%	245	65
New York	Philadelphia	3,582	8%	-716	-7%	125	-25
New York	San Francisco	3,221	7%	1,856	18%	590	340
New York	Phoenix	2,846	6%	1,436	14%	555	280
New York	Toronto	2,799	6%	1,088	10%	450	175
New York	Seattle	2,792	6%	467	4%	448	75
Columbus (Ohio)	New York	2,483	6%	1,536	14%	202	125
Total Domestic routes		**44,534**		**10,596**		**272**	**53**

Figure 3-9:
Before
and after
applying
table design
principles.

If possible, consider using modern-looking fonts such as Calibri and Segoe UI in your reports and dashboards. Fonts such as Times New Roman or Arial can make your reports look old compared with the rounded edges of the more trendy fonts used now. This change in font perception is primarily driven by popular online sites that often use fonts with rounded edges.

Getting Fancy with Custom Number Formatting

You can apply number formatting to cells in several ways. Most people just use the convenient number commands found on the Home tab. By using these commands, you can quickly apply some default formatting (number, percent, currency, and so on) and just be done with it, but a better way is to use the Format Cells dialog box, in which you have the ability to create your own custom number formatting.

Number formatting basics

Follow these steps to apply basic number formatting:

1. **Right-click a range of cells and select Format Cells.**

   The Format Cells dialog box appears.

2. **Open the Number tab and choose a starting format that makes the most sense for your scenario.**

   In Figure 3-10, the format chosen is Number and the selected options are to use a comma separator, to include no decimal places, and to enclose negative numbers in parentheses.

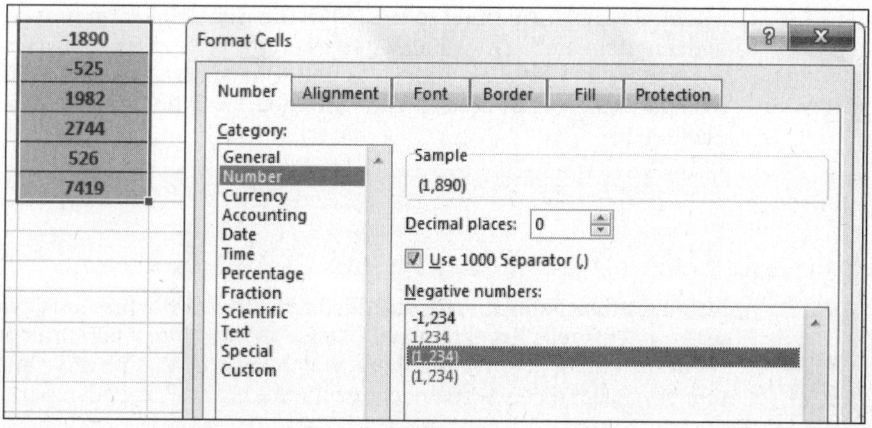

Figure 3-10:
Choose a
base format.

| -1890 |
| -525 |
| 1982 |
| 2744 |
| 526 |
| 7419 |

Format Cells

Number | Alignment | Font | Border | Fill | Protection

Category:

General
Number
Currency
Accounting
Date
Time
Percentage
Fraction
Scientific
Text
Special
Custom

Sample
(1,890)

Decimal places: 0

☑ Use 1000 Separator (,)

Negative numbers:

-1,234
1,234
(1,234)
(1,234)

3. Click the Custom option as shown in Figure 3-11.

Excel takes you to a screen that exposes the syntax that makes up the format you selected. Here, you can edit the syntax in the Type input box to customize the number format.

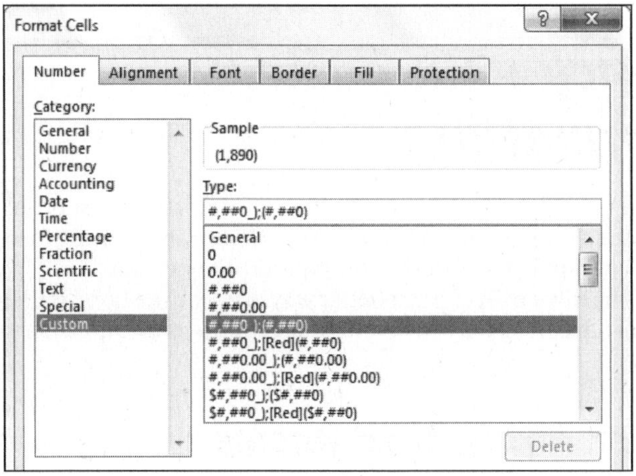

Figure 3-11:
The Type input box allows you to customize the syntax for the number format.

Format Cells
Number	Alignment	Font	Border	Fill	Protection

Category:
General
Number
Currency
Accounting
Date
Time
Percentage
Fraction
Scientific
Text
Special
Custom

Sample
(1,890)

Type:
#,##0_);(#,##0)

General
0
0.00
#,##0
#,##0.00
#,##0_);(#,##0)
#,##0_);[Red](#,##0)
#,##0.00_);(#,##0.00)
#,##0.00_);[Red](#,##0.00)
$#,##0_);($#,##0)
$#,##0_);[Red]($#,##0)

Delete

The number formatting syntax tells Excel how a number should look in various scenarios. Number formatting syntax consists of different individual number formats separated by semicolons.

In this case, you see:

```
#,##0_);(#,##0)
```

Here you see two different formats: the format to the left of the semicolon, and the format to the right of the semicolon.

By default, any formatting to the left of the first semicolon is applied to positive numbers and any formatting to the right of the first semicolon is applied to negative numbers. So with this choice, negative numbers will be formatted with parentheses, whereas positive numbers will be formatted as a simple number, like

```
(1,890)
```

```
1,982
```

Note that the syntax for the positive formatting in the previous example ends with _). This tells Excel to leave a space the width of a parenthesis character at the end of positive numbers, which ensures that positive and negative numbers align nicely when negative numbers are wrapped in parentheses.

You can edit the syntax in the Type input box so that the numbers are formatted differently. For example, try changing the syntax to

```
+#,##0;-#,##0
```

When this syntax is applied, positive numbers will start with the + symbol and negative numbers will start with a – symbol. Like so:

```
+1,200
```

```
-15,000
```

This comes in handy when formatting percentages. For instance, you can apply a custom percent format by entering the following syntax into the Type input box:

```
+0%;-0%
```

This syntax gives you percentages that look like this:

```
+43%
```

```
-54%
```

You can get fancy and wrap your negative percentages with parentheses with this syntax:

```
0%_);(0%)
```

This syntax gives you percentages that look like this:

```
43%
```

```
(54%)
```

If you include only one format syntax, meaning you don't add a second formatting option with the use of a semicolon separator, that one format will be applied to all numbers — negative or positive.

Formatting numbers in thousands and millions

Earlier in this chapter, you format your revenue numbers to appear in thousands. This allows us to present cleaner numbers and avoid inundating your audience with overlarge numbers. To show your numbers in thousands, highlight them, right-click, and select Format Cells.

After the Format Cells dialog box opens, click the Custom option to get to the screen shown in Figure 3-12.

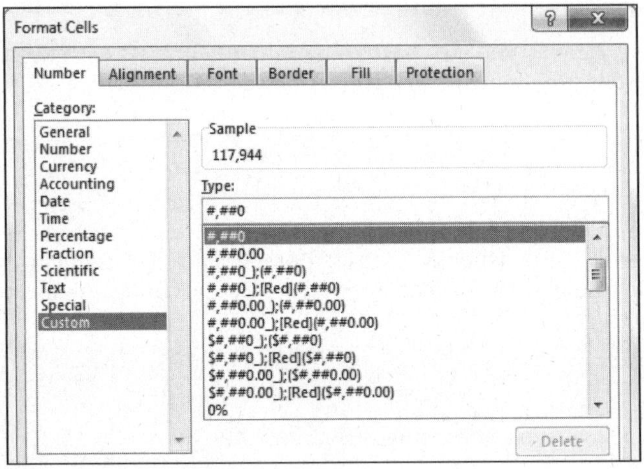

Figure 3-12: Go to the Custom screen of the Format Cells dialog box.

In the Type input box, add a comma after the format syntax.

```
#,##0,
```

After confirming your changes, your numbers will automatically appear in the thousands place!

The beautiful thing here is that this technique doesn't change the integrity or truncate your numeric values in any way. Excel is simply applying a cosmetic effect to the number. To see what this means, take a look at Figure 3-13.

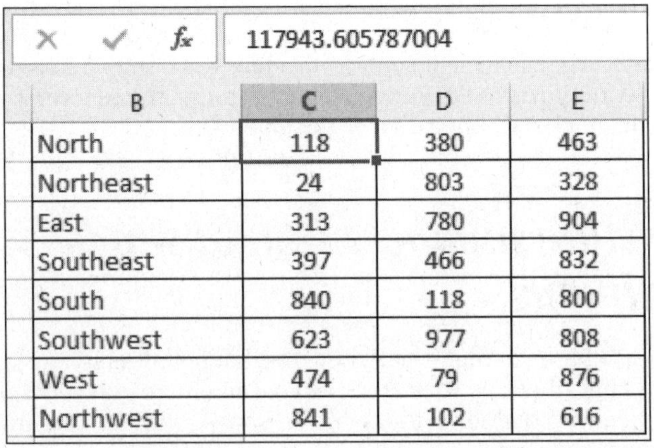

Figure 3-13: Formatting numbers applies only a cosmetic look. Look in the formula bar to see the real, unformatted number.

× ✓ *fx*	117943.605787004		
B	C	D	E
North	118	380	463
Northeast	24	803	328
East	313	780	904
Southeast	397	466	832
South	840	118	800
Southwest	623	977	808
West	474	79	876
Northwest	841	102	616

The selected cell has been formatted to show in thousands; you see 118. But if you look in the formula bar above it, you'll see the real unformatted number (117943.605787004). The 118 you are seeing in the cell is a cosmetically formatted version of the real number shown in the formula bar.

Custom number formatting has obvious advantages over using other techniques to format numbers to thousands. For instance, many beginning analysts would convert numbers to thousands by dividing them by 1,000 in a formula. But that changes the integrity of the number dramatically. When you perform a mathematical operation into a cell, you are literally changing the value represented in that cell. This forces you to carefully keep track of and maintain the formulas you introduced to simply achieve a cosmetic effect. Using custom number formatting avoids that by changing only how the number looks, keeping the actual number intact.

If needed, you can even indicate that the number is in thousands by adding "k" to the number syntax.

```
#,##0,"k"
```

This would show your numbers like this:

```
118k
```

```
318k
```

You can use this technique on both positive and negative numbers.

```
#,##0,"k"; (#,##0,"k")
```

After applying this syntax, your negative numbers also appear in thousands.

```
118k
```

```
(318k)
```

Need to show numbers in millions? Easy. Simply add two commas to the number format syntax in the Type input box.

```
#,##0.00,, "m"
```

Note the use of the extra decimal places (.00). When converting numbers to millions, it's often useful to show additional precision points, as in

```
24.65 m
```

Hiding and suppressing zeroes

In addition to formatting positive and negative numbers, Excel allows you to provide a format for zeroes. You do this by adding another semicolon to your custom number syntax. By default, any format syntax placed after the second semicolon is applied to any number that evaluates to zero.

For example, the following syntax applies a format that shows n/a for any cells that contain zeroes.

```
#,##0_);(#,##0);"n/a"
```

You can also use this to suppress zeroes entirely. If you add the second semicolon but don't follow it with any syntax, cells containing zeroes will appear blank.

```
#,##0_);(#,##0);
```

Again, custom number formatting only affects the cosmetic look of the cell. The actual data in the cell is not affected. Figure 3-14 demonstrates this. The selected cell is formatted so that zeroes appear as n/a, but if you look at the formula bar, you can see the actual unformatted cell contents.

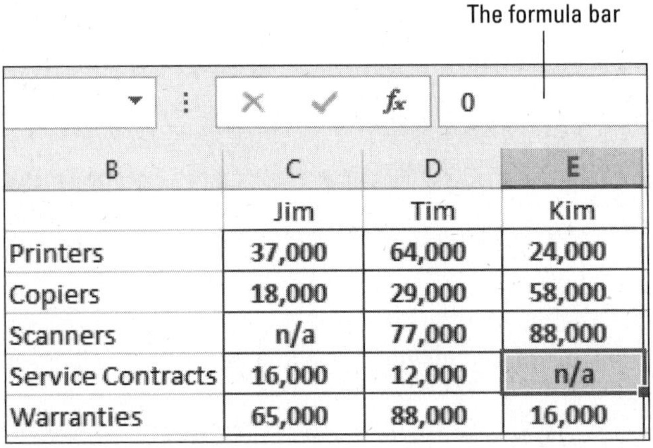

The formula bar

Figure 3-14:
Custom
number
formatting
that shows
zeroes as
n/a.

B	C	D	E
	Jim	Tim	Kim
Printers	37,000	64,000	24,000
Copiers	18,000	29,000	58,000
Scanners	n/a	77,000	88,000
Service Contracts	16,000	12,000	n/a
Warranties	65,000	88,000	16,000

Applying custom format colors

Have you ever set the formatting on a cell so that negative numbers appear red? If you have, you essentially applied a custom format color. In addition to controlling the look of your numbers with custom number formatting, you can also control their color.

In this example, you format the percentages so that positive percentages appear blue with a + symbol, whereas negative percentages appear red with a – symbol. Enter this syntax in the Type input box shown in Figure 3-11.

```
[Blue]+0%; [Red]-0%
```

Notice that all it takes to apply a color is to enter the color name wrapped in square brackets [ ].

Now, there are only certain colors — the eight Visual Basic colors — you can call out by name like this. These colors make up the first eight colors of the default Excel color pallet:

[Black]

[Blue]

[Cyan]

[Green]

[Magenta]

[Red]

[White]

[Yellow]

Formatting dates and times

Custom number formatting isn't just for numbers. You can also format dates and times. As you can see in Figure 3-15, you use the same dialog box to apply date and time formats using the Type input box.

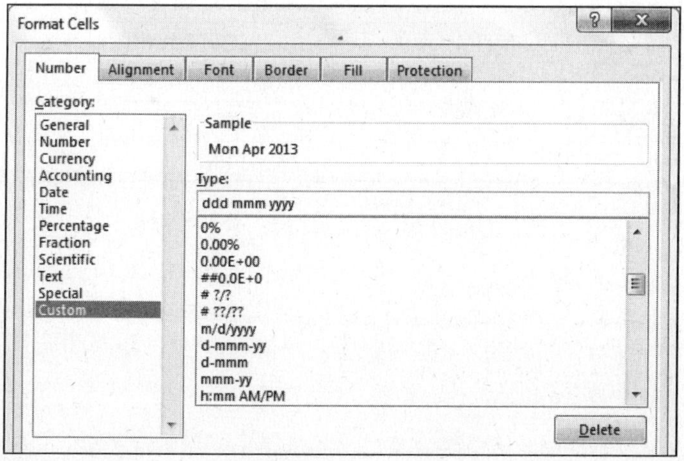

Figure 3-15: Dates and times can also be formatted using the Format Cells dialog box.

Figure 3-15 demonstrates that date and time formatting involves little more than stringing date-specific or time-specific syntax together. The syntax used is fairly intuitive. For example, ddd is the syntax for the three-letter day, mmm is the syntax for the three-letter month, and yyyy is the syntax for the four-digit year.

There are several variations on the format for days, months, years, hours, and minutes. It's worthwhile to take some time and experiment with different combinations of syntax strings.

Table 3-1 lists some common date and time format codes you can use as starter syntax for your reports and dashboards.

Table 3-1	Common Date and Time Format Codes
Format Code	*1/31/2014 7:42:53 PM Displays As*
M	1
Mm	01
mmm	Jan
mmmm	January
mmmmm	J
dd	31
ddd	Thu
dddd	Thursday
Yy	14
yyyy	2014
mmm-yy	Jan-14
dd/mm/yyyy	31/01/2014
dddd mmm yyyy	Thursday Jan 2014
mm-dd-yyyy h:mm AM/PM	01-31-2014 7:42 PM
h AM/PM	7 PM
h:mm AM/PM	7:42 PM
h:mm:ss AM/PM	7:42:53 PM

Chapter 4

Sparking Inspiration with Sparklines

In This Chapter

▶ Understanding the Excel Sparkline feature

▶ Adding sparklines to a worksheet

▶ Customizing sparklines

▶ Working with groups of sparklines

This chapter introduces you to sparklines. These magically named visualizations are essentially mini word-sized charts placed in and among the textual data in tables. Sparklines enable you to see trends and patterns within your data at a glance using minimal real estate on your dashboard.

Before getting into the nuts and bolts of using sparklines, it's important to understand just how they can enhance your reporting. This chapter introduces you to the concept of sparklines and then shows you how to customize and add them to your tables.

Introducing Sparklines

As mentioned in Chapter 3, much of the reporting done in Excel is table-based, in which precise numbers are more important than pretty charts. However, in table-based reporting, you often lose the ability to show important aspects of the data such as trends. The number of columns needed to show adequate trend data in a table makes it impractical to do so. Any attempt to add trend data to a table usually does nothing more than render your report unreadable.

Take the example in Figure 4-1. The data here represents a compact KPI (key performance indicator) summary designed to be an at-a-glance view of key metrics. Although the table compares various time periods (in columns D, E, and F), it does so only by averaging, which tells us nothing about trends over time. It quickly becomes evident that seeing a full year trend would be helpful.

◢A	B	C	D	E	F	H	I
1	Compact KPI Summary		Current Month	Last 3 Mo Avg	Last 12 mo Avg	Target	% of Target
2	Finance Metrics	$ Revenues	$18,134 K	$17,985 K	$17,728 K	$18,000 K	101%
3		$ Expenses	$11,358 K	$11,186 K	$11,580 K	$12,600 K	90%
4		$ Profits	$6,776 K	$6,799 K	$6,147 K	$5,400 K	125%
5		% Market Share	44%	46%	45%	52%	85%
6	Flight Metircs	Flights	446	447	449	500	89%
7		Passengers	63 K	62 K	61 K	65 K	97%
8		Miles	346 K	347 K	349 K	395 K	88%
9		Passenger Miles	31,206 K	31,376 K	31,510 K	36,000 K	87%
10		Cancelled Flights	9	9	10	15	60%
11		Late Arrivals	63	71	64	45	141%
12		Minutes Late	1,302	1,472	1,337	1,000	130%
13		$ Fuel Costs	$1,293 K	$1,332 K	$1,326 K	$1,080 K	120%
14		Customer Satisfaction	4.52	4.5	4.5	4.80	94%
15		Flight Utilization	92%	91%	91%	94%	98%

Figure 4-1: Although this KPI summary is useful, it lacks the ability show a full-year trend.

Figure 4-2 illustrates the same KPI summary with Excel sparklines added to visually show the 12-month trend. With the sparklines added, you can see the broader story behind each metric. For example, based solely on the numbers, the Passengers metric appears to be slightly up from the average. But the sparkline tells the story of a heroic comeback from a huge hit at the beginning of the year.

◢A	B	C	D	E	F	G	H	I
1	Compact KPI Summary		Current Month	Last 3 Mo Avg	Last 12 mo Avg	12 Month Trend	Target	% of Target
2	Finance Metrics	$ Revenues	$18,134 K	$17,985 K	$17,728 K		$18,000 K	101%
3		$ Expenses	$11,358 K	$11,186 K	$11,580 K		$12,600 K	90%
4		$ Profits	$6,776 K	$6,799 K	$6,147 K		$5,400 K	125%
5		% Market Share	44%	46%	45%		52%	85%
6	Flight Metircs	Flights	446	447	449		500	89%
7		Passengers	63 K	62 K	61 K		65 K	97%
8		Miles	346 K	347 K	349 K		395 K	88%
9		Passenger Miles	31,206 K	31,376 K	31,510 K		36,000 K	87%
10		Cancelled Flights	9	9	10		15	60%
11		Late Arrivals	63	71	64		45	141%
12		Minutes Late	1,302	1,472	1,337		1,000	130%
13		$ Fuel Costs	$1,293 K	$1,332 K	$1,326 K		$1,080 K	120%
14		Customer Satisfaction	4.52	4.5	4.5		4.80	94%
15		Flight Utilization	92%	91%	91%		94%	98%

Figure 4-2: Sparklines allow you to add trending in a compact space, enabling you to see a broader picture for each metric.

Again, it's not about adding flash and pizzaz to your tables. It's about building the most effective message in the limited space you have. Sparklines are another tool you can use to add another dimension to your table-based reports.

Sparklines are available only with Excel 2010 and Excel 2013. If you open a workbook with sparklines using a previous version of Excel, the sparkline cells will be empty. If your organization is not fully using Excel 2010 or 2013, you may want to search for alternatives to the built-in Excel sparklines. Many third-party add-ins bring sparkline features to earlier versions of Excel. Some of these products support additional sparkline types, and most have customization options. Search the web for *sparklines excel*, and you'll find several add-ins to choose from.

Understanding Sparklines

Although sparklines look like miniature charts (and can sometimes take the place of a chart), this feature is completely separate from the Excel chart feature (covered in Chapters 7, 8, and 9 of this book). For example, charts are placed on a worksheet's drawing layer, and a single chart can display several series of data. In contrast, a sparkline is displayed inside of a worksheet cell, and displays only one series of data.

Excel 2013 supports three types of sparklines: Line, Column, and Win/Loss. Figure 4-3 shows examples of each type of sparkline graphic, displayed in column H. Each sparkline depicts the six data points to the left.

	A	B	C	D	E	F	G	H
1	**Line Sparklines**							
2	**Fund Number**	**Jan**	**Feb**	**Mar**	**Apr**	**May**	**Jun**	**Sparklines**
3	A-13	103.98	98.92	88.12	86.34	75.58	71.2	
4	C-09	212.74	218.7	202.18	198.56	190.12	181.74	
5	K-88	75.74	73.68	69.86	60.34	64.92	59.46	
6	W-91	91.78	95.44	98.1	99.46	98.68	105.86	
7	M-03	324.48	309.14	313.1	287.82	276.24	260.9	
8								
9	**Column Sparklines**							
10	**Fund Number**	**Jan**	**Feb**	**Mar**	**Apr**	**May**	**Jun**	**Sparklines**
11	A-13	103.98	98.92	88.12	86.34	75.58	71.2	
12	C-09	212.74	218.7	202.18	198.56	190.12	181.74	
13	K-88	75.74	73.68	69.86	60.34	64.92	59.46	
14	W-91	91.78	95.44	98.1	99.46	98.68	105.86	
15	M-03	324.48	309.14	313.1	287.82	276.24	260.9	
16								
17	**Win/Loss Sparklines**							
18	**Fund Number**	**Jan**	**Feb**	**Mar**	**Apr**	**May**	**Jun**	**Sparklines**
19	A-13	0	-5.06	-10.8	-1.78	-10.76	-4.38	
20	C-09	0	5.96	-16.52	-3.62	-8.44	-8.38	
21	K-88	0	-2.06	-3.82	-9.52	4.58	-5.46	
22	W-91	0	3.66	2.66	1.36	-0.78	7.18	
23	M-03	0	-15.34	3.96	-25.28	-11.58	-15.34	

Figure 4-3:
Three types of sparklines.

✓ **Line:** Similar to a line chart, the Line type of sparkline can appear with or without a marker for each data point. The first group in Figure 4-3 shows Line sparklines with markers. A quick glance reveals that with the exception of Fund Number W-91, the funds have been losing value over the six-month period.

✓ **Column:** Similar to a column chart, the second group shows the same data with Column sparklines.

✓ **Win/Loss:** A Win/Loss sparkline is a binary-type chart that displays each data point as a high block or a low block. The third group shows Win/Loss sparklines. Notice that the data is different. Each cell displays the change from the previous month. In the sparkline, each data point is depicted as a high block (win) or a low block (loss). In this example, a positive change from the previous month is a win, and a negative change from the previous month is a loss.

Creating sparklines

Figure 4-4 shows some weather data that you can summarize with sparklines. To create sparkline graphics for the values in these nine rows, follow these steps:

1. **Select the data range that you want to summarize. In this example, select B4:M12.**

   If you are creating multiple sparklines, select all the data.

Figure 4-4:
Data that
you want
to sum-
marize with
sparkline
graphics.

	A	B	C	D	E	F	G	H	I	J	K	L	M
1	**Average Monthly Precipitation (Inches)**												
2													
3		Jan	Feb	Mar	Apr	May	Jun	Jul	Aug	Sep	Oct	Nov	Dec
4	ASHEVILLE, NC	4.06	3.83	4.59	3.50	4.41	4.38	3.87	4.30	3.72	3.17	3.82	3.39
5	BAKERSFIELD, CA	1.18	1.21	1.41	0.45	0.24	0.12	0.00	0.08	0.15	0.30	0.59	0.76
6	BATON ROUGE, LA	6.19	5.10	5.07	5.56	5.34	5.33	5.96	5.86	4.84	3.81	4.76	5.26
7	BILLINGS, MT	0.81	0.57	1.12	1.74	2.48	1.89	1.28	0.85	1.34	1.26	0.75	0.67
8	DAYTONA BEACH, FL	3.13	2.74	3.84	2.54	3.26	5.69	5.17	6.09	6.61	4.48	3.03	2.71
9	EUGENE, OR	7.65	6.35	5.80	3.66	2.66	1.53	0.64	0.99	1.54	3.35	8.44	8.29
10	HONOLULU,HI	2.73	2.35	1.89	1.11	0.78	0.43	0.50	0.46	0.74	2.18	2.26	2.85
11	ST. LOUIS, MO	2.14	2.28	3.60	3.69	4.11	3.76	3.90	2.98	2.96	2.76	3.71	2.86
12	TUCSON, AZ	0.99	0.88	0.81	0.28	0.24	0.24	2.07	2.30	1.45	1.21	0.67	1.03

2. **With the data selected, click the Insert tab on the Ribbon and find the Sparklines group. There, select any one of the three sparkline types: Line, Column, or Win/Loss. In this case, select the Column option.**

   Excel displays the Create Sparklines dialog box, as shown in Figure 4-5.

Figure 4-5:
Use the
Create
Sparklines
dialog box
to specify
the data
range and
the loca-
tion for the
sparkline
graphics.

3. **Specify the data range and the location for the sparklines. For this example, specify N4:N12 as the Location Range.**

   Typically, you'll put the sparklines next to the data, but that's not required. Most of the time, you'll use an empty range to hold the sparklines. However, Excel does not prevent you from inserting sparklines into filled-in cells. The sparkline location that you specify must match the source data in terms of number of rows or number of columns.

4. **Click OK.**

   Excel creates the sparklines graphics of the type you specified, as shown in Figure 4-6.

   The sparklines are linked to the data, so if you change any of the values in the data range, the sparkline graphic will update.

Figure 4-6:
Column
sparklines
summarize
the precipi-
tation data
for nine
cities.

	A	B	C	D	E	F	G	H	I	J	K	L	M	N
1	**Average Monthly Precipitation (Inches)**													
2														
3		Jan	Feb	Mar	Apr	May	Jun	Jul	Aug	Sep	Oct	Nov	Dec	
4	ASHEVILLE, NC	4.06	3.83	4.59	3.50	4.41	4.38	3.87	4.30	3.72	3.17	3.82	3.39	
5	BAKERSFIELD, CA	1.18	1.21	1.41	0.45	0.24	0.12	0.00	0.08	0.15	0.30	0.59	0.76	
6	BATON ROUGE, LA	6.19	5.10	5.07	5.56	5.34	5.33	5.96	5.86	4.84	3.81	4.76	5.26	
7	BILLINGS, MT	0.81	0.57	1.12	1.74	2.48	1.89	1.28	0.85	1.34	1.26	0.75	0.67	
8	DAYTONA BEACH, FL	3.13	2.74	3.84	2.54	3.26	5.69	5.17	6.09	6.61	4.48	3.03	2.71	
9	EUGENE, OR	7.65	6.35	5.80	3.66	2.66	1.53	0.64	0.99	1.54	3.35	8.44	8.29	
10	HONOLULU,HI	2.73	2.35	1.89	1.11	0.78	0.43	0.50	0.46	0.74	2.18	2.26	2.85	
11	ST. LOUIS, MO	2.14	2.28	3.60	3.69	4.11	3.76	3.90	2.98	2.96	2.76	3.71	2.86	
12	TUCSON, AZ	0.99	0.88	0.81	0.28	0.24	0.24	2.07	2.30	1.45	1.21	0.67	1.03	

Most of the time, you'll create sparklines on the same sheet that contains the data. If you want to create sparklines on a different sheet, start by activating the sheet where the sparklines will be displayed. Then, in the Create Sparklines dialog box, specify the source data either by selecting the cell range or by typing the complete sheet reference (for example, Sheet1!A1:C12). The Create Sparklines dialog box lets you specify a different sheet for the Data Range, but not for the Location Range.

Understanding sparkline groups

Most of the time, you'll probably create a group of sparklines — one for each row or column of data. A worksheet can hold any number of sparkline groups. Excel remembers each group, and you can work with the group as a single unit. For example, you can select one sparkline in a group and then modify the formatting of all sparklines in the group. When you select one sparkline cell, Excel displays an outline of all the other sparklines in the group.

You can, however, perform some operations on an individual sparkline in a group:

- ✔ **Change the sparkline's data source.** Click the sparkline cell and go to the Sparkline Tools tab on the Ribbon. There you can click Design➪Sparkline➪Edit Data➪Edit Single Sparkline's Data. Excel displays a dialog box that lets you change the data source for the selected sparkline.

- ✔ **Delete the sparkline.** Click the sparkline, click the Sparkline Tools tab on the Ribbon, and then select Design➪Group➪Clear➪Clear Selected Sparklines.

Both of these operations are available from the shortcut menu that appears when you right-click a sparkline cell.

You can also ungroup a set of sparklines. Select any sparkline in the group and select Design➪Group➪Ungroup from the Sparkline Tools tab. After you ungroup a set of sparklines, you can work with each sparkline individually.

You can add a new sparkline to an existing group by first selecting any sparkline in the existing group, and then selecting Design➪Edit Data➪Edit Group Location & Data. This activates the Edit Sparklines dialog box. Simply edit the Data Range and Location Range to include the new data you want added.

Customizing Sparklines

When you activate a cell that contains a sparkline, Excel displays an outline around all the sparklines in its group. You can then use the commands on the Sparkline Tools⇨Design tab to customize the group of sparklines.

Sizing and merging sparkline cells

When you change the width or height of a cell that contains a sparkline, the sparkline adjusts to fill the new cell size. In addition, you can put a sparkline into merged cells. To merge cells, select at least two cells and choose Home⇨Alignment⇨Merge & Center.

Figure 4-7 shows the same sparkline displayed at four sizes resulting from changing column width and row height, and from merging cells.

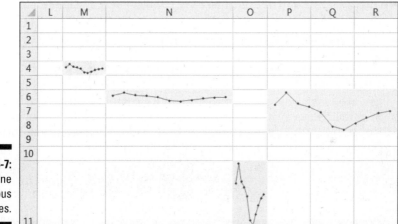

Figure 4-7:
A sparkline
at various
sizes.

It's important to note that a skewed aspect ratio can distort your visualizations, exaggerating the trend in sparklines that are too tall, and flattening the trend in sparklines that are too wide. Generally speaking, the most appropriate aspect ratio for a chart is one where the width of the chart is about twice as long as the height. In Figure 4-7, the sparkline with the most appropriate aspect ratio is the one located in cell M4.

If you merge cells, and the merged cells occupy more than one row or one column, Excel won't let you insert a group of sparklines into those merged cells. Rather, you need to insert the sparklines into a normal range (with no merged cells), and then merge the cells.

You can also put a sparkline in non-empty cells, including merged cells. Figure 4-8 shows two sparklines that occupy merged cells alongside text that describes the graphics.

	A	B	C	D	E	F	G	H	I
1		Western	Eastern						
2	Jan	76	76		WESTERN REGION: Following a slow start, sales in the 2nd half picked up considerably, and exceeded expectations.				
3	Feb	67	84						
4	Mar	69	79						
5	Apr	71	89						
6	May	87	98						
7	Jun	99	86						
8	Jul	109	83						
9	Aug	143	82		EASTERN REGION: Sales were steady throughout the year, significantly below the levels in the Western Region.				
10	Sep	156	87						
11	Oct	178	85						
12	Nov	198	89						
13	Dec	185	81						
14									

Figure 4-8: Sparklines in merged cells (E2:I7 and E9:I14).

Handling hidden or missing data

In some cases, you just want to present a sparkline visualization without the numbers. One way to do this is to hide the rows or columns that contain the data. Figure 4-9 shows a table with the values displayed, and the same table with the values hidden (by hiding the columns).

Figure 4-9: Sparklines can use data in hidden rows or columns.

Product Line	Jan	Feb	Mar	Apr	May	Jun	6-Month Trend		Product Line	6-Month Trend
Women's shoes	87	92	101	121	89	88			Women's shoes	
Men's shoes	67	66	73	59	54	61			Men's shoes	
Children's shoes	92	101	114	125	109	111			Children's shoes	
Women's hats	76	71	65	73	65	51			Women's hats	
Men's hats	12	15	18	26	13	12			Men's hats	
Children's hats	44	46	48	44	42	41			Children's hats	

By default, if you hide rows or columns that contain data used in a sparkline graphic, the hidden data does not appear in the sparkline. In addition, blank cells are displayed as a gap in the graphic.

To change these default settings, go to the Sparkline Tools tab on the Ribbon, and select Design⇨Sparkline⇨Edit Data⇨Hidden & Empty Cells. In the Hidden and Empty Cell Settings dialog box, specify how to handle hidden data and empty cells.

Changing the sparkline type

As mentioned earlier in this chapter, Excel supports three sparkline types: Line, Column, and Win/Loss. After you create a sparkline or group of sparklines, you can easily change the type by clicking the sparkline and selecting one of the three icons located under Sparkline Tools⇨Design⇨Type. If the selected sparkline is part of a group, all sparklines in the group are changed to the new type.

If you've customized the appearance, Excel remembers your customization settings for each sparkline type if you switch among different sparkline types.

Changing sparkline colors and line width

After you create a sparkline, changing the color is easy. Simply click the sparkline, click to open the Sparkline Tools tab on the Ribbon, and select Design⇨Style. There you find various options to change the color and style of your sparkline.

For Line sparklines, you can also specify the line width. Choose Sparkline Tools⇨Design⇨Style⇨Sparkline Color⇨Weight.

Colors used in sparkline graphics are tied to the document theme. If you change the theme (by choosing Page Layout⇨Themes⇨Themes), the sparkline colors then change to the new theme colors.

Using color to emphasize key data points

Use the commands under Sparkline Tools⇨Design⇨Show to customize the sparklines to emphasize key aspects of the data. The options in the Show group are:

- **High Point:** Apply a different color to the highest data point in the sparkline.
- **Low Point:** Apply a different color to the lowest data point in the sparkline.
- **Negative Points:** Apply a different color to negative values in the sparkline.
- **First Point:** Apply a different color to the first data point in the sparkline.
- **Last Point:** Apply a different color to the last data point in the sparkline.
- **Markers:** Show data markers in the sparkline. This option is available only for Line sparklines.

You can control the color of the sparkline by using the Marker Color control in the Sparkline Tools⇨Design⇨Style group. Unfortunately, you cannot change the size of the markers in Line sparklines.

Adjusting sparkline axis scaling

When you create one or more sparklines, they all use (by default) automatic axis scaling. In other words, Excel determines the minimum and maximum vertical axis values for each sparkline in the group based on the numeric range of the sparkline data.

The Sparkline Tools⇨Design⇨Group⇨Axis command lets you override this automatic behavior and control the minimum and maximum value for each sparkline, or for a group of sparklines. For even more control, you can use the Custom Value option and specify the minimum and maximum for the sparkline group.

Axis scaling can make a huge difference in the sparklines. Figure 4-10 shows two groups of sparklines. The group at the top uses the default axis settings (Automatic For Each Sparkline option). Each sparkline in this group shows the six-month trend for the product, but there is no indication of the magnitude of the values.

Figure 4-10: The bottom group of sparklines shows the effect of using the same axis minimum and maximum values for all sparklines in a group.

⬦	A	B	C	D	E	F	G	H
1								
2		Jan	Feb	Mar	Apr	May	Jun	Sparklines
3	Product A	100	103	103	115	122	125	
4	Product B	300	295	300	312	307	322	
5	Product C	600	597	599	606	620	618	
6								
7								
8								
9		Jan	Feb	Mar	Apr	May	Jun	Sparklines
10	Product A	100	103	103	115	122	125	
11	Product B	300	295	300	312	307	322	
12	Product C	600	597	599	606	620	618	

The sparkline group at the bottom (which uses the same data), uses the Same For All Sparklines setting for the minimum and maximum axis values. With these settings in effect, the magnitude of the values across the products is apparent — but the trend across the months within a product is not apparent.

The axis scaling option you choose depends upon what aspect of the data you want to emphasize.

Faking a reference line

One useful feature that's missing in the Excel 2013 implementation of sparklines is a reference line. For example, it might be useful to show performance relative to a goal. If the goal is displayed as a reference line in a sparkline, the viewer can quickly see whether the performance for a period exceeded the goal.

One approach is to write formulas that transform the data and then use a sparkline axis as a fake reference line. Figure 4-11 shows an example. Students have a monthly reading goal of 500 pages. The range of data shows the actual pages read, with sparklines in column H. The sparklines show the six-month page data, but it's impossible to tell who exceeded the goal, and when they did it.

	A	B	C	D	E	F	G	H
1	**Pages Read**							
2	Monthly Goal:		500					
3								
4					*Pages Read*			
5	**Student**	**Jan**	**Feb**	**Mar**	**Apr**	**May**	**Jun**	**Sparklines**
6	Ann	450	412	632	663	702	512	
7	Bob	309	215	194	189	678	256	
8	Chuck	608	783	765	832	483	763	
9	Dave	409	415	522	598	421	433	
10	Ellen	790	893	577	802	874	763	
11	Frank	211	59	0	0	185	230	
12	Giselle	785	764	701	784	214	185	
13	Henry	350	367	560	583	784	663	

Figure 4-11: Sparklines display the number of pages read per month.

The lower set of sparklines in Figure 4-12 shows another approach: Transforming the data such that meeting the goal is expressed as a 1, and failing to meet the goal is expressed as a -1. The following formula (in cell B18) transforms the original data:

```
=IF(B6>$C$2,1,-1)
```

	A	B	C	D	E	F	G	H
4				Pages Read				
5	Student	Jan	Feb	Mar	Apr	May	Jun	Sparklines
6	Ann	450	412	632	663	702	512	
7	Bob	309	215	194	189	678	256	
8	Chuck	608	783	765	832	483	763	
9	Dave	409	415	522	598	421	433	
10	Ellen	790	893	577	802	874	763	
11	Frank	211	59	0	0	185	230	
12	Giselle	785	764	701	784	214	185	
13	Henry	350	367	560	583	784	663	
14								
15								
16				Pages Read (Did or Did Not Meet Goal)				
17	Student	Jan	Feb	Mar	Apr	May	Jun	Sparklines
18	Ann	-1	-1	1	1	1	1	
19	Bob	-1	-1	-1	-1	1	-1	
20	Chuck	1	1	1	1	-1	1	
21	Dave	-1	-1	1	1	-1	-1	
22	Ellen	1	1	1	1	1	1	
23	Frank	-1	-1	-1	-1	-1	-1	
24	Giselle	1	1	1	1	-1	-1	
25	Henry	-1	-1	1	1	1	1	

Figure 4-12: Using Win/ Loss sparklines to display goal status.

This formula was copied to the other cells in B18:G25 range.

Using the transformed data, Win/Loss sparklines are used to visualize the results. This approach is better than the original, but it doesn't convey any magnitude differences. For example, you cannot tell whether the student missed the goal by 1 page or by 500 pages.

Figure 4-13 shows a better approach. Here, the original data is transformed by subtracting the goal from the pages read. The formula in cell B30 is:

```
=B6-C$2
```

	A	B	C	D	E	F	G	H
1	Pages Read							
2	Monthly Goal:		500					
3								
28				Pages Read (Relative to Goal)				
29	Student	Jan	Feb	Mar	Apr	May	Jun	Sparklines
30	Ann	-50	-88	132	163	202	12	
31	Bob	-191	-285	-306	-311	178	-244	
32	Chuck	108	283	265	332	-17	263	
33	Dave	-91	-85	22	98	-79	-67	
34	Ellen	290	393	77	302	374	263	
35	Frank	-289	-441	-500	-500	-315	-270	
36	Giselle	285	264	201	284	-286	-315	
37	Henry	-150	-133	60	83	284	163	

Figure 4-13: The axis in the sparklines represents the goal.

This formula was copied to the other cells in the B30:G37 range, and a group of Line sparklines display the resulting values. This group has the Show Axis setting enabled, and also uses Negative Point markers so the negative values (failure to meet the goal) clearly stand out.

Specifying a date axis

By default, data displayed in a sparkline is assumed to be at equal intervals. For example, a sparkline might display a daily account balance, sales by month, or profits by year. But what if the data aren't at equal intervals?

Figure 4-14 shows data, by date, along with a sparklines graphic created from column B. Notice that some dates are missing, but the sparkline shows the columns as if the values were spaced at equal intervals.

	A	B	C	D	E
1	Date	Amount			
2	1/1/2010	154			
3	1/2/2010	201			
4	1/3/2010	245			
5	1/4/2010	176			
6	1/11/2010	267			
7	1/12/2010	289			
8	1/13/2010	331			
9	1/14/2010	365			
10	1/18/2010	298			
11	1/19/2010	424			
12					

Figure 4-14: The sparkline displays the values as if they are at equal time intervals.

To better depict this type of time-based data, the solution is to specify a date axis. Select the sparkline and choose Sparkline Tools⇨Design⇨Group⇨Axis⇨Date Axis Type.

Excel displays a dialog box asking for the range that contains the corresponding dates. In this example, specify range A2:A11.

Click OK, and the sparkline displays gaps for the missing dates, as shown in Figure 4-15.

◢	A	B	C	D	E
1	**Date**	**Amount**			
2	1/1/2010	154			
3	1/2/2010	201			
4	1/3/2010	245			
5	1/4/2010	176			
6	1/11/2010	267			
7	1/12/2010	289			
8	1/13/2010	331			
9	1/14/2010	365			
10	1/18/2010	298			
11	1/19/2010	424			
12					

Figure 4-15: After specifying a date axis, the sparkline shows the values accurately.

Autoupdating sparkline ranges

If a sparkline uses data in a normal range of cells, adding new data to the beginning or end of the range does not force the sparkline to use the new data. You need to use the Edit Sparklines dialog box to update the data range (Sparkline Tools⇨Design⇨Sparkline⇨Edit Data).

However, if the sparkline data is in a column within a table object (created using Insert⇨Tables⇨Table as described in Chapter 2), then the sparkline uses new data that's added to the end of the table without requiring an update.

Figure 4-16 shows an example. The sparkline was created using the data in the Rate column of the table. When you add the new rate for September, the sparkline automatically updates its data range.

◢	A	B	C	D	E
1	**End of month interest rates**				
2					
3		Month ▾	Rate ▾		
4		Jan	5.20%		
5		Feb	5.02%		
6		Mar	4.97%		
7		Apr	4.99%		
8		May	4.89%		
9		Jun	4.72%		
10		Jul	4.68%		
11		Aug	4.61%		
12					

Figure 4-16: Creating a sparkline from data in a table.

Chapter 5

Formatting Your Way to Visualizations

Visualization is the presentation of abstract concepts or data in visual terms through some sort of graphical imagery. A traffic light, for example, is a visualization of the abstract concepts of stop and go.

In the business world, visualizations help us communication and process the meaning of data faster than simple tables of numbers. Excel offers business analysts a wide array of features that can be used to add visualizations to dashboards and reports.

In this chapter, you explore some of the formatting techniques you can leverage to add layers of visualizations that can turn your data into meaningful views.

Enhancing Reports with Conditional Formatting

Conditional formatting is the term given to Excel's capability to dynamically change the formatting of a value, cell, or range of cells based on a set of conditions you define. Conditional formatting adds a level of visualization that allows you to look at your Excel reports and make split-second determinations on which values are "good" and which are "bad," simply based on formatting.

In this section, you are introduced to the world of conditional formatting, learning how to leverage this functionality to enhance your reports and dashboards.

Applying basic conditional formatting

Thanks to the many pre-defined scenarios offered with Excel 2013, you can apply some basic conditional formatting with a few clicks of the mouse. To get a first taste of what you can do, click the Conditional Formatting button found on the Home tab of the Ribbon, as shown in Figure 5-1.

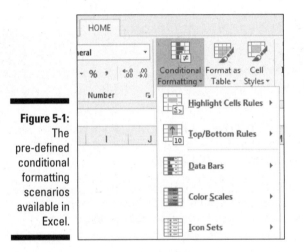

Figure 5-1:
The pre-defined conditional formatting scenarios available in Excel.

As you can see, there are five categories of pre-defined scenarios: Highlight Cells Rules, Top/Bottom Rules, Data Bars, Color Scales, and Icon Sets.

Take a moment to review what each category of pre-defined scenarios allows you to do.

Using the Highlight Cells Rules

The formatting scenarios under the Highlight Cells Rules category, shown in Figure 5-2, allow you to highlight those cells whose values meet a specific condition.

The thing to remember about these scenarios is that they work very much like an IF ... THEN ... ELSE statement. That is to say, if the condition is met, the cell is formatted and if the condition is not met, the cell remains untouched.

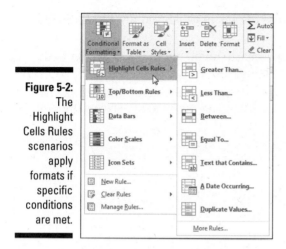

Figure 5-2:
The
Highlight
Cells Rules
scenarios
apply
formats if
specific
conditions
are met.

The scenarios under the Highlight Cells Rules category are pretty self-explanatory. Here is a breakdown of each scenario:

✓ **Greater Than:** This scenario allows you to conditionally format a cell whose value is greater than a specified amount. For instance, you can tell Excel to format those cells that contain a value greater than 50.

✓ **Less Than:** This scenario allows you to conditionally format a cell whose value is less than a specified amount. For instance, you can tell Excel to format those cells that contain a value less than 100.

✓ **Between:** This scenario allows you to conditionally format a cell whose value is between two given amounts. For example, you can tell Excel to format those cells that contain a value between 50 and 100.

✓ **Equal To:** This scenario allows you to conditionally format a cell whose value is equal to a given amount. For example, you can tell Excel to format those cells that contain a value that is exactly 50.

✓ **Text That Contains:** This scenario allows you to conditionally format a cell whose contents contain any form of a given text you specify as a criterion. For example, you can tell Excel to format those cells that contain the text "North."

✓ **A Date Occurring:** This scenario allows you to conditionally format a cell whose contents contain a date occurring in a specified period relative to today's date. For example, Yesterday, Last Week, Last Month, Next Month, Next Week, and so on.

✓ **Duplicate Values:** This scenario allows you to conditionally format both duplicate values and unique values in a given range of cells. This rule was designed more for data cleanup than dashboarding, enabling you to quickly identify either duplicates or unique values in your dataset.

Take a moment to go through an example of how to apply one of these scenarios. In this simple example, you highlight all values greater than a certain amount.

1. **Start by selecting the range of cells to which you need to apply the conditional formatting.**

2. **Choose the Greater Than scenario found under the Highlight Cells Rules category shown in Figure 5-2.**

   This opens the dialog box shown in Figure 5-3. In this dialog box, the idea is to define a value that will trigger the conditional formatting.

Figure 5-3:
Each scenario has its own dialog box you can use to define the trigger values and the format for each rule.

Greater Than		
Format cells that are GREATER THAN:		
400	with	Light Red Fill with Dark Red Text
	OK	Cancel

3. **Either type the value (400 in this example) or reference a cell that contains the trigger value. Also in this dialog box, use the drop-down box to specify the format you want applied.**

4. **Click the OK button.**

   Immediately, Excel applies the formatting rule to the selected cells; see Figure 5-4.

	Greater Than 400
Jan	100
Feb	-100
Mar	200
Apr	250
May	-50
Jun	350
Jul	400
Aug	450
Sep	500
Oct	550
Nov	600
Dec	650

Figure 5-4:
Cells greater than 400 are formatted.

The benefit of a conditional formatting rule is that Excel automatically reevaluates the rule each time a cell is changed (provided that cell has a conditional formatting rule applied to it). For instance, if I were to change any of the low values to 450, the formatting for that value would automatically change because all of the cells in the dataset have the formatting applied to it.

Applying Top/Bottom Rules

The formatting scenarios under the Top/Bottom Rules category, shown in Figure 5-5, allow you to highlight those cells whose values meet a given threshold.

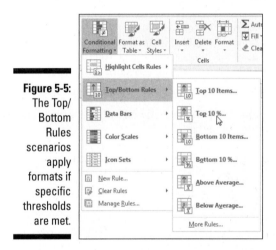

Figure 5-5: The Top/Bottom Rules scenarios apply formats if specific thresholds are met.

Like the Highlight Cells Rules, these scenarios work like IF ... THEN ... ELSE statements — meaning, if the condition is met, the cell is formatted, and if the condition is not met, the cell remains untouched.

Here is a breakdown of each scenario under the Top/Bottom Rules category:

- ✔ **Top 10 Items:** Although the name doesn't suggest it, this scenario allows you to specify any number of cells to highlight based on individual cell values (not just ten). For example, you can highlight the top five cells whose values are among the five largest numbers of all the cells selected.

- ✔ **Top 10 %:** This scenario is similar to the Top 10 Items scenario: Only the selected cells are evaluated on a percentage basis. Again, don't let the name fool you; the percent selection does not have to be ten. For instance, you can highlight the cells whose values make up the top 20% of the total values of all the selected cells.

- ✔ **Bottom 10 Items:** This scenario allows you to specify the number of cells to highlight based on the lowest individual cell values. Again, don't let the name fool you: You can specify any number of cells to highlight — not just ten. For example, you can highlight the bottom 15 cells whose values are within the 15 smallest numbers among all the cells selected.

✔ **Bottom 10 %:** This scenario is similar to the Bottom 10 Items scenario. However, in this scenario, only the selected cells are evaluated on a percentage basis. For instance, you can highlight the cells whose values make up the bottom 15% of the total values of all the selected cells.

✔ **Above Average:** This scenario allows you to conditionally format each cell whose value is above the average of all cells selected.

✔ **Below Average:** Allows you to conditionally format each cell whose value is below the average of all cells selected.

To avoid overlapping different conditional formatting scenarios, you may want to clear any conditional formatting you've previously applied before applying a new scenario. To clear the conditional formatting for a given range of cells, select the cells and select Conditional Formatting from the Home tab of the Ribbon. Here you find the Clear Rules selection. Click Clear Rules and select whether you want to clear conditional formatting for the entire sheet or only the selected workbook.

In the following example, you conditionally format all cells whose values are within the top 40% of the total values of all cells.

1. **Start by selecting the range of cells to which you need to apply the conditional formatting.**

2. **Choose the Top 10 % scenario found under the Top/Bottom Rules category; refer to Figure 5-5.**

   This opens the Top 10% dialog box shown in Figure 5-6. The idea here is to define the threshold that that will trigger the conditional formatting.

Figure 5-6: Each scenario has its own dialog box you can use to define the trigger values and the format for each scenario.

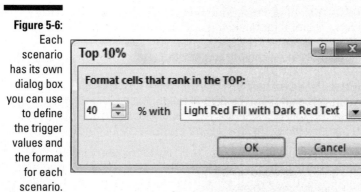

3. **In this example, enter 40. Also in this dialog box, use the drop-down box to specify the format you want applied.**

4. **Click OK. Immediately, Excel applies the formatting scenario to the selected cells. See Figure 5-7.**

Figure 5-7:
With con-
ditional for-
matting, you
can easily
see that
September
through
December
makes up
40% of the
total value
in this
dataset.

	Within Top 40%
Jan	100
Feb	-100
Mar	200
Apr	250
May	-50
Jun	350
Jul	400
Aug	450
Sep	500
Oct	550
Nov	600
Dec	650

Creating Data Bars

Data Bars fill each cell you are formatting with mini-bars in varying length, indicating the value in each cell relative to other formatted cells. Excel essentially takes the largest and smallest values in the selected range and calculates the length for each bar. To apply Data Bars to a range, do the following:

1. **Select the target range of cells to which you need to apply the conditional formatting.**

2. **Choose Data Bars from the Conditional Formatting menu on the Home tab, as demonstrated in Figure 5-8.**

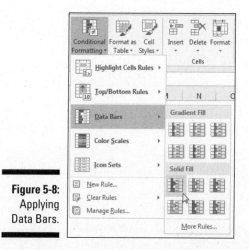

Figure 5-8:
Applying
Data Bars.

As you can see in Figure 5-9, the result is essentially a mini-chart within the cells you selected. Also note that by default the Data Bars scenario accounts for negative numbers nicely by changing the direction of the bar and inverting the color to red.

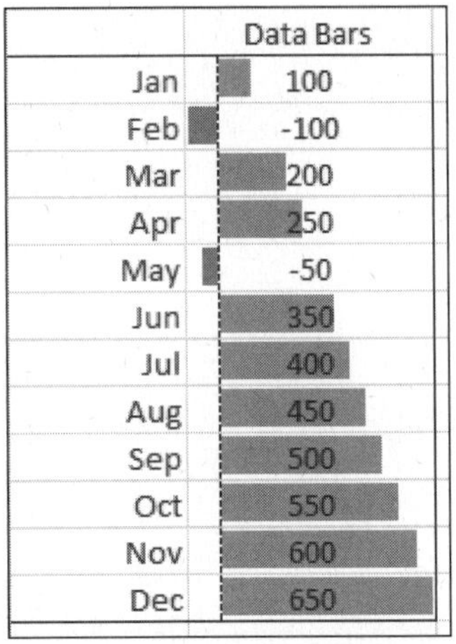

	Data Bars	
Jan		100
Feb		-100
Mar		200
Apr		250
May		-50
Jun		350
Jul		400
Aug		450
Sep		500
Oct		550
Nov		600
Dec		650

Figure 5-9: Conditional formatting with Data Bars.

Applying Color Scales

Color Scales fill each cell you are formatting with a color varying in scale based on the value in each cell relative to other formatted cells. Excel essentially takes the largest and smallest values in the selected range and determines the color for each cell. To apply Color Scales to a range, do the following:

1. **Select the target range of cells to which you need to apply the conditional formatting.**

2. **Choose Color Scales from the Conditional Formatting menu on the Home tab. See Figure 5-10.**

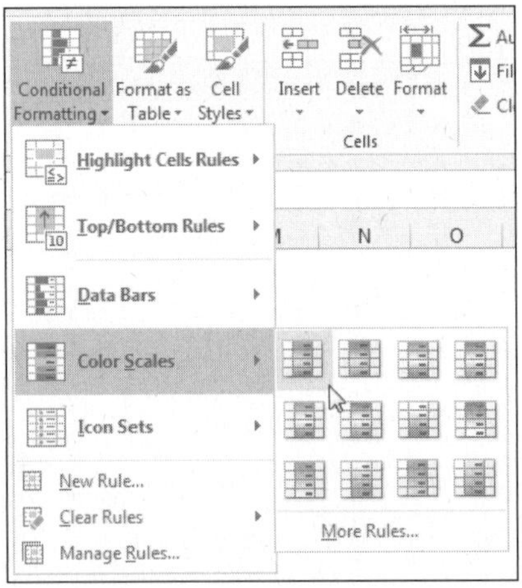

Figure 5-10: Applying Color Scales.

As you can see in Figure 5-11, the result is a kind of heat-map within the cells you selected.

Color Scales	
Jan	100
Feb	-100
Mar	200
Apr	250
May	-50
Jun	350
Jul	400
Aug	450
Sep	500
Oct	550
Nov	600
Dec	650

Figure 5-11:
Conditional
formatting
with Color
Scales.

Using Icon Sets

Icon Sets are sets of symbols that are inserted in each cell you are formatting. Excel determines which symbol to use based on the value in each cell relative to other formatted cells. To apply an Icon Set to a range, do the following:

1. **Select the target range of cells to which you need to apply the conditional formatting.**

2. **Choose Icon Sets from the Conditional Formatting menu on the Home tab. As you can see in Figure 5-12, you can choose from a menu of Icon Sets varying in shape and color.**

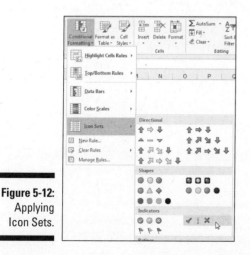

Figure 5-12:
Applying
Icon Sets.

Figure 5-13 illustrates how each cell is formatted with a symbol indicating each cell's value based on the other cells.

Icon Sets		
Jan	✖	100
Feb	✖	-100
Mar	!	200
Apr	!	250
May	✖	-50
Jun	!	350
Jul	!	400
Aug	✔	450
Sep	✔	500
Oct	✔	550
Nov	✔	600
Dec	✔	650

Figure 5-13:
Conditional
formatting
with Icon
Sets.

Adding your own formatting rules manually

You don't have to use one of the pre-defined scenarios offered by Excel. Excel gives you the flexibility to create your own formatting rules manually. Creating your own formatting rules helps you better control how cells are formatted and allows you to do things you wouldn't be able to do with the pre-defined scenarios.

For example, a useful conditional formatting rule is to tag all above-average values with a Check icon and all below-average values with an X icon. Figure 5-14 demonstrates this.

Figure 5-14:
With a
custom for-
matting rule,
you can tag
the above-
average
values with
a check and
the below
average
values with
an X.

	A	B	C
1	REGION	MARKET	Sales
2	North	Great Lakes	✖ 70,261
3	North	New England	✔ 217,858
4	North	New York North	✖ 157,774
5	North	New York South	✖ 53,670
6	North	North Carolina	✖ 124,600
7	North	Ohio	✖ 100,512
8	North	Shenandoah Valley	✖ 149,742
9	South	Florida	✖ 111,606
10	South	Gulf Coast	✔ 253,703
11	South	Illinois	✖ 129,148
12	South	Indiana	✖ 152,471
13	South	Kentucky	✔ 224,524
14	South	South Carolina	✔ 249,535
15	South	Tennessee	✔ 307,490
16	South	Texas	✔ 180,167

Although it's true that the Above Average and Below Average scenarios built into Excel allow you to format cell and font attributes, they don't enable the use of Icon Sets. You can imagine why Icon Sets would be better on a dashboard than just color variances. Icons and shapes do a much better job at conveying your message, especially when your dashboard is printed in black and white.

To get started in creating your first custom formatting rule, open the Chapter 5 Samples file found among the sample files on this book's companion website. After the file is open, go to the Create Rule by Hand tab, then follow these steps:

1. **Select the target range of cells to which you need to apply the conditional formatting and select New Rule as demonstrated in Figure 5-15.**

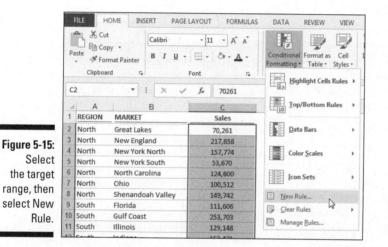

Figure 5-15:
Select the target range, then select New Rule.

This opens the New Formatting Rule dialog box shown in Figure 5-16. As you look through the rule types at the top of the dialog box, you may recognize some of them from the pre-defined scenario choices discussed earlier in this chapter. The types are as follows:

- *Format All Cells Based on Their Values:* This selection measures the values in the selected range against each other. This selection is handy for finding general anomalies in your dataset.

- *Format Only Cells That Contain:* This selection applies conditional formatting to those cells that meet specific criteria you define. This selection is perfect for comparing values against a defined benchmark.

- *Format Only Top or Bottom Ranked Values:* This selection applies conditional formatting to those cells that are ranked in the top or bottom Nth number or percent of all the values in the range.

- *Format Only Values That Are Above or Below Average:* This applies conditional formatting to those values that are mathematically above or below the average of all values in the selected range.

- *Use a Formula to Determine Which Cells to Format:* This selection evaluates values based on a formula you specify. If a particular value evaluates to true, then the conditional formatting is applied to that cell. This selection is typically used when applying conditions based on the results of an advanced formula or mathematical operation.

Data Bars, Color Scales, and Icon Sets can be used only with the Format All Cells Based on Their Values rule type.

2. **Ensure that the Format All Cells Based on Their Values rule type is selected, then use the Format Style drop-down box to switch to Icon Sets.**

3. **Click the Icon Style drop-down box to select your desired Icon Set.**

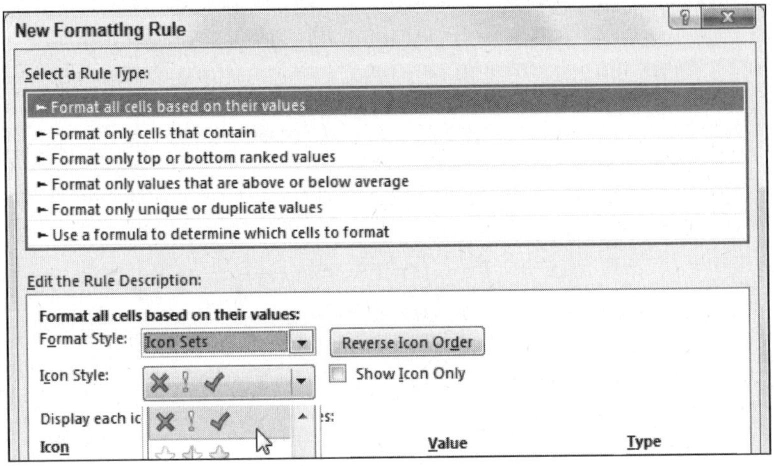

Figure 5-16:
Select the
Format All
Cells Based
on Their
Values rule,
then use
the Format
Style drop-
down box
to switch to
Icon Sets.

> **New Formatting Rule**
>
> Select a Rule Type:
> ► Format all cells based on their values
> ► Format only cells that contain
> ► Format only top or bottom ranked values
> ► Format only values that are above or below average
> ► Format only unique or duplicate values
> ► Use a formula to determine which cells to format
>
> Edit the Rule Description:
>
> Format all cells based on their values:
> Format Style: Icon Sets ▼   Reverse Icon Order
> Icon Style: ✖ ❗ ✔ ▼   ☐ Show Icon Only
> Display each ic ✖ ❗ ✔ ▲ es:
> Icon   Value   Type

4. **Change both Type drop-down boxes to Formula.**

5. **In each Value box, enter** =Average($C$2:$C$22).

This tells Excel that the value in each cell must be greater than the average of the entire dataset in order to get the Check icon.

At this point, your dialog box looks similar to the one in Figure 5-17.

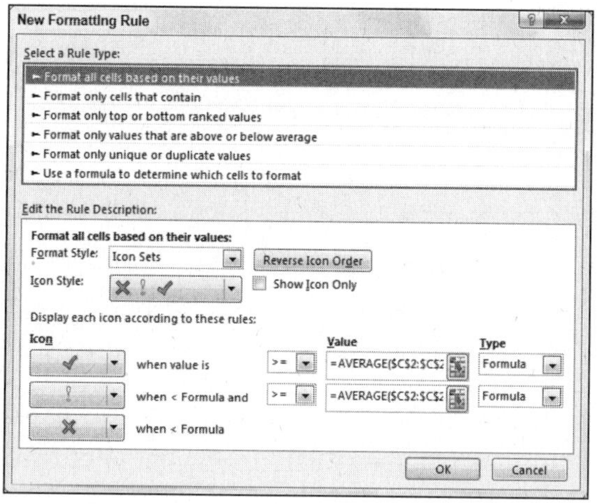

Figure 5-17:
Change
the Type
drop-down
boxes to
Formula and
enter the
appropriate
formulas in
the Value
boxes.

6. **Click OK to apply your conditional formatting.**

It's worth taking some time to understand how this conditional formatting rule works. Excel assesses every cell in your target range to see if its contents match the logic in each Value box in order (top box first). If a cell contains a number or text that evaluates true to the first Value box, the first icon is applied and Excel moves on to the next cell in your range. If not, Excel continues down each Value box until one of them evaluates to true. If the cell being assessed does not fit any of the logic placed in the Value boxes, Excel automatically tags that cell with the last icon.

In this example, you want your cells to get a Check icon only if the value of that cell is greater than (or equal to) the average of the total values. Otherwise, you want Excel to skip right to the X icon and apply the X.

Show only one icon

In many cases, you may not need to show all icons when applying the Icon Set. In fact, showing too many icons at one time may serve only to obstruct the data you're trying to convey on your dashboard.

In the earlier example, you apply a Check icon to values above the average for the range, and an X icon to all below-average values; see Figure 5-18. However, in the real world, you often need only to bring attention to the below-average values. This way, your eyes aren't inundated with superfluous icons.

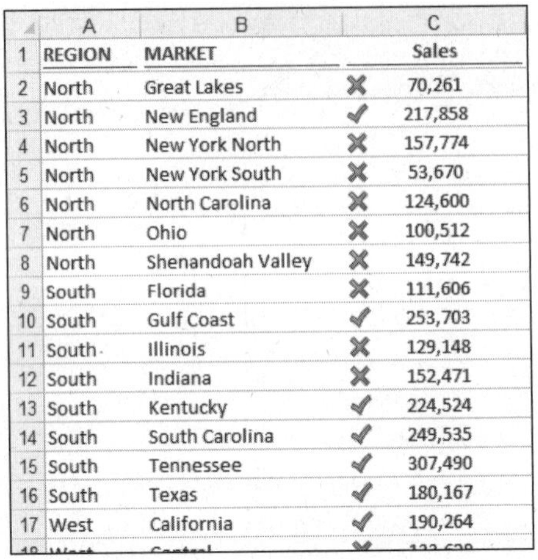

	A	B	C
1	REGION	MARKET	Sales
2	North	Great Lakes	✗ 70,261
3	North	New England	✓ 217,858
4	North	New York North	✗ 157,774
5	North	New York South	✗ 53,670
6	North	North Carolina	✗ 124,600
7	North	Ohio	✗ 100,512
8	North	Shenandoah Valley	✗ 149,742
9	South	Florida	✗ 111,606
10	South	Gulf Coast	✓ 253,703
11	South	Illinois	✗ 129,148
12	South	Indiana	✗ 152,471
13	South	Kentucky	✓ 224,524
14	South	South Carolina	✓ 249,535
15	South	Tennessee	✓ 307,490
16	South	Texas	✓ 180,167
17	West	California	✓ 190,264

Figure 5-18:
Too many icons can hide the items you want to draw attention to.

Excel provides a clever mechanism to allow you to stop evaluating and formatting values if a condition is true.

In this example, you want to remove the Check icons. The cells that contain those icons all have values above the average for the range. Therefore, you first need to add a condition for all cells whose values are above average. To do so, follow these steps:

1. **Select the target range of cells, then go to the Home tab and select Conditional Formatting➪Manage Rules.**

   This opens the Conditional Formatting Rules Manager dialog box shown in Figure 5-19.

2. **Click the New Rule button to start a new rule.**

   The New Formatting Rule dialog box appears.

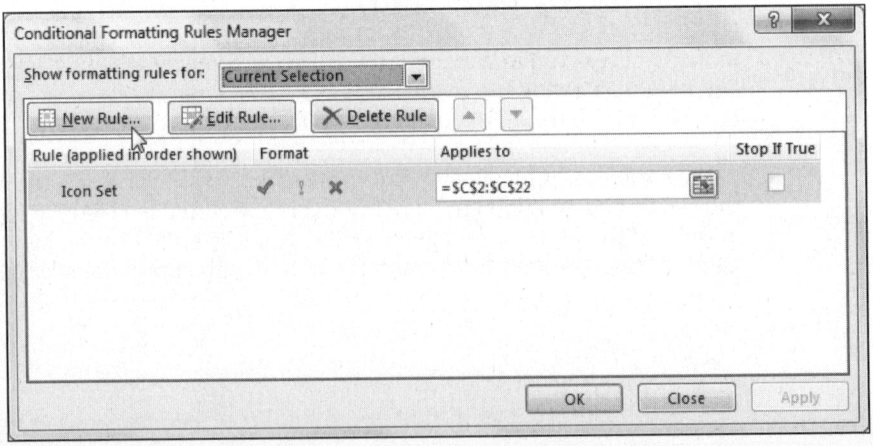

Figure 5-19:
Open the Conditional Formatting Rules Manager and click New Rule.

3. **Click the Format Only Cells That Contain rule type. Then configure the rule so that the format applies only to cell values greater than the average; see Figure 5-20.**

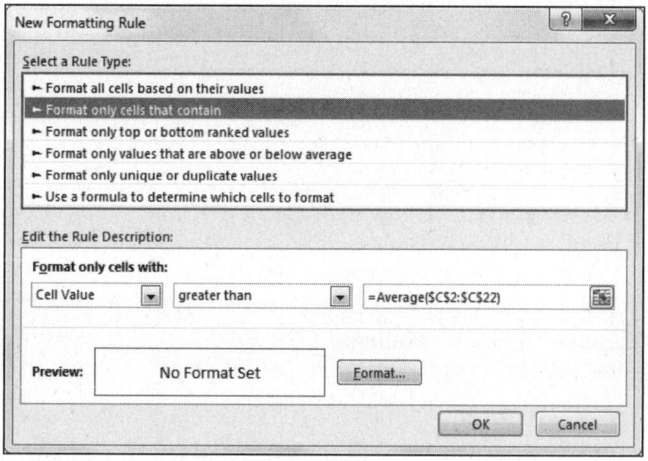

Figure 5-20:
This new rule is meant to apply to any cell value that you don't want format-ted — in this case, any value that's greater than the aver-age of your range.

4. **Click OK without changing any of the formatting options.**

5. **Back in the Conditional Formatting Rules Manager, select the Stop If True check box, as demonstrated in Figure 5-21.**

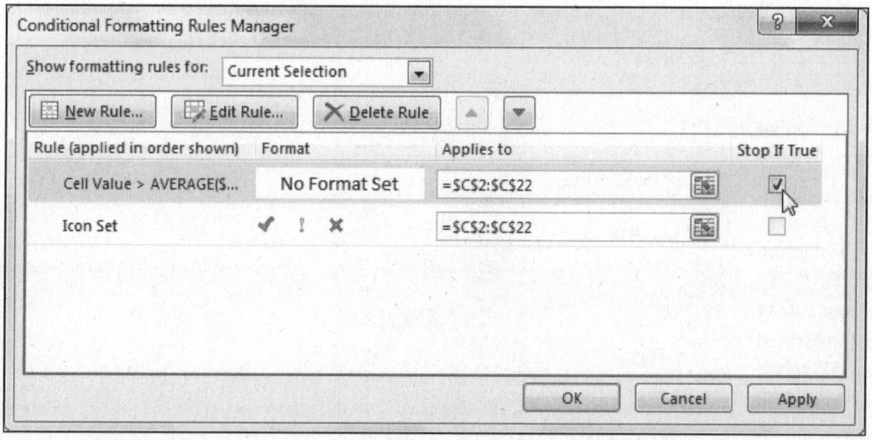

Figure 5-21:
Click Stop If True to tell Excel to stop evaluating those cells that meet the first condition.

6. Click OK to apply your changes.

As you can see in Figure 5-22, only the X icons are now shown. Again, this allows your audience to focus on the exceptions rather than determining which icons are good and bad.

	A	B		C
1	REGION	MARKET		Sales
2	North	Great Lakes	✗	70,261
3	North	New England		217,858
4	North	New York North	✗	157,774
5	North	New York South	✗	53,670
6	North	North Carolina	✗	124,600
7	North	Ohio	✗	100,512
8	North	Shenandoah Valley	✗	149,742
9	South	Florida	✗	111,606
10	South	Gulf Coast		253,703
11	South	Illinois	✗	129,148
12	South	Indiana	✗	152,471
13	South	Kentucky		224,524
14	South	South Carolina		249,535
15	South	Tennessee		307,490
16	South	Texas		180,167
17	West	California		190,264

Figure 5-22: This table is now formatted to show only one icon.

Show Data Bars and icons outside of cells

Although Data Bars and Icon Sets give you a snazzy way of adding visualizations to your dashboards, you don't have a lot of say in where they appear within your cell. Take a look at Figure 5-23 to see what I mean.

	A	B
1	MARKET	Sales
2	Great Lakes	70,261
3	New England	217,858
4	New York North	157,774
5	New York South	53,670
6	Ohio	100,512
7	Shenandoah Valley	149,742
8	South Carolina	249,535
9	Florida	111,606
10	Gulf Coast	253,703
11	Illinois	129,148
12	Indiana	152,471
13	Kentucky	224,524
14	North Carolina	124,600
15	Tennessee	307,490

Figure 5-23: Showing Data Bars inside the same cell as your values can make it difficult to analyze the data.

By default, the Data Bars are placed directly inside each cell, which in this case almost obfuscates the data. From a dashboarding perspective, this is less than ideal for two reasons. First, the numbers can get lost in the colors of the Data Bars, making them difficult to read — especially when printed in black-and-white. Second, it's difficult to see the ends of each bar.

The solution to this problem is to show the Data Bars *outside* the cell that contains the value. Here's how:

1. **To the right of each cell, enter a formula that references the cell that contains your data value. For example, if your data is in B2, go to cell C2 and enter** =B2.

2. **Apply the Data Bar conditional formatting to the formulas you just created.**

3. **Select the formatted range of cells and select Manage Rules under the Conditional Formatting button on the Home tab of the Ribbon.**

4. **In the dialog box that opens, click the Edit Rule button.**

5. **Select the Show Bar Only option, as demonstrated in Figure 5-24.**

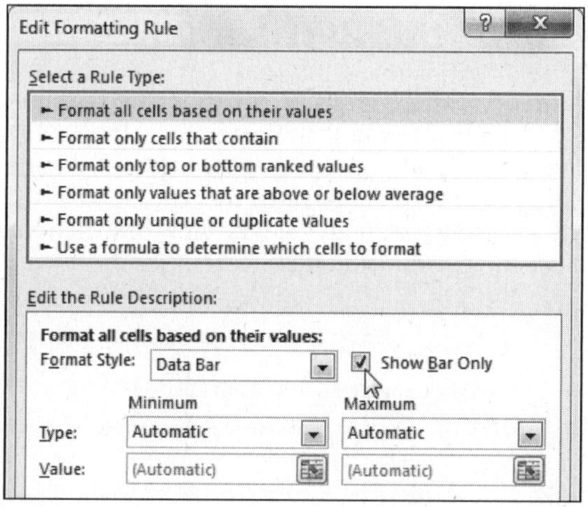

Figure 5-24:
Edit the
formatting
rule to show
only the
Data Bars,
not the data.

6. **Click OK to apply your change.**

The reward for your efforts is a cleaner view that's much better suited for reporting in a dashboard environment. Figure 5-25 illustrates the improvement gained with this technique.

	A	B	C
1	MARKET	Sales	
2	Great Lakes	70,261	
3	New England	217,858	
4	New York North	157,774	
5	New York South	53,670	
6	Ohio	100,512	
7	Shenandoah Valley	149,742	
8	South Carolina	249,535	
9	Florida	111,606	
10	Gulf Coast	253,703	
11	Illinois	129,148	
12	Indiana	152,471	
13	Kentucky	224,524	
14	North Carolina	124,600	
15	Tennessee	307,490	

Figure 5-25: Data Bars cleanly placed next to the data values.

Using the same technique, you can separate Icon Sets from the data — allowing you to position the icons where they best suit your dashboard.

Representing trends with Icon Sets

In a dashboard environment, there may not always be enough space available to add a chart that shows trending. In these cases, Icon Sets are an ideal replacement, enabling you to visually represent the overall trending without taking up a lot of space. Figure 5-26 illustrates this with a table that provides a nice visual element, allowing for an at-a-glance view of which markets are up, down, and flat over the previous month.

	A	B	C	D	E
1	REGION	MARKET	Previous Month	Current Month	Variance
2	North	Great Lakes	70,261	72,505	⬆ 3.2%
3	North	New England	217,858	283,324	⬆ 30.0%
4	North	New York North	157,774	148,790	⬇ -5.7%
5	North	New York South	53,670	68,009	⬆ 26.7%
6	North	Ohio	100,512	98,308	➡ -2.2%
7	North	Shenandoah Valley	149,742	200,076	⬆ 33.6%
8	South	South Carolina	249,535	229,473	⬇ -8.0%
9	South	Florida	111,606	136,104	⬆ 22.0%
10	South	Gulf Coast	253,703	245,881	⬇ -3.1%
11	South	Illinois	129,148	131,538	➡ 1.9%
12	South	Indiana	152,471	151,699	➡ -0.5%
13	South	Kentucky	224,524	225,461	➡ 0.4%
14	North	North Carolina	124,600	130,791	⬆ 5.0%
15	South	Tennessee	307,490	268,010	⬇ -12.8%

Figure 5-26: Conditional Formatting Icon Sets enable trending visualizations.

You may want to do the same type of thing with your reports. The key is to create a formula that gives you a variance or trending of some sort.

To achieve this type of view, follow these steps:

1. **Select the target range of cells to which you need to apply the conditional formatting. In this case, the target range will be the cells that hold your variance formulas.**

2. **Choose Icon Sets from the Conditional Formatting menu on the Home tab, and then choose the most appropriate icons for your situation. For this example, choose the set with three arrows shown in Figure 5-27.**

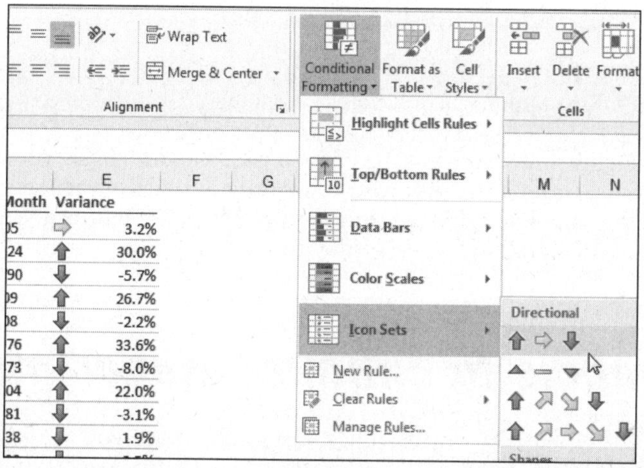

Figure 5-27: The up arrow indicates an upward trend; the down arrow indicates a downward trend; and the right arrow indicates a flat trend.

In most cases, you'll want to adjust the thresholds that define what up, down, and flat mean. Imagine that you need any variance above 3% to be tagged with an up arrow, any variance below -3% to be tagged with a down arrow, and all others to show flat.

3. **Select the target range of cells and select Manage Rules under the Conditional Formatting button on the Home tab of the Ribbon.**

4. **In the dialog box that opens, click the Edit Rule button.**

5. **Adjust the properties as shown in Figure 5-28.**

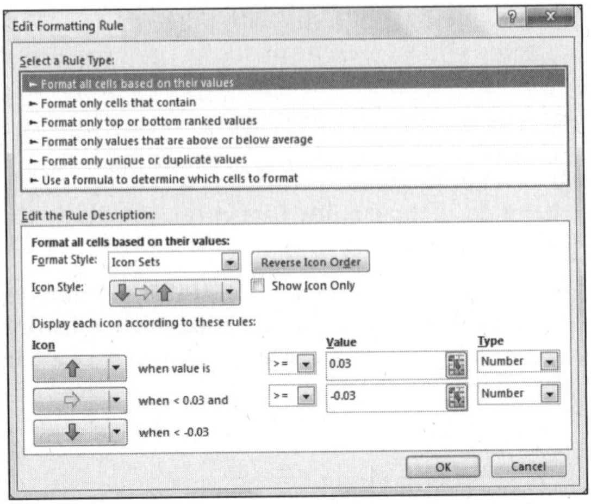

Figure 5-28:
You can
adjust the
thresholds
that define
what up,
down, and
flat mean.

6. **Click OK to apply your change.**

Notice in Figure 5-28 that the Type property for the formatting rule is set to Number even though the data you're working with (the variances) are percentages. You'll find that working with the Number setting gives you more control and predictability when setting thresholds.

Using Symbols to Enhance Reporting

Symbols are essentially tiny graphics, not unlike those you see when you use the Wingdings, Webdings, or other fancy fonts. However, symbols are not really fonts. They're Unicode characters. *Unicode characters* are a set of industry standard text elements designed to provide a reliable character-set that remains viable on any platform regardless of international font differences.

One example of a commonly used symbol is the copyright symbol (©). This symbol is a Unicode character. You can use this symbol on a Chinese, Turkish, French, and American PC and it will reliably be available with no international differences.

In terms of Excel presentations, Unicode characters (or symbols) can be used in places where conditional formatting cannot. For instance, in the chart labels that you see in Figure 5-29, the x-axis shows some trending arrows that allow for an extra layer of analysis. This couldn't be done with conditional formatting.

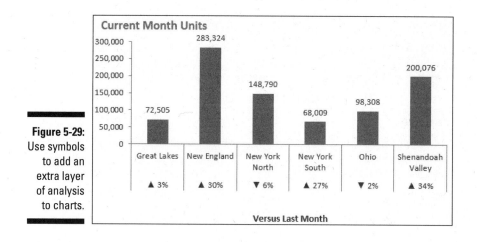

Figure 5-29:
Use symbols
to add an
extra layer
of analysis
to charts.

Let's take some time to review the steps that led to the chart in Figure 5-29.

Start with the data shown in Figure 5-30. Note that you have a designated cell — C1 in this case — to hold any symbols you're going to use. This cell isn't really all that important. It's just a holding cell for the symbols you'll insert. Now, follow these steps:

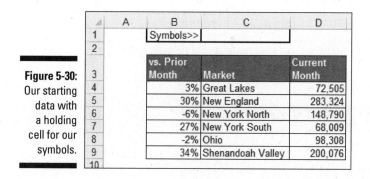

Figure 5-30:
Our starting
data with
a holding
cell for our
symbols.

1. **Click in C1 and then select the Symbol command on the Insert tab.**

   The Symbol dialog box shown in Figure 5-31 opens.

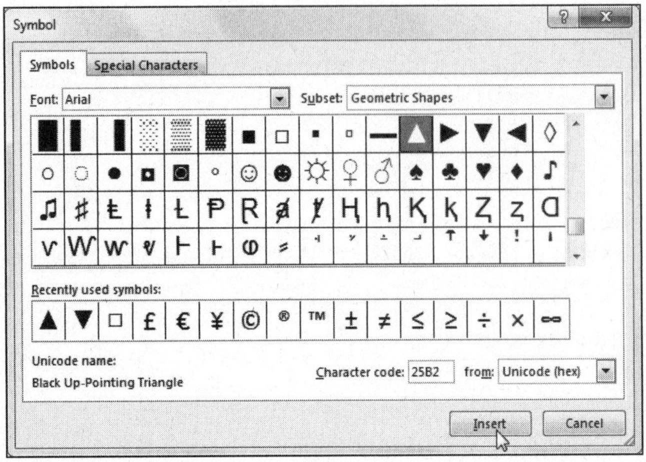

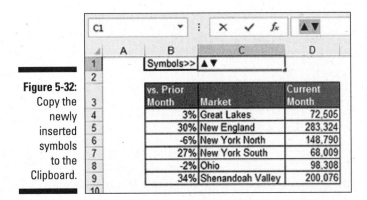

Figure 5-31:
Use the
Symbol
dialog box
to insert
the desired
symbols into
your holding
cell.

2. **Find and select your desired symbols by clicking the Insert button after each symbol. In this scenario, select the down-pointing triangle, and click Insert. Then click the up-pointing triangle and click Insert. Close the dialog box when you're done.**

   At this point, you have the up triangle and down triangle symbols in cell C1, as shown in Figure 5-32.

Figure 5-32:
Copy the
newly
inserted
symbols
to the
Clipboard.

3. **Click the C1 cell, go to the Formula bar, and copy the two symbols by highlighting them and pressing Ctrl+C on your keyboard.**

4. **Go to your data table, right-click the percentages, and then select Format Cells.**

5. **In the Format Cells dialog box, create a new custom format by pasting the up- and down-triangle symbols into the appropriate syntax parts; see Figure 5-33. In this case, any positive percentage will be preceded with the up-triangle symbol, and any negative percentage will be preceded with the down-triangle symbol.**

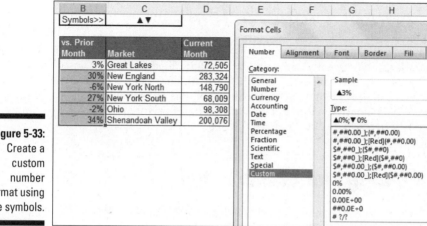

Figure 5-33:
Create a
custom
number
format using
the symbols.

Not familiar with custom number formatting? Chapter 3 covers the ins and outs of custom number formatting in detail.

6. Click OK.

The symbols are now part of your number formatting! Figure 5-34 illustrates what your percentages look like. Change any number from positive to negative (or vice versa) and Excel automatically applies the appropriate symbol.

	A	B	C	D
1		Symbols>>	▲▼	
2				
3		vs. Prior Month	Market	Current Month
4		▲3%	Great Lakes	72,505
5		▲30%	New England	283,324
6		▼ 6%	New York North	148,790
7		▲27%	New York South	68,009
8		▼ 2%	Ohio	98,308
9		▲34%	Shenandoah Valley	200,076

Figure 5-34:
Your
symbols are
now part of
your number
formatting.

Because charts automatically adopt number formatting, a chart created from this data will show the symbols as part of the labels. Simply use this data as the source for the chart.

This is just one way to use symbols in your reporting. With this basic technique, you can insert symbols to add visual appeal to tables, pivot tables, formulas, or any other object you can think of.

The Magical Camera Tool

Excel's Camera tool enables you to take a live picture of a range of cells that updates dynamically while the data in that range updates. If you've never heard of it, don't feel too bad. This nifty tool has been hidden away in the last few versions of Excel. Although Microsoft has chosen not to include this tool on the mainstream Ribbon, it's actually quite useful for those of us building dashboards and reports.

Finding the Camera tool

Before you can use the Camera tool, you have to find it and add it to your Quick Access toolbar.

 The Quick Access toolbar is a customizable toolbar in which you can store frequently used commands so that they're always accessible with just one click. You can add commands to the Quick Access toolbar by dragging them directly from the Ribbon or by going through the Customize menu.

Follow these steps to add the Camera tool to the Quick Access toolbar:

1. **Click the File button.**

2. **Open the Excel Options dialog box by clicking the Options button.**

3. **Click the Quick Access Toolbar button.**

4. **In the Choose Commands From drop-down list, select Commands Not in the Ribbon.**

5. **Scroll down the alphabetical list of commands shown in Figure 5-35 and find Camera; double-click it to add it to the Quick Access toolbar.**

Figure 5-35: Add the Camera tool to the Quick Access toolbar.

Excel Options

General	![] Customize the Quick Access Toolbar.
Formulas	
Proofing	Choose commands from: ⓘ
Save	Commands Not in the Ribbon
Language	
Advanced	
Customize Ribbon	
Quick Access Toolbar	
Add-Ins	
Trust Center	

Customize Quick Access Too

For all documents (default)

- Button (Form Control)
- Calculate Full
- Calculator
- Camera
- ✓ Check Box (ActiveX Control)
- ✓ Check Box (Form Control)
- Check for Updates
- Close All
- × Close Window
- Collapse the Ribbon

- Save
- Undo
- Redo
- New

Add >>

<< Remove

6. Click OK.

When you've taken these steps, you'll see the Camera tool in your Quick Access toolbar, as shown in Figure 5-36.

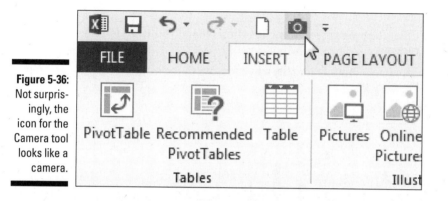

Figure 5-36: Not surprisingly, the icon for the Camera tool looks like a camera.

Using the Camera tool

To use the Camera tool, you simply highlight a range of cells to then capture everything in that range in a live picture. The cool thing about the Camera tool is that you're not limited to showing a single cell's value like you are with a linked text box. And because the picture is live, any updates made to the source range automatically changes the picture.

Take a moment to walk through this basic demonstration of the Camera tool. In Figure 5-37, you see some simple numbers and a chart based on those numbers. The goal here is to create a live picture of the range that holds both the numbers and the chart. Just follow these steps:

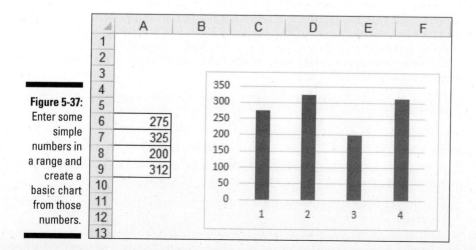

Figure 5-37: Enter some simple numbers in a range and create a basic chart from those numbers.

1. **Highlight the range that contains the information you want to capture. In this scenario, you select B3:F13 to capture the area with the chart.**

2. **Select the Camera tool icon in the Quick Access toolbar.**

   You add the Camera tool to the Quick Access toolbar in the preceding section.

3. **Click the worksheet in the location where you want to place the picture.**

   Excel immediately creates a live picture of the entire range, as shown in Figure 5-38.

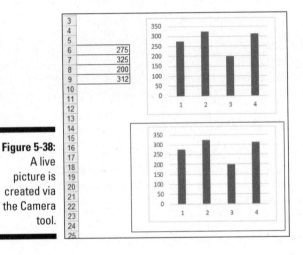

Figure 5-38:
A live picture is created via the Camera tool.

Changing any number in the original range automatically causes the picture to update.

By default, the picture that's created has a border around it. To remove the border, right-click the picture and select Format Picture. This opens the Format Picture dialog box. In the Colors and Lines tab, you see a Line Color drop-down list. Here you can select No Color, thereby removing the border. On a similar note, to get a picture without gridlines, simply remove the gridlines from the source range.

Enhancing a dashboard with the Camera tool

Here are a few ways to go beyond the basics and use the Camera tool to enhance your dashboards and reports:

✔ **Consolidating disparate ranges into one print area:** Sometimes a data model gets so complex that it's difficult to keep all the final data in one printable area. This often forces you to print multiple pages inconsistent in layout and size. Given that dashboards are most effective when contained in a compact area that can be printed in a page or two, complex data models prove to be problematic when it comes to layout and design.

You can use the Camera tool in these situations to create live pictures of various ranges that you can place on a single page. Figure 5-39 shows a workbook that contains data from various worksheets. The secret here is that these are nothing more than linked pictures created by the Camera tool.

As you can see, you can create and manage multiple analyses on different tabs and then bring together all your presentation pieces into a nicely formatted presentation layer.

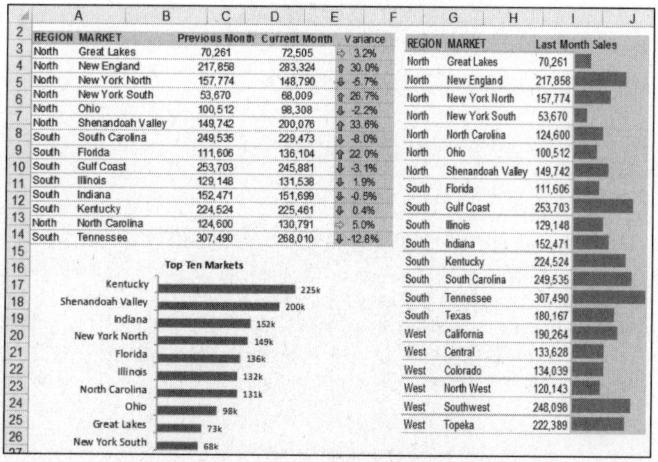

Figure 5-39: Use the Camera tool to get multiple source ranges into a compact area.

✔ **Rotating objects to save time:** Again, because the Camera tool outputs pictures, you can rotate the pictures in situations in which placing the copied range on its side can help save time. A great example is a chart. Certain charts are relatively easy to create in a vertical orientation but extremely difficult to create in a horizontal orientation.

The Camera tool to the rescue! When the live picture of the chart is created, all you have to do is change the alignment of the chart labels and then rotate the picture using the rotate handle to create a horizontal version.

✔ **Creating small charts:** When you create pictures with the Camera Tool, you can resize and move the pictures around freely. This gives you the freedom to test different layouts and chart sizes without the need to work around column widths, hidden rows, or other such nonsense.

Chapter 6

The Pivotal Pivot Table

I know what you're thinking. Am I supposed to be jumping right in with pivot tables? My answer is an emphatic yes!

In Chapter 2, I introduce the concept of reporting models that separate the data, analysis, and presentation layers. As you discover in this chapter, pivot tables lend themselves nicely to this concept. With pivot tables, you can build reporting models that are not only easy to set up, but also can be refreshed with a simple press of a button. This allows you to spend less time maintaining your dashboards and reports and more time doing other useful things. No utility in the whole of Excel allows you to achieve this efficient data model better than a pivot table.

Pivot tables have a reputation for being complicated, but if you're new to pivot tables, relax a bit. After going through this introduction, you'll be pleasantly surprised at how easy it is to create and use pivot tables. Later, you'll find some time-saving techniques to help create useful pivot-driven views for your dashboards and reports.

An Introduction to the Pivot Table

A *pivot table* is a robust tool that allows you to create an interactive view of your dataset, commonly referred to as a *pivot table report*. With a pivot table report, you can quickly and easily categorize your data into groups, summarize large amounts of data into meaningful analyses, and interactively perform a wide variety of calculations.

Pivot tables get their name from the way they allow you to drag and drop fields within the pivot table report to dynamically change (or *pivot*) perspective and give you an entirely new analysis using the same data source.

Think of a pivot table as an object you can point at your dataset. When you look at your dataset through a pivot table, you can see your data from different perspectives. The dataset itself doesn't change, and it's not connected to the pivot table. The pivot table is simply a tool you're using to dynamically change analyses, apply varying calculations, and interactively drill down to the detail records.

The reason a pivot table is so well suited for dashboarding and reporting is that you can refresh the analyses shown through your pivot table simply by updating the dataset it's pointed to. This allows you to set up your analysis and presentation layers only one time; then, to refresh your reporting mechanism, all you have to do is press a button.

Let's start this exploration of pivot tables with a lesson on the anatomy of a pivot table.

The Four Areas of a Pivot Table

A pivot table is composed of four areas. The data you place in these areas defines both the utility and appearance of the pivot table. Take a moment to understand the function of each of these four areas.

Values area

The *values area*, as shown in Figure 6-1, is the large rectangular area below and to the right of the column and row headings. In the example in Figure 6-1, the values area contains a sum of the values in the Sales Amount field.

Region	(All) ▾			
Sales Amount	Segment ▾			
Market ▾	Accessories	Bikes	Clothing	Components
Australia	23,974	1,351,873	43,232	203,791
Canada	119,303	11,714,700	383,022	2,246,255
Central	46,551	6,782,978	155,874	947,448
France	48,942	3,597,879	129,508	871,125
Germany	35,681	1,602,487	75,593	337,787
Northeast	51,246	5,690,285	163,442	1,051,702
Northwest	53,308	10,484,495	201,052	1,784,207
Southeast	45,736	6,737,556	165,689	959,337
Southwest	110,080	15,430,281	364,099	2,693,568
United Kingdom	43,180	3,435,134	120,225	712,588

Figure 6-1: The values area of a pivot table calculates and counts data.

↑
Values area

The values area calculates and counts data. The data fields that you drag and drop here are typically those that you want to measure — fields, such as Sum of Revenue, Count of Units, or Average of Price.

Row area

The *row area* is shown in Figure 6-2. Placing a data field into the row area displays the unique values from that field down the rows of the left side of the pivot table. The row area typically has at least one field, although it's possible to have no fields.

Figure 6-2:
The row area of a pivot table gives you a row-oriented perspective.

Region	(All) ▼			
Sales Amount	Segment ▼			
Market ▼	Accessories	Bikes	Clothing	Components
Australia	23,974	1,351,873	43,232	203,791
Canada	119,303	11,714,700	383,022	2,246,255
Central	46,551	6,782,978	155,874	947,448
France	48,942	3,597,879	129,508	871,125
Germany	35,681	1,602,487	75,593	337,787
Northeast	51,246	5,690,285	163,442	1,051,702
Northwest	53,308	10,484,495	201,052	1,784,207
Southeast	45,736	6,737,556	165,689	959,337
Southwest	110,080	15,430,281	364,099	2,693,568
United Kingdom	43,180	3,435,134	120,225	712,588

↑
Row area

The types of data fields that you would drop here include those that you want to group and categorize, such as Products, Names, and Locations.

Column area

The *column area* is composed of headings that stretch across the top of columns in the pivot table.

As you can see in Figure 6-3, the column area stretches across the top of the columns. In this example, it contains the unique list of business segments.

Placing a data field into the column area displays the unique values from that field in a column-oriented perspective. The column area is ideal for creating a data matrix or showing trends over time.

Column area

Sales Amount	Segment			
Market	Accessories	Bikes	Clothing	Components
Australia	23,974	1,351,873	43,232	203,791
Canada	119,303	11,714,700	383,022	2,246,255
Central	46,551	6,782,978	155,874	947,448
France	48,942	3,597,879	129,508	871,125
Germany	35,681	1,602,487	75,593	337,787
Northeast	51,246	5,690,285	163,442	1,051,702
Northwest	53,308	10,484,495	201,052	1,784,207
Southeast	45,736	6,737,556	165,689	959,337
Southwest	110,080	15,430,281	364,099	2,693,568
United Kingdom	43,180	3,435,134	120,225	712,588

Region (All)

Figure 6-3: The column area of a pivot table gives you a column-oriented perspective.

Filter area

The *filter area* is an optional set of one or more drop-downs at the top of the pivot table. In Figure 6-4, the filter area contains the Region field, and the pivot table is set to show all regions.

Filter area

Region (All)

Sales Amount	Segment			
Market	Accessories	Bikes	Clothing	Components
Australia	23,974	1,351,873	43,232	203,791
Canada	119,303	11,714,700	383,022	2,246,255
Central	46,551	6,782,978	155,874	947,448
France	48,942	3,597,879	129,508	871,125
Germany	35,681	1,602,487	75,593	337,787
Northeast	51,246	5,690,285	163,442	1,051,702
Northwest	53,308	10,484,495	201,052	1,784,207
Southeast	45,736	6,737,556	165,689	959,337
Southwest	110,080	15,430,281	364,099	2,693,568
United Kingdom	43,180	3,435,134	120,225	712,588

Figure 6-4: The filter area allows you to easily apply filters to your pivot table report.

Placing data fields into the filter area allows you to filter the entire pivot table based on your selections. The types of data fields that you'd drop here include those that you want to isolate and focus on; for example, Region, Line of Business, and Employees.

Creating Your First Pivot Table

If you've followed along so far, you now have a good understanding of the basic structure of a pivot table, so let's quit all the talking and use the following steps to walk through the creation of your first pivot table:

You can find the sample file for this chapter on this book's companion website.

1. **Click any single cell inside your *data source* — the table you'll use to feed the pivot table.**

2. **Select the Insert tab on the Ribbon. Here, find the PivotTable icon, as shown in Figure 6-5. Choose PivotTable from the drop-down list beneath the icon.**

FILE	HOME	INSERT	PAGE LAYOUT	FORMULAS

PivotTable Recommended Table   Pictures Online   Shapes ▾
            PivotTables   Pictures   SmartArt
                                                         Screenshot ▾
            Tables   Illustrations

A1   fx   Region

	A	B	C	
1	Region	SubRegion	Market	Customer
2	North America	United States	Southeast	Trusted Cata
3	North America	United States	Southeast	Trusted Cata
4	North America	United States	Southeast	Trusted Cata
5	North America	United States	Southeast	Trusted Cata

Figure 6-5: Start a pivot table via the Insert tab.

This activates the Create PivotTable dialog box, as shown in Figure 6-6. As you can see, this dialog box asks you to specify the location of your source data and the place you want to put the pivot table.

Notice that in the Create PivotTable dialog box, Excel makes an attempt to fill in the range of your data for you. In most cases, Excel gets this right. However, always make sure the correct range is selected.

You will also note in Figure 6-6 that the default location for a new pivot table is New Worksheet. This means your pivot table will be placed in a new worksheet within the current workbook. You can change this by selecting the Existing Worksheet option and specifying the worksheet where you want the pivot table placed.

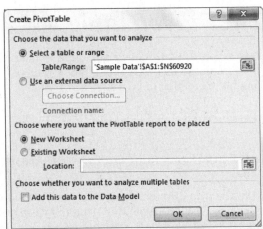

Figure 6-6:
The Create
PivotTable
dialog box.

3. Click OK.

At this point, you have an empty pivot table report on a new worksheet. Next to the empty pivot table, you see the PivotTable Fields dialog box, shown in Figure 6-7.

The idea here is to add the fields you need into the pivot table by using the four *drop zones* found in the PivotTable Field List — Filters, Columns, Rows and Values. Pleasantly enough, these drop zones correspond to the four areas of the pivot table you review at the beginning of this chapter.

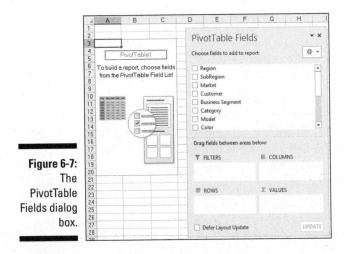

Figure 6-7:
The
PivotTable
Fields dialog
box.

If clicking the pivot table doesn't activate the PivotTable Fields dialog box, you can manually activate it by right-clicking anywhere inside the pivot table and selecting Show Field List.

Now, before you go wild and start dropping fields into the various drop zones, it's important that you ask yourself two questions; "What am I measuring?" and "How do I want to see it?" The answers to these questions give you some guidance when determining which fields go where.

For your first pivot table report, you want to measure the dollar sales by market. This automatically tells you that you will need to work with the Sales Amount field and the Market field.

How do you want to see that? You want markets to go down the left side of the report and sales amount to be calculated next to each market. Remembering the four areas of the pivot table, you'll need to add the Market field to the Rows drop zone, and the Sales Amount field to the Values drop zone.

4. **Select the Market check box in the list, as demonstrated in Figure 6-8.**

   Now that you have regions in your pivot table, it's time to add the dollar sales.

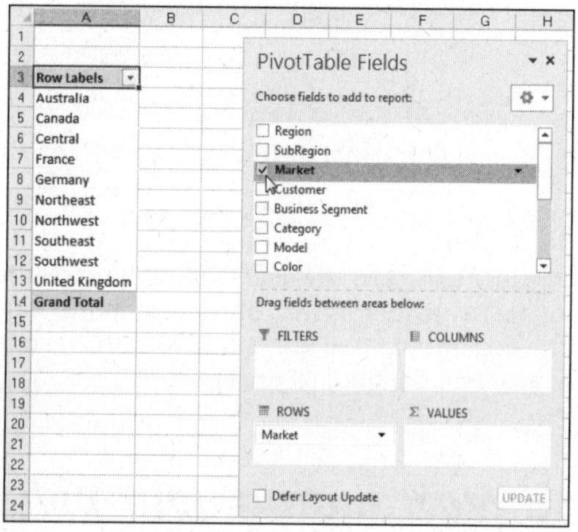

Figure 6-8: Select the Market check box.

5. **Select the Sales Amount check box in the list, as demonstrated in Figure 6-9.**

   Selecting a check box that is *non-numeric* (text or date) automatically places that field into the row area of the pivot table. Selecting a check box that is *numeric* automatically places that field in the values area of the pivot table.

   What happens if you need fields in the other areas of the pivot table? Well, instead of selecting the field's check box, you can drag any field directly to the different drop zones.

   One more thing: When you add fields to the drop zones, you may find it difficult to see all the fields in each drop zone. You can expand the PivotTable Fields dialog box by clicking and dragging the borders of the dialog box.

◢	A	B	C	D	E	F	G
1							
2			PivotTable Fields				▼ ✕
3	**Row Labels** ▼	**Sum of Sales Amount**	Choose fields to add to report:				⚙ ▾
4	Australia	1622869.422					
5	Canada	14463280.15	☐ SalesDate				▲
6	Central	7932851.609	☐ SalesPeriod				
7	France	4647454.207	☐ ListPrice				
8	Germany	2051547.728	☐ UnitPrice				
9	Northeast	6956673.913	☐ OrderQty				
10	Northwest	12523062.94	✓ **Sales Amount**				▼
11	Southeast	7908318.256	MORE TABLES...				▼
12	Southwest	18598026.98					
13	United Kingdom	4311126.886	Drag fields between areas below:				
14	**Grand Total**	**81015212.09**					
15			▼ FILTERS		▥ COLUMNS		
16							
17							
18							
19			≡ ROWS		Σ VALUES		
20							
21			Market	▼	Sum of Sales Amount	▼	
22							
23			☐ Defer Layout Update			UPDATE	
24							

Figure 6-9:
Add the
Sales
Amount field
by selecting
its check
box.

As you can see, you have just analyzed the sales for each market in just five steps! That's an amazing feat considering you start with more than 60,000 rows of data. With a little formatting, this modest pivot table can become the starting point for a management dashboard or report.

Changing and rearranging your pivot table

Now here's the wonderful thing about pivot tables: You can add as many layers of analysis as made possible by the fields in your source data table. Say that you want to show the dollar sales each market earned by business segment. Because your pivot table already contains the Market and Sales Amount fields, all you have to add is the Business Segment field.

So, simply click anywhere on your pivot table to reactivate the PivotTable Fields dialog box and then select the Business Segment check box. Figure 6-10 illustrates what your pivot table should look like now.

If clicking the pivot table doesn't activate the PivotTable Fields dialog box, you can manually activate it by right-clicking anywhere inside the pivot table and selecting Show Field List.

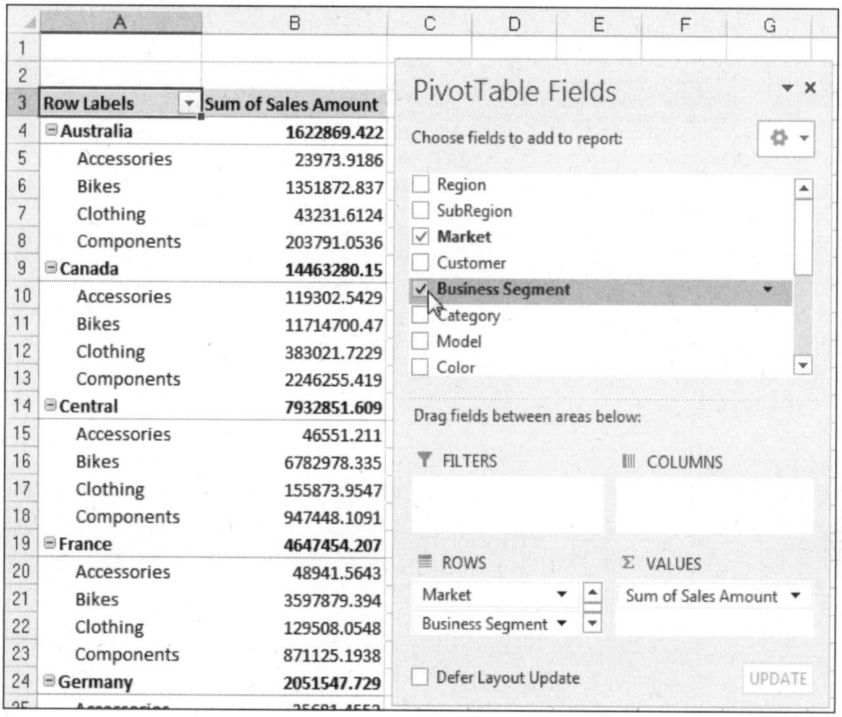

Figure 6-10:
Adding a
layer of
analysis is
as easy as
bringing
in another
field.

Imagine that your manager says that this layout doesn't work for him. He wants to see business segments going across the top of the pivot table report. No problem. Simply drag the Business Segment field from the Rows drop zone to the Columns drop zone. As you can see in Figure 6-11, this instantly restructures the pivot table to his specifications.

Adding a report filter

Often, you're asked to produce reports for one particular region, market, product, and so on. Instead of working hours and hours building separate reports for every possible analysis scenario, you can leverage pivot tables to help create multiple views of the same data. For example, you can do so by creating a region filter in your pivot table.

Click anywhere on your pivot table to reactivate the PivotTable Fields dialog box and then drag the Region field to the Filters drop zone. This adds a drop-down selector to your pivot table, shown in Figure 6-12. You can then use this selector to analyze one particular region at a time.

	A	B	C	D	E	F	G	H
1								
2								
3	Sum of Sales Amount	Column Labels						
4	Row Labels	Accessories	Bikes	Clothing				
5	Australia	23973.9186	1351872.837	43231.6				
6	Canada	119302.5429	11714700.47	383021.7				
7	Central	46551.211	6782978.335	155873.9				
8	France	48941.5643	3597879.394	129508.0				
9	Germany	35681.4552	1602487.163	75592.5				
10	Northeast	51245.8881	5690284.732	163441.7				
11	Northwest	53308.4547	10484495.02	201052.0				
12	Southeast	45736.1077	6737555.913	165689.0				
13	Southwest	110079.5882	15430280.58	364098.8				
14	United Kingdom	43180.2218	3435134.262	120224.4				
15	Grand Total	578000.9525	66827668.7	1801734				

PivotTable Fields

Choose fields to add to report:

- ☐ Region
- ☐ SubRegion
- ☑ **Market**
- ☐ Customer
- ☑ **Business Segment**
- ☐ Category
- ☐ Model
- ☐ Color

Drag fields between areas below:

▼ FILTERS	||| COLUMNS
	Business Segment ▼

≡ ROWS	Σ VALUES
Market ▼	Sum of Sales Amount ▼

☐ Defer Layout Update   UPDATE

Figure 6-11: Your business segments are now column oriented.

	A	B	C	D	E	F	G	H
1	Region	North America						
2								
3	Sum of Sales Amount	Column Labels						
4	Row Labels	Accessories	Bikes	Clothing				
5	Canada	119302.5429	11714700.47	383021.7				
6	Central	46551.211	6782978.335	155873.9				
7	Northeast	51245.8881	5690284.732	163441.7				
8	Northwest	53308.4547	10484495.02	201052.0				
9	Southeast	45736.1077	6737555.913	165689.0				
10	Southwest	110079.5882	15430280.58	364098.8				
11	Grand Total	426223.7926	56840295.04	1433177				

PivotTable Fields

Choose fields to add to report:

- ☑ **Region**
- ☐ SubRegion
- ☑ **Market**
- ☐ Customer
- ☑ **Business Segment**
- ☐ Category
- ☐ Model
- ☐ Color

Drag fields between areas below:

▼ FILTERS	||| COLUMNS
Region ▼	Business Segment ▼

≡ ROWS	Σ VALUES
Market ▼	Sum of Sales Amount ▼

☐ Defer Layout Update   UPDATE

Figure 6-12: Using pivot tables to analyze regions.

Keeping your pivot table fresh

In Hollywood, it's important to stay fresh and relevant. As boring as your pivot tables may seem, they'll eventually become the stars of your reports and dashboards. So it's just as important to keep your pivot tables fresh and relevant.

As time goes by, your data may change and grow with newly added rows and columns. The action of updating your pivot table with these changes is *refreshing* your data.

Your pivot table report can be refreshed by simply right-clicking inside your pivot table report and selecting Refresh, as demonstrated in Figure 6-13.

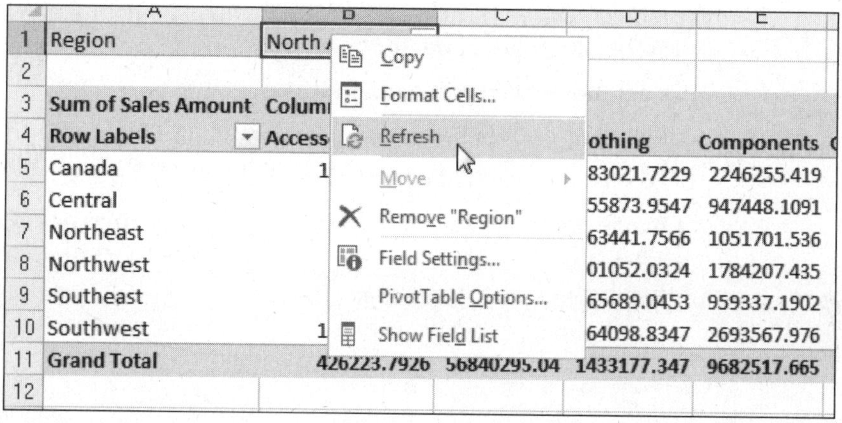

Figure 6-13: Refreshing your pivot table captures changes made to your data.

Pivot tables and spreadsheet bloat

It's important to understand that pivot tables come with space and memory implications for your reporting processes. When you create a pivot table, Excel takes a snapshot of your dataset and stores it in a pivot cache. A *pivot cache* is essentially a memory container that holds this snapshot of your dataset. Each pivot table report you create from a separate data source creates its own pivot cache, which increases your workbook's memory usage and file size. The increase in memory usage and file size depends on the size of the original data source that's being duplicated to create the pivot cache.

Simple enough, right? Well here's the rub: You often need to create separate pivot tables from the same data source in order to analyze the same data in different ways. If you create two pivot tables from the data source, a new pivot cache is automatically created even though one may already exist for the dataset being used. This means that you're bloating your spreadsheet with redundant data each time you create a new pivot table using the same dataset.

To work around this potential problem, you can employ Copy and then Paste. That's right; simply copying a pivot table and pasting it somewhere else will create another pivot table, *without* duplicating the pivot cache. This allows you to create multiple pivot tables that use the same source data, with negligible increase in memory and file size.

Sometimes, *you're* the data source that feeds your pivot table changes in structure. For example, you may have added or deleted rows or columns from your data table. These types of changes affect the range of your data source, not just a few data items in the table.

In these cases, performing a simple Refresh of your pivot table won't do. You have to update the range being captured by the pivot table. Here's how:

1. **Click anywhere inside your pivot table to activate the PivotTable Tools context tab in the Ribbon.**

2. **Select the Analyze tab on the Ribbon.**

3. **Click Change Data Source, as demonstrated in Figure 6-14.**

   The Change PivotTable Data Source dialog box appears.

4. **Change the range selection to include any new rows or columns. See Figure 6-15.**

5. **Click OK to apply the change.**

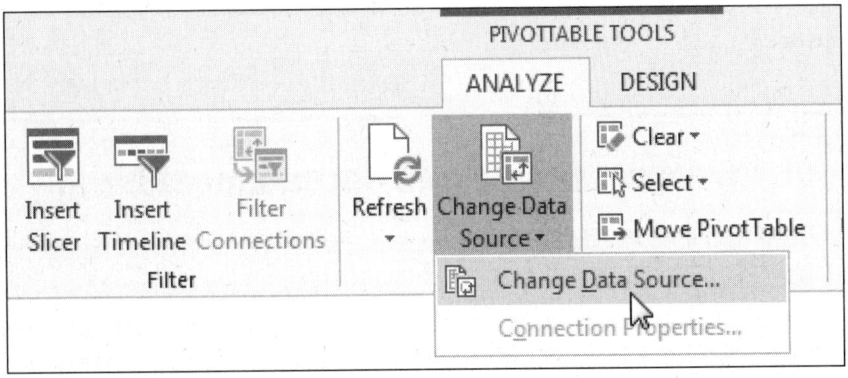

Figure 6-14: Changing the range that feeds your pivot table.

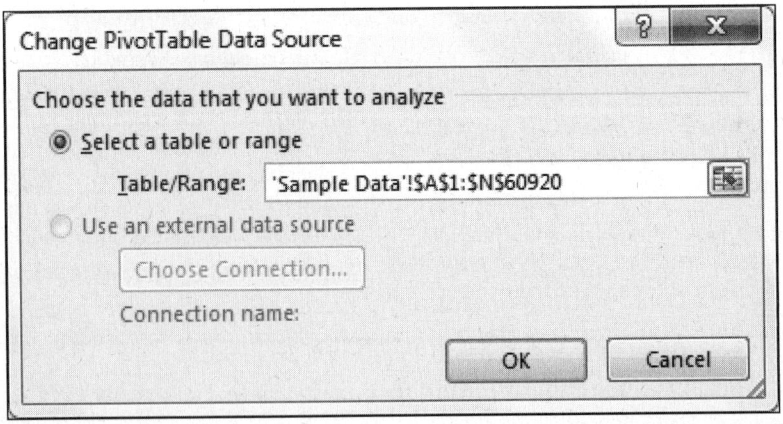

Figure 6-15: Select the new range that feeds your pivot table.

Customizing Your Pivot Table Reports

The pivot tables you create often need to be tweaked to get the look and feel you're looking for. In this section, I cover some of the options you can adjust to customize your pivot tables to suit your reporting needs.

Changing the pivot table layout

Excel gives you a choice in the layout of your data in a pivot table. The three layouts, shown side by side in Figure 6-16, are the Compact Form, Outline Form, and Tabular Form. Although no layout stands out as better than the others, I prefer using the Tabular Form layout because it seems easiest to read, and it's the layout that most people who have seen pivot tables are used to.

Figure 6-16:
The three layouts for a pivot table report.

Compact Form Layout		Outline Form Layout			Tabular Form Layout		
Row Labels ↓	Sales	Market ↓	Segment ↓	Sales	Market ↓	Segment ↓	Sales
⊟Australia	1622869.422	⊟Australia		1622869.422	⊟Australia	Accessories	23973.9186
Accessories	23973.9186		Accessories	23973.9186		Bikes	1351872.837
Bikes	1351872.837		Bikes	1351872.837		Clothing	43231.6124
Clothing	43231.6124		Clothing	43231.6124		Components	203791.0536
Components	203791.0536		Components	203791.0536	Australia Total		1622869.422
⊟Canada	14463280.15	⊟Canada		14463280.15	⊟Canada	Accessories	119302.5429
Accessories	119302.5429		Accessories	119302.5429		Bikes	11714700.47
Bikes	11714700.47		Bikes	11714700.47		Clothing	383021.7229
Clothing	383021.7229		Clothing	383021.7229		Components	2246255.419
Components	2246255.419		Components	2246255.419	Canada Total		14463280.15
⊟Central	7932851.609	⊟Central		7932851.609	⊟Central	Accessories	46551.211
Accessories	46551.211		Accessories	46551.211		Bikes	6782978.335
Bikes	6782978.335		Bikes	6782978.335		Clothing	155873.9547
Clothing	155873.9547		Clothing	155873.9547		Components	947448.1091
Components	947448.1091		Components	947448.1091	Central Total		7932851.609
⊟France	4647454.207	⊟France		4647454.207	⊟France	Accessories	48941.5643
Accessories	48941.5643		Accessories	48941.5643		Bikes	3597879.394
Bikes	3597879.394		Bikes	3597879.394		Clothing	129508.0548
Clothing	129508.0548		Clothing	129508.0548		Components	871125.1938
Components	871125.1938		Components	871125.1938	France Total		4647454.207
⊟Germany	2051547.729	⊟Germany		2051547.729	⊟Germany	Accessories	35681.4552
Accessories	35681.4552		Accessories	35681.4552		Bikes	1602487.163
Bikes	1602487.163		Bikes	1602487.163		Clothing	75592.5945
Clothing	75592.5945		Clothing	75592.5945		Components	337786.516
Components	337786.516		Components	337786.516	Germany Total		2051547.729

The layout you choose not only affects the look and feel of your reporting mechanisms, but it may also affect the way you build and interact with any dashboard models based on your pivot tables.

Changing the layout of a pivot table is easy. Follow these steps:

1. **Click anywhere inside your pivot table to activate the PivotTable Tools context tab on the Ribbon.**

2. **Select the Design tab on the Ribbon.**

3. **Click the Report Layout icon and choose the layout you like. See Figure 6-17.**

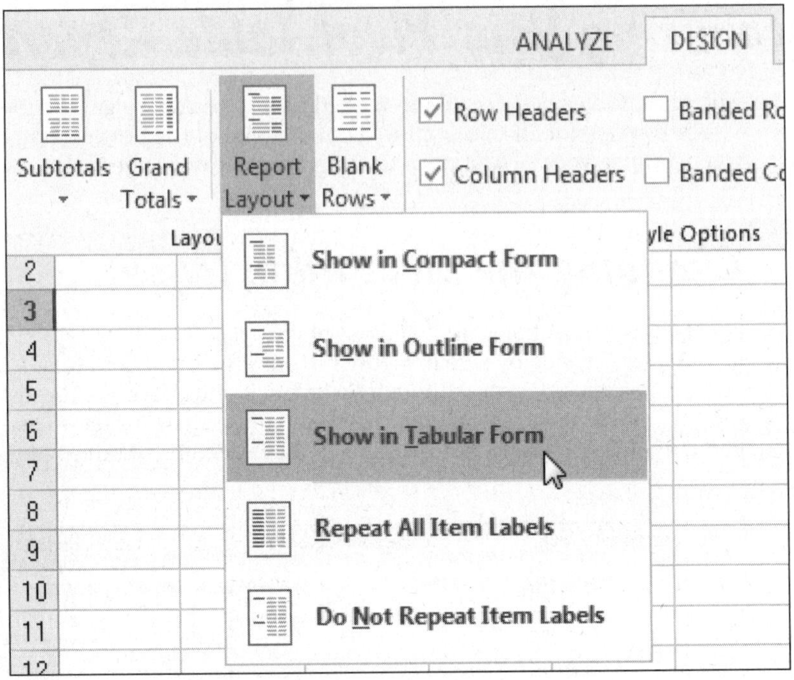

Figure 6-17:
Changing
the layout
for your
pivot table.

Customizing field names

Notice that every field in your pivot table has a name. The fields in the row, column, and filter areas inherit their names from the data labels in your source table. The fields in the values area are given a name, such as Sum of Sales Amount.

Sometimes you might prefer the name Total Sales instead of the unattractive default name, like Sum of Sales Amount. In these situations, the ability to change your field names is handy. To change a field name, do the following:

1. **Right-click any value within the target field.**

   For example, if you want to change the name of the field Sum of Sales Amount, you right-click any value under that field.

2. **Select Value Field Settings, as shown in Figure 6-18.**

   The Value Field Settings dialog box appears.

   Note that if you were changing the name of a field in the row or column area, this selection is Field Settings.

3. **Enter the new name in the Custom Name input box, shown in Figure 6-19.**

4. **Click OK to apply the change.**

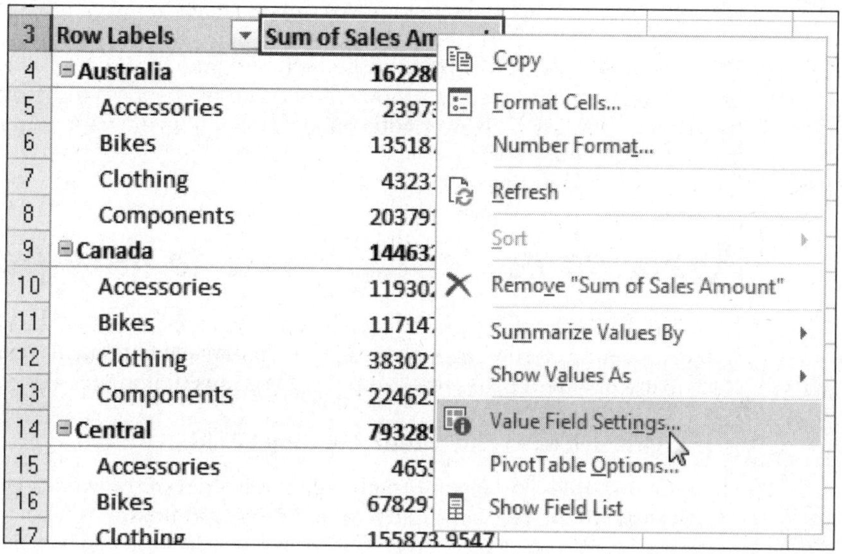

3	Row Labels ▼	Sum of Sales Am..		
4	⊟ **Australia**	162280	📋	Copy
5	Accessories	23973	▦	Format Cells...
6	Bikes	135187		Number Format...
7	Clothing	43231	⟳	Refresh
8	Components	203791		
9	⊟ **Canada**	144632		Sort ▸
10	Accessories	119302	✕	Remove "Sum of Sales Amount"
11	Bikes	117147		Summarize Values By ▸
12	Clothing	383021		Show Values As ▸
13	Components	224625		
14	⊟ **Central**	793285	▦	Value Field Settings...
15	Accessories	4655		PivotTable Options...
16	Bikes	678297	▦	Show Field List
17	Clothing	155873.9547		

Figure 6-18:
Right-click any value in the target field to select the Value Field Settings option.

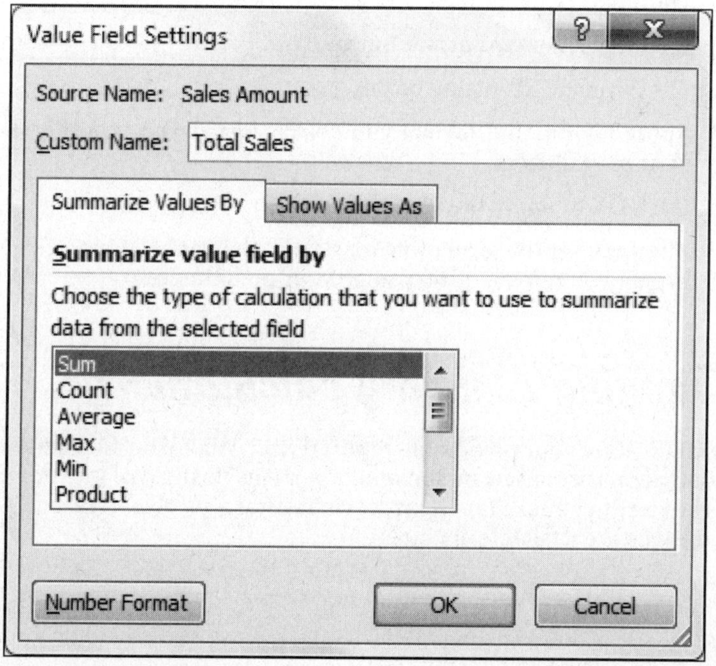

Value Field Settings ? ✕

Source Name: Sales Amount

Custom Name: Total Sales

Summarize Values By | Show Values As

Summarize value field by

Choose the type of calculation that you want to use to summarize data from the selected field

- Sum
- Count
- Average
- Max
- Min
- Product

Number Format | OK | Cancel

Figure 6-19:
Use the Custom Name input box to change the name of the field.

If you use the name of the data label used in your source table, you receive an error. For example, if you rename Sum of Sales Amount as Sales Amount, you get an error message because there's already a Sales Amount field in the source data table. Well, this is kinda lame, especially if Sales Amount is exactly what you want to name the field in your pivot table.

To get around this, you can name the field and add a space to the end of the name. Excel considers Sales Amount (followed by a space) to be different from Sales Amount. This way you can use the name you want, and no one will notice it's any different.

Applying numeric formats to data fields

Numbers in pivot tables can be formatted to fit your needs — that is, formatted as currency, percentage, or number. You can easily control the numeric formatting of a field using the Value Field Settings dialog box. Here's how:

1. **Right-click any value within the target field.**

   For example, if you want to change the format of the values in the Sales Amount field, right-click any value under that field.

2. **Select Value Field Settings.**

   The Value Field Settings dialog box appears.

3. **Click the Number Format button.**

   The Format Cells dialog box opens.

4. **Apply the number format you desire, just as you typically would on your spreadsheet.**

5. **Click OK to apply the changes.**

   After you set the formatting for a field, the applied formatting will persist even if you refresh or rearrange your pivot table.

Changing summary calculations

When creating your pivot table report, Excel will, by default, summarize your data by either counting or summing the items. Instead of Sum or Count, you might want to choose functions, such as Average, Min, Max, and so on. In all, 11 options are available, including

- ✔ **Sum:** Adds all numeric data.
- ✔ **Count:** Counts all data items within a given field, including numeric-, text-, and date-formatted cells.
- ✔ **Average:** Calculates an average for the target data items.

✔ **Max:** Displays the largest value in the target data items.

✔ **Min:** Displays the smallest value in the target data items.

✔ **Product:** Multiplies all target data items together.

✔ **Count Nums:** Counts only the numeric cells in the target data items.

✔ **StdDevP and StdDev:** Calculates the standard deviation for the target data items. Use StdDevP if your dataset contains the complete population. Use StdDev if your dataset contains a sample of the population.

✔ **VarP and Var:** Calculates the statistical variance for the target data items. Use VarP if your data contains a complete population. If your data contains only a sampling of the complete population, use Var to estimate the variance.

You can easily change the summary calculation for any given field by taking the following actions:

1. **Right-click any value within the target field.**

2. **Select Value Field Settings.**

   The Value Field Settings dialog box appears.

3. **Choose the type of calculation you want to use from the list of calculations. See Figure 6-20.**

4. **Click OK to apply the changes.**

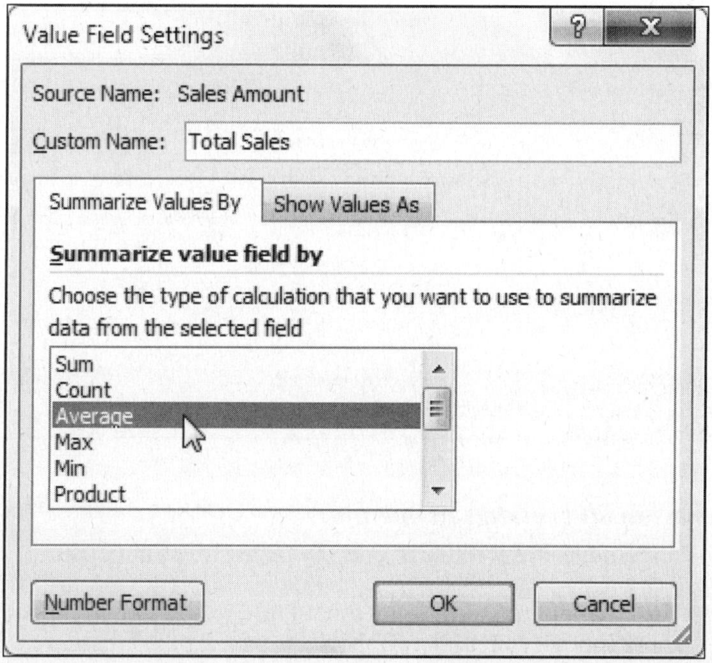

Figure 6-20:
Changing
the type of
summary
calculation
used in a
field.

Did you know that a single blank cell causes Excel to count instead of sum? That's right. If all the cells in a column contain numeric data, Excel chooses Sum. If just one cell is either blank or contains text, Excel chooses Count.

Be sure to pay attention to the fields that you place into the values area of the pivot table. If the field name starts with Count Of, Excel's counting the items in the field instead of summing the values.

Suppressing subtotals

Notice that each time you add a field to your pivot table, Excel adds a subtotal for that field. There may be times however, when the inclusion of subtotals either doesn't make sense or just hinders a clear view of your pivot table report. For example, Figure 6-21 shows a pivot table in which the subtotals inundate the report with totals that hide the real data you're trying to report.

	A	B	C	D	E
1	Region	SubRegion	Market	Business Segment	Sum of Sales Amount
2	North America	United States	Central	Accessories	46,551
3				Bikes	6,782,978
4				Clothing	155,874
5				Components	947,448
6			Central Total		7,932,852
7			Northeast	Accessories	51,246
8				Bikes	5,690,285
9				Clothing	163,442
10				Components	1,051,702
11			Northeast Total		6,956,674
12			Northwest	Accessories	53,308
13				Bikes	10,484,495
14				Clothing	201,052
15				Components	1,784,207
16			Northwest Total		12,523,063
17			Southeast	Accessories	45,736
18				Bikes	6,737,556
19				Clothing	165,689
20				Components	959,337
21			Southeast Total		7,908,318
22			Southwest	Accessories	110,080
23				Bikes	15,430,281
24				Clothing	364,099
25				Components	2,693,568
26			Southwest Total		18,598,027
27		United States Total			53,918,934
28	North America Total				53,918,934

Figure 6-21: Subtotals sometimes muddle the data you're trying to show.

Removing all subtotals at one time

You can remove all subtotals at once by taking these actions:

1. **Click anywhere inside your pivot table to activate the PivotTable Tools context tab on the Ribbon.**

2. **Select the Design tab on the Ribbon.**

3. **Click the Subtotals icon and select Do Not Show Subtotals, as shown in Figure 6-22.**

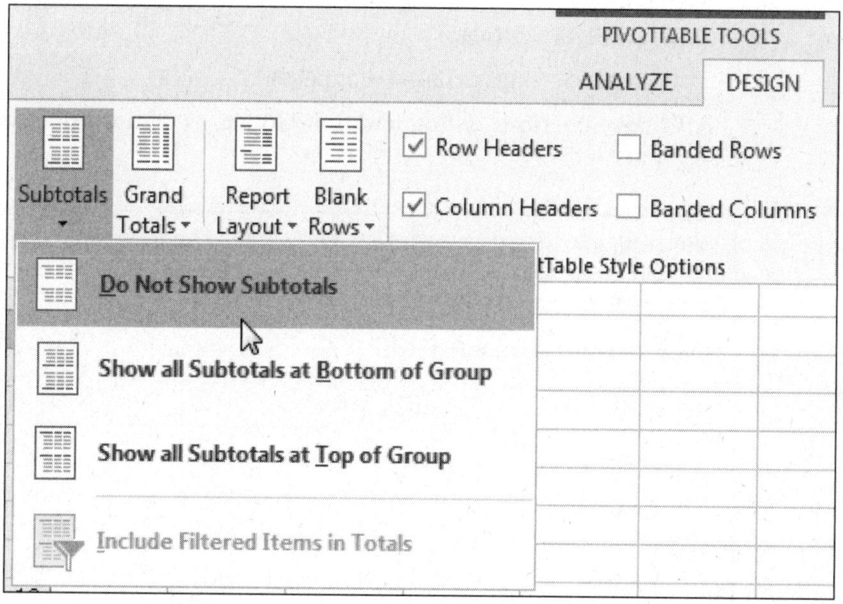

Figure 6-22:
Use the Do
Not Show
Subtotals
option to
remove all
subtotals at
once.

As you can see in Figure 6-23, the same report without subtotals is much more pleasant to review.

	A	B	C	D	E
1	Region	SubRegion	Market	Business Segment	Sum of Sales Amount
2	North America	United States	Central	Accessories	46,551
3				Bikes	6,782,978
4				Clothing	155,874
5				Components	947,448
6			Northeast	Accessories	51,246
7				Bikes	5,690,285
8				Clothing	163,442
9				Components	1,051,702
10			Northwest	Accessories	53,308
11				Bikes	10,484,495
12				Clothing	201,052
13				Components	1,784,207
14			Southeast	Accessories	45,736
15				Bikes	6,737,556
16				Clothing	165,689
17				Components	959,337
18			Southwest	Accessories	110,080
19				Bikes	15,430,281
20				Clothing	364,099
21				Components	2,693,568
22	Grand Total				53,918,934

Figure 6-23:
The report
shown in
Figure 6-21
without
subtotals.

Removing the subtotals for only one field

Maybe you want to remove the subtotals for only one field? In such a case, you can take the following actions:

1. **Right-click any value within the target field.**

2. **Select Field Settings.**

   The Field Settings dialog box appears.

3. **Choose the None option under Subtotals, as demonstrated in Figure 6-24.**

4. **Click OK to apply the changes.**

Removing grand totals

There may be instances when you want to remove the grand totals from your pivot table.

1. **Right-click anywhere on your pivot table.**

2. **Select PivotTable Options.**

    The PivotTable Options dialog box appears.

3. **Click the Totals & Filters tab.**

4. **Click the Show Grand Totals for Rows check box to deselect it.**

5. **Click the Show Grand Totals for Columns check box to deselect it.**

Showing and hiding data items

A pivot table summarizes and displays all the records in your source data table. There may be situations however, when you want to inhibit certain data items from being included in your pivot table summary. In these situations, you can choose to hide a data item.

In terms of pivot tables, hiding doesn't just mean preventing the data item from being shown on the report. Hiding a data item also prevents it from being factored into the summary calculations.

In the pivot table illustrated in Figure 6-25, I show sales amounts for all Business Segments by Market. In this example, I want to show totals without taking sales from the Bikes segment into consideration. In other words, I want to hide the Bikes segment.

	A	B	C
1	Market	Business Segment	Sum of Sales Amount
2	⊟ Australia	Accessories	$23,974
3		Bikes	$1,351,873
4		Clothing	$43,232
5		Components	$203,791
6	Australia Total		$1,622,869
7	⊟ Canada	Accessories	$119,303
8		Bikes	$11,714,700
9		Clothing	$383,022
10		Components	$2,246,255
11	Canada Total		$14,463,280
12	⊟ Central	Accessories	$46,551
13		Bikes	$6,782,978
14		Clothing	$155,874
15		Components	$947,448
16	Central Total		$7,932,852
17	⊟ France	Accessories	$48,942

Figure 6-25: To remove Bikes from this analysis . . .

I can hide the Bikes Business Segment by clicking the Business Segment drop-down list arrow and deselecting the Bikes check box, as shown in Figure 6-26.

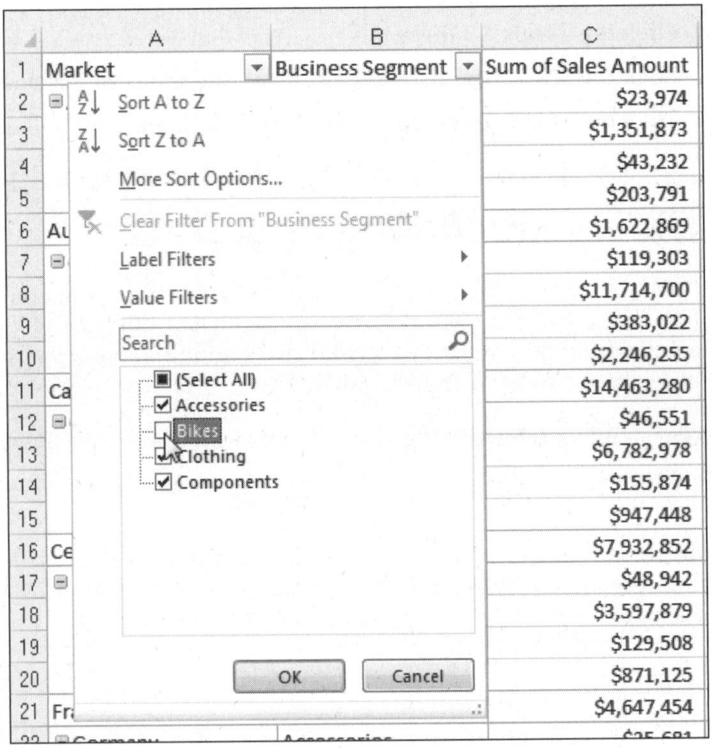

Figure 6-26:
... deselect
the Bikes
check box.

After choosing OK to close the selection box, the pivot table instantly recal-culates, leaving out the Bikes segment. As you can see in Figure 6-27, the Market total sales now reflect the sales without Bikes.

I can just as quickly reinstate all hidden data items for my field. I simply click the Business Segment drop-down list arrow and click the Select All check box, as shown in Figure 6-28.

Hiding or showing items without data

By default, your pivot table shows only data items that have data. This inher-ent behavior may cause unintended problems for your data analysis.

Look at Figure 6-29, which shows a pivot table with the SalesPeriod field in the row area and the Region field in the filter area. Note that the Region field is set to (All), and every sales period appears in the report.

If I choose Europe in the filter area, only a portion of all the sales periods will show. See Figure 6-30. The pivot table will show only those sales periods that apply to the Europe region.

	A	B	C
1	Market ▾	Business Segment ⊤	Sum of Sales Amount
2	⊟Australia	Accessories	$23,974
3		Clothing	$43,232
4		Components	$203,791
5	Australia Total		$270,997
6	⊟Canada	Accessories	$119,303
7		Clothing	$383,022
8		Components	$2,246,255
9	Canada Total		$2,748,580
10	⊟Central	Accessories	$46,551
11		Clothing	$155,874
12		Components	$947,448
13	Central Total		$1,149,873
14	⊟France	Accessories	$48,942

Figure 6-27: The analysis from Figure 6-25 without the Bikes segment.

	A	B	C
1	Market ▾	Business Segment ⊤	Sum of Sales Amount
2		↓ Sort A to Z	$23,974
3		↓ Sort Z to A	$43,232
4		More Sort Options...	$203,791
5	Au		$270,997
6		Clear Filter From "Business Segment"	$119,303
7		Label Filters ▸	$383,022
8		Value Filters ▸	$2,246,255
9	Ca		$2,748,580
10		Search	$46,551
11		☑(Select All)	$155,874
12		☑Accessories	$947,448
13	Ce	☑Bikes	$1,149,873
14		☑Clothing	$48,942
15		☑Components	$129,508
16			$871,125
17	Fr		$1,049,575
18			$35,681
19			$75,593
20		OK Cancel	$337,787
21	Ge		$449,061

Figure 6-28: Clicking the Select All check box forces all data items in that field to become unhidden.

	A	B
1	Region	(All) ▼
2		
3	SalesPeriod ▼	Sum of Sales Amount
4	01/01/08	$713,230
5	02/01/08	$1,900,797
6	03/01/08	$1,455,282
7	04/01/08	$883,011
8	05/01/08	$2,269,722
9	06/01/08	$1,137,250
10	07/01/08	$2,411,569
11	08/01/08	$3,615,926
12	09/01/08	$2,894,658
13	10/01/08	$1,804,184
14	11/01/08	$3,055,007

Figure 6-29: All sales periods are showing.

	A	B
1	Region	Europe ▼
2		
3	SalesPeriod ▼	Sum of Sales Amount
4	07/01/08	$180,241
5	08/01/08	$448,373
6	09/01/08	$373,122
7	10/01/08	$119,384
8	11/01/08	$330,026
9	12/01/08	$254,011
10	01/01/09	$71,313
11	02/01/09	$264,487
12	03/01/09	$177,006
13	04/01/09	$105,153
14	05/01/09	$300,602

Figure 6-30: Filtering for the Europe region causes some of the sales periods to disappear.

Displaying only those items with data could cause trouble if I plan on using this pivot table as the feeder for my charts or other dashboard components. From a dashboarding-and-reporting perspective, it isn't ideal if half the year's data disappeared each time customers selected Europe.

Here's how you can prevent Excel from hiding pivot items without data:

1. **Right-click any value within the target field.**

   In this example, the target field is the SalesPeriod field.

2. **Select Field Settings.**

   The Field Settings dialog box appears.

3. **Select the Layout & Print tab in the Field Settings dialog box.**

4. **Select the Show Items with No Data option, as shown in Figure 6-31.**

5. **Click OK to apply the change.**

As you can see in Figure 6-32, after choosing the Show Items with No Data option, all the sales periods appear whether the selected region had sales that period or not.

Now that I'm confident that the structure of the pivot table is locked, I can use it to feed charts and other components on my dashboard.

◢	A	B
1	Region	Europe ▼
2		
3	SalesPeriod ▼	Sum of Sales Amount
4	01/01/08	
5	02/01/08	
6	03/01/08	
7	04/01/08	
8	05/01/08	
9	06/01/08	
10	07/01/08	$180,241
11	08/01/08	$448,373
12	09/01/08	$373,122
13	10/01/08	$119,384
14	11/01/08	$330,026

Figure 6-32: All sales periods are now displayed, even if there is no data to be shown.

Sorting your pivot table

By default, items in each pivot field are sorted in ascending sequence based on the item name. Excel gives you the freedom to change the sort order of the items in your pivot table.

Like many actions you can perform in Excel, there are lots of different ways to sort data within a pivot table. The easiest way, and the way that I use the most, is to apply the sort directly in the pivot table. Here's how:

1. **Right-click any value within the *target field* — the field you need to sort.**

   In the example shown in Figure 6-33, I want to sort by Sales Amount.

4	Bib-Shorts	$168,003		
5	Bike Racks	$200,077	📋	Copy
6	Bottles and Cages	$7,555	⊞	Format Cells...
7	Bottom Brackets	$51,826		Number Format...
8	Brakes	$66,062		
9	Caps	$31,824	🔄	Refresh
10	Chains	$9,386		Sort ▶ ▲↓ Sort Smallest to Largest
11	Cleaners	$11,300	✕	Remove "Sum of Sales Amount" ▼↓ Sort Largest to Smallest
12	Cranksets	$204,065		Summarize Values By ▶ 🔲 More Sort Options...
13	Derailleurs	$70,263		Show Values As ▶
14	Forks	$77,969		
15	Gloves	$211,942	⁺	Show Details
16	Handlebars	$170,657	🔲	Value Field Settings...

Figure 6-33: Applying a sort to a pivot table field.

2. **Select Sort and then select the sort direction.**

   The changes take effect immediately and persist while you work with your pivot table.

Creating Useful Pivot-Driven Views

At this point in your exploration of pivot tables, you have covered enough of the fundamentals to start creating your own pivot table reports. In this last section, I share with you a few of the techniques I use to create some of the more useful report views. Although you could create these views by hand, creating them with pivot tables helps save you hours of work and allows you to more easily update and maintain them.

Producing top and bottom views

You'll often find that managers are interested in the top and bottom of things: the top 50 customers, the bottom 5 sales reps, the top 10 products. Although you may think this is because managers have the attention span of a four-year-old, there's a more logical reason for focusing on the outliers.

Dashboarding and reporting is often about showing actionable data. If you, as a manager, know who the bottom ten revenue-generating accounts are, you could apply your effort and resources in building up those accounts. Because you most likely wouldn't have the resources to focus on all accounts, viewing a manageable subset of accounts would be more useful.

Luckily, pivot tables make it easy to filter your data for the top five, the bottom ten, or any conceivable combination of top or bottom records. Here's an example.

Imagine that in your company, the Accessories Business Segment is a high-margin business — you make the most profit for each dollar of sales in the Accessories segment. To increase sales, your manager wants to focus on the 50 customers who spend the least amount of money on accessories. He obviously wants to spend his time and resources on getting those customers to buy more accessories. Here's what to do:

1. **Build a pivot table with Business Segment in the filter area, Customer in the row area, and Sales Amount in the values area; see Figure 6-34. For cosmetic value, change the layout to Tabular Form. See the earlier section "Changing the pivot table layout," to find out how to do that.**

   You can find the sample file for this chapter on this book's companion website.

2. **Right-click any customer name in the Customer field, select Filter, and then Top 10 — as demonstrated in Figure 6-35.**

   Don't let the label *Top 10* confuse you. You can use the Top 10 option to filter both top and bottom records.

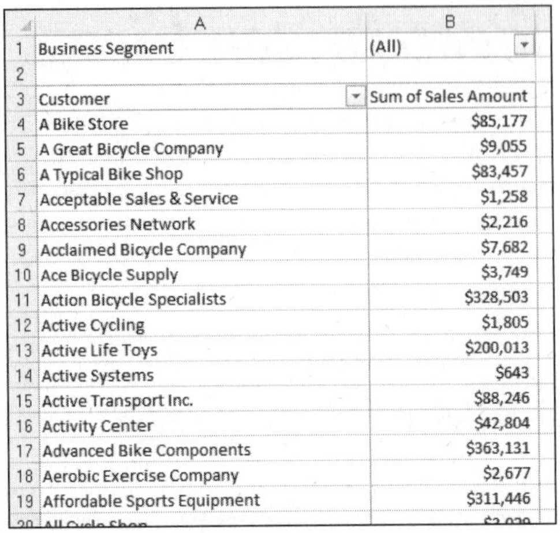

	A	B
1	Business Segment	(All)
2		
3	Customer	Sum of Sales Amount
4	A Bike Store	$85,177
5	A Great Bicycle Company	$9,055
6	A Typical Bike Shop	$83,457
7	Acceptable Sales & Service	$1,258
8	Accessories Network	$2,216
9	Acclaimed Bicycle Company	$7,682
10	Ace Bicycle Supply	$3,749
11	Action Bicycle Specialists	$328,503
12	Active Cycling	$1,805
13	Active Life Toys	$200,013
14	Active Systems	$643
15	Active Transport Inc.	$88,246
16	Activity Center	$42,804
17	Advanced Bike Components	$363,131
18	Aerobic Exercise Company	$2,677
19	Affordable Sports Equipment	$311,446

Figure 6-34: Build this pivot table to start.

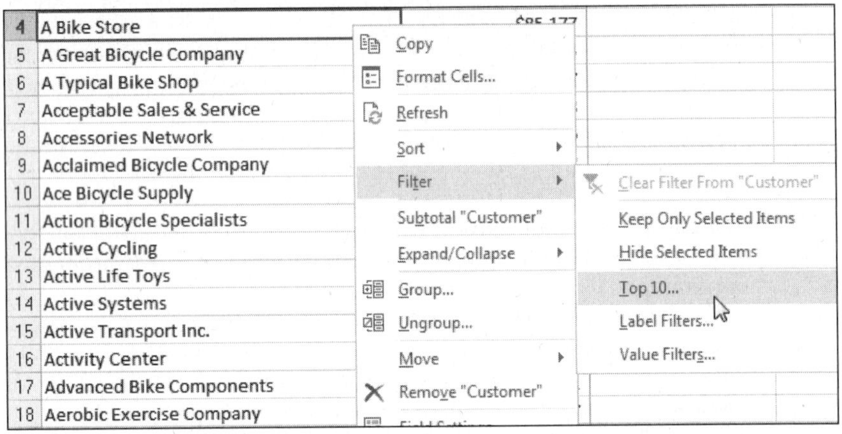

Figure 6-35: Select the Top 10 filter option.

3. **In the Top 10 Filter dialog box, as illustrated in Figure 6-36, you simply have to define the view you're looking for. In this example, you want the bottom 50 items (customers), as defined by the Sum of Sales Amount field.**

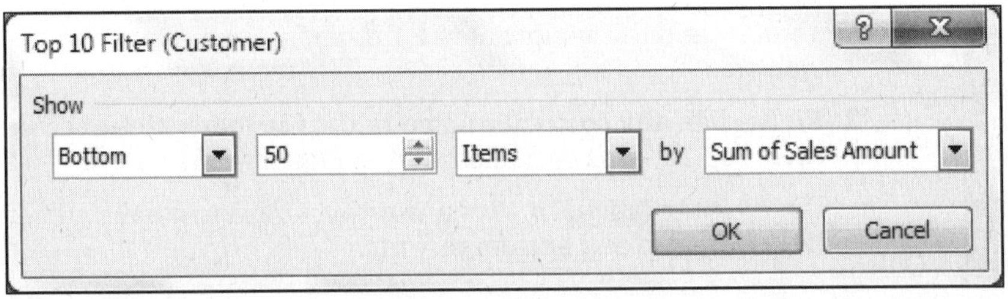

Figure 6-36: Specify the filter you want to apply.

4. **Click OK to apply the filter.**
5. **In the filter area, click the drop-down button for the Business Segment field and select the check box for the filter item Accessories, as shown in Figure 6-37.**

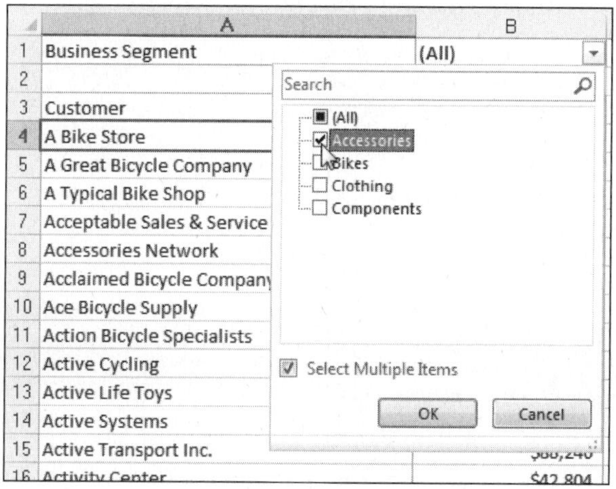

Figure 6-37: Filter your pivot table report to show Accessories.

At this point, you have exactly what your manager asked for — the 50 customers who spend the least amount of money on accessories. You can go a step further and format the report a bit by sorting on the Sum of Sales Amount and applying a currency format to the numbers. See Figure 6-38.

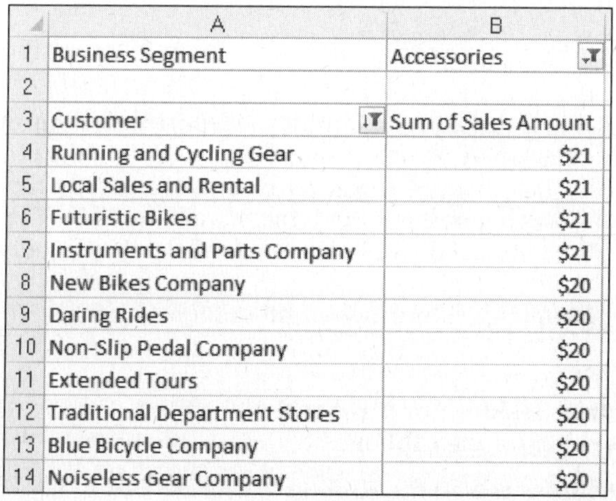

	A	B
1	Business Segment	Accessories
2		
3	Customer	Sum of Sales Amount
4	Running and Cycling Gear	$21
5	Local Sales and Rental	$21
6	Futuristic Bikes	$21
7	Instruments and Parts Company	$21
8	New Bikes Company	$20
9	Daring Rides	$20
10	Non-Slip Pedal Company	$20
11	Extended Tours	$20
12	Traditional Department Stores	$20
13	Blue Bicycle Company	$20
14	Noiseless Gear Company	$20

Figure 6-38: Your final report.

Note that because you built this view using a pivot table, you can easily adapt your newly created report to create a whole new view. For example, you can add the SubRegion field — shown in Figure 6-39 — to the filter area to get the 50 United Kingdom customers who spend the least amount of money on accessories. This, my friends, is the power of using pivot tables for the basis of your dashboards and reports. Continue to play around with the Top 10 filter option to see what kind of reports you can come up with.

	A	B
1	Business Segment	Accessories ⊤
2	SubRegion	United Kingdom ⊤
3		
4	Customer ⊤	Sum of Sales Amount
5	Vigorous Sports Store	$3
6	Closest Bicycle Store	$3
7	Exclusive Bicycle Mart	$15
8	Extended Tours	$20
9	Instruments and Parts Company	$21
10	Tachometers and Accessories	$23
11	Metropolitan Bicycle Supply	$26
12	Number One Bike Co.	$30
13	Nearby Cycle Shop	$36
14	Metro Metals Co.	$46
15	Cycles Wholesaler & Mfg.	$376
16	Cycling Goods	$433
17	Exceptional Cycle Services	$758
18	Channel Outlet	$918
19	Express Bike Services	$1,718
20	Downhill Bicycle Specialists	$1,915
21	Uttermost Bike Shop	$3,807
22	Bulk Discount Store	$4,067
23	Commerce Bicycle Specialists	$4,436
24	Action Bicycle Specialists	$4,861
25	Exhibition Showroom	$5,723
26	Riding Cycles	$6,459
27	Prosperous Tours	$7,487

Figure 6-39: You can easily adapt this report to produce any combination of views.

You may notice that in Figure 6-39, the bottom 50 report is showing only 23 records. This is because there are fewer than 50 customers in the United Kingdom market that have accessories sales. Because I asked for the bottom 50, Excel shows up to 50 accounts, but fewer if there are fewer than 50. If there's a tie for any rank in the bottom 50, Excel shows you all the tied records.

You can remove the applied filters in your pivot tables by taking these actions:

1. **Click anywhere inside your pivot table to activate the PivotTable Tools context tab on the Ribbon.**

2. **Select the Options tab on the Ribbon.**

3. **Click the Clear icon and select Clear Filters, as demonstrated in Figure 6-40.**

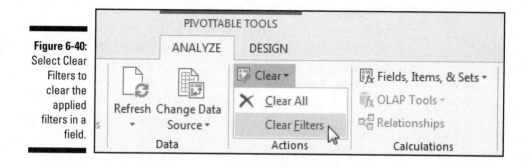

Creating views by month, quarter, and year

Raw transactional data is rarely aggregated by month, quarter, or year for you. This type of data is often captured by the day. However, managers often want reports by month or quarters instead of detail by day. Fortunately, pivot tables make it easy to group date fields into various time dimensions. Here's how:

1. **Build a pivot table with Sales Date in the row area and Sales Amount in the values area, similar to the one in Figure 6-41.**

	A	B	C
1	Business Segment	(All)	
2	SubRegion	(All)	
3			
4	SalesDate	Sum of Sales Amount	
5	01/01/08	$22,889	
6	01/02/08	$26,794	
7	01/03/08	$14,118	
8	01/04/08	$19,905	
9	01/05/08	$26,170	
10	01/06/08	$11,550	
11	01/07/08	$47,136	
12	01/08/08	$9,646	
13	01/09/08	$25,337	
14	01/10/08	$12,577	
15	01/11/08	$31,988	
16	01/12/08	$33,923	
17	01/13/08	$37,343	
18	01/14/08	$42,444	

Figure 6-41:
Build this
pivot table
to start.

2. **Right-click any date and select Group, as demonstrated in Figure 6-42.**

   The Grouping dialog box appears, as shown in Figure 6-43.

3. Select the time dimensions you want. In this example, select Months, Quarters and Years.

4. Click OK to apply the change.

Here are several interesting things to note about the resulting pivot table. First, notice that Quarters and Years have been added to your field list. Keep in mind that your source data hasn't changed to include these new fields; instead, these fields are now part of your pivot table. Another interesting thing to note is that by default, the Years and Quarters fields are automatically added next to the original date field in the pivot table layout, as shown in Figure 6-44.

	A	B	C	D
1	Business Segment	(All)		
2	SubRegion	(All)		
3				
4	Years	Quarters	SalesDate	Sum of Sales Amount
5	⊟2008	⊟Qtr1	Jan	$713,230
6			Feb	$1,682,318
7			Mar	$1,673,760
8		⊟Qtr2	Apr	$872,568
9			May	$2,280,165
10			Jun	$1,102,021
11		⊟Qtr3	Jul	$2,446,798
12			Aug	$3,615,926
13			Sep	$2,826,440
14		⊟Qtr4	Oct	$1,872,402
15			Nov	$2,939,785
16			Dec	$2,303,436
17	⊟2009	⊟Qtr1	Jan	$1,318,597
18			Feb	$2,166,151
19			Mar	$1,784,231
20		⊟Qtr2	Apr	$1,829,387

Figure 6-44: Adding Years and Quarters fields.

After your date field is grouped, you can use each added time grouping just as you would any other field in your pivot table. In Figure 6-45, I use the newly created time groupings to show sales for each market by quarter for 2010.

	A	B	C	D	E	F
1	Business Segment	(All)				
2	SubRegion	(All)				
3						
4	Sum of Sales Amount	Years	Quarters			
5		⊟2010				Grand Total
6	Market	Qtr1	Qtr2	Qtr3	Qtr4	
7	Australia	$340,522	$236,578	$170,142		$747,242
8	Canada	$1,024,564	$1,114,589	$884,516	$886,391	$3,910,059
9	Central	$626,424	$481,199	$565,002	$608,210	$2,280,836
10	France	$597,773	$680,722	$101,901		$1,380,396
11	Germany	$406,367	$399,498	$100,772		$906,637
12	Northeast	$475,563	$508,589	$288,912	$353,648	$1,626,712
13	Northwest	$1,166,061	$1,162,232	$931,871	$1,072,927	$4,333,091
14	Southeast	$500,399	$532,449	$719,666	$872,692	$2,625,207
15	Southwest	$1,441,357	$1,457,835	$1,069,882	$1,109,502	$5,078,576
16	United Kingdom	$542,587	$511,905	$225,600		$1,280,092
17	Grand Total	$7,121,616	$7,085,597	$5,058,264	$4,903,371	$24,168,848

Figure 6-45: You can use your newly created time dimensions just like a typical pivot field.

Creating a percent distribution view

A percent distribution (or percent contribution) view allows you to see how much of the total is made up of a specific data item. This view is useful when you're trying to measure the general impact of a particular item.

The pivot table, as shown in Figure 6-46, gives you a view into the percent of sales that comes from each business segment. Here, you can tell that bikes make up 81 percent of Canada's sales whereas only 77 percent of France's sales come from bikes.

Figure 6-46:
This view shows percent of total for the row.

Sum of Sales Amount	Business S ▾				
Market	▾	Accessories	Bikes	Clothing	Components
Australia		1.48%	83.30%	2.66%	12.56%
Canada		0.82%	81.00%	2.65%	15.53%
Central		0.59%	85.50%	1.96%	11.94%
France		1.05%	77.42%	2.79%	18.74%
Germany		1.74%	78.11%	3.68%	16.46%

Here are the steps to create this type of view:

1. **Right-click any value within the target field.**

   For example, if you want to change the settings for the Sales Amount field, right-click any value under that field.

2. **Select Value Field Settings.**

   The Value Field Settings dialog box appears.

3. **Click the Show Values As tab.**

4. **Select % of Row Total from the drop-down list.**

5. **Click OK to apply your change.**

The pivot table in Figure 6-47 gives you a view into the percent of sales that comes from each market. Here, you have the same type of view, but this time, you use the % of Column Total option.

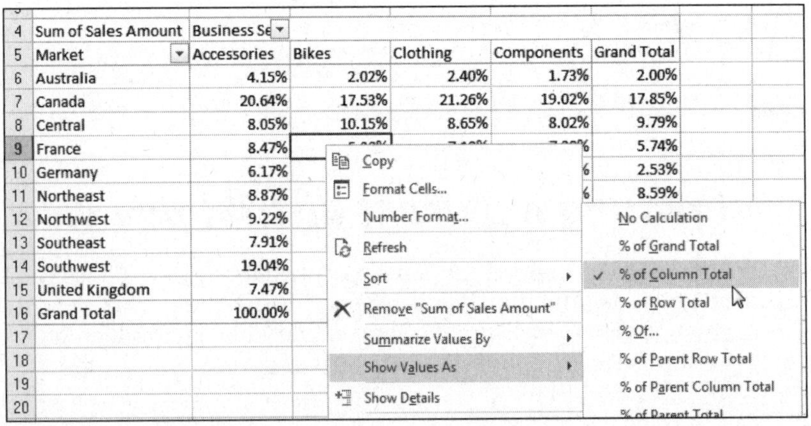

Figure 6-47:
This view shows percent of total for the column.

Sum of Sales Amount	Business Se ▾				
Market	▾	Accessories	Bikes	Clothing	Components	Grand Total
Australia		4.15%	2.02%	2.40%	1.73%	2.00%
Canada		20.64%	17.53%	21.26%	19.02%	17.85%
Central		8.05%	10.15%	8.65%	8.02%	9.79%
France		8.47%				5.74%
Germany		6.17%				2.53%
Northeast		8.87%				8.59%
Northwest		9.22%				No Calculation
Southeast		7.91%				% of Grand Total
Southwest		19.04%				✓ % of Column Total
United Kingdom		7.47%		Sort		% of Row Total
Grand Total		100.00%		Remove "Sum of Sales Amount"		% Of...
				Summarize Values By		% of Parent Row Total
				Show Values As		% of Parent Column Total
				Show Details		% of Parent Total

Copy
Format Cells...
Number Format...
Refresh

Again, remember that because you built these views in a pivot table, you have the flexibility to slice the data by region, bring in new fields, rearrange data, and most importantly, refresh this view when new data comes in.

Creating a YTD totals view

Sometimes it's useful to capture a running-totals view to analyze the movement of numbers on a year-to-date (YTD) basis. Figure 6-48 illustrates a pivot table that shows a running total of revenue by month for each year. In this view, you can see where the YTD sales stand at any given month in each year. For example, you can see that in August 2010, revenues were about a million dollars lower than the same point in 2009.

			2008	2009	2010
2	SubRegion	(All)			
3					
4	Sum of Sales Amount	Years			
5	SalesDate	2008	2009	2010	
6	Jan	$713,230	$1,318,597	$1,670,606	
7	Feb	$2,395,549	$3,484,749	$4,192,484	
8	Mar	$4,069,309	$5,268,979	$7,121,616	
9	Apr	$4,941,877	$7,098,366	$9,290,064	
10	May	$7,222,042	$10,020,068	$12,670,668	
11	Jun	$8,324,063	$11,952,318	$14,207,214	
12	Jul	$10,770,861	$14,741,281	$16,588,415	
13	Aug	$14,386,786	$19,055,823	$18,128,489	
14	Sep	$17,213,226	$23,036,113	$19,265,477	
15	Oct	$19,085,628	$25,506,056	$20,139,655	
16	Nov	$22,025,413	$28,833,967	$22,408,366	
17	Dec	$24,328,849	$32,517,515	$24,168,848	
18	Grand Total				
19					

Value Field Settings

Source Name: Sales Amount

Custom Name: Sum of Sales Amount

Summarize Values By | Show Values As

Show values as

Running Total In

Base field:
SalesDate
SalesPeriod
ListPrice
UnitPrice
OrderQty
Sales Amount

Base item:

Number Format | OK

Figure 6-48: This view shows a running total of sales for each month.

In the sample data for this chapter, you don't see Months and Years. You have to create them by grouping the SalesDate field. Feel free to review the section, "Creating views by month, quarter, and year," earlier in this chapter to find out how.

To create this type of view, take these actions:

1. **Right-click any value within the target field.**

   For example, if you want to change the settings for the Sales Amount field, right-click any value under that field.

2. **Select Value Field Settings.**

   The Value Field Settings dialog box appears.

3. **Click the Show Values As tab.**

4. **Select Running Total In from the drop-down list.**

5. **In the Base Field list, select the field that you want the running totals to be calculated against.**

   In most cases, this would be a time series such as, in this example, the SalesDate field.

6. **Click OK to apply your change.**

Creating a month-over-month variance view

Another commonly requested view is a month-over-month variance. How did this month's sales compare to last month's sales? The best way to create these types of views is to show the raw number and the percent variance together.

In that light, you can start creating this view by building a pivot table similar to the one shown in Figure 6-49. Notice that you bring in the Sales Amount field twice. One of these remains untouched, showing the raw data. The other is changed to show the month-over-month variance.

	A	B	C
1			
2	SubRegion	(All)	
3			
4		Values	
5	SalesDate	Sum of Sales Amount	Sum of Sales Amount2
6	Jan	$3,702,433	$3,702,433
7	Feb	$6,370,348	$6,370,348
8	Mar	$6,387,124	$6,387,124
9	Apr	$4,870,403	$4,870,403
10	May	$8,582,470	$8,582,470
11	Jun	$4,570,817	$4,570,817
12	Jul	$7,616,962	$7,616,962
13	Aug	$9,470,541	$9,470,541
14	Sep	$7,943,719	$7,943,719
15	Oct	$5,216,523	$5,216,523
16	Nov	$8,536,406	$8,536,406
17	Dec	$7,747,467	$7,747,467
18	Grand Total	$81,015,212	$81,015,212

Figure 6-49: Build a pivot table that contains the Sum of Sales Amount twice.

Figure 6-50 illustrates the settings that convert the second Sum of Sales Amount field into a month-over-month variance calculation.

2	SubRegion	(All)	▼
3			
4		Values	
5	SalesDate ↓	Sum of Sales Amount	Sum of Sales Amount2
6	Jan	$3,702,433	
7	Feb	$6,370,348	72.06%
8	Mar	$6,387,124	0.26%
9	Apr	$4,870,403	-23.75%
10	May	$8,582,470	76.22%
11	Jun	$4,570,817	-46.74%
12	Jul	$7,616,962	66.64%
13	Aug	$9,470,541	24.33%
14	Sep	$7,943,719	-16.12%
15	Oct	$5,216,523	-34.33%
16	Nov	$8,536,406	63.64%
17	Dec	$7,747,467	-9.24%
18	Grand Total	$81,015,212	
19			
20			
21			

Value Field Settings

Source Name: Sales Amount

Custom Name: Sum of Sales Amount2

Summarize Values By | Show Values As

Show values as

% Difference From

Base field:
Customer
Business Segment
Category
Model
Color
Sale:Date
SalesPeriod
ListPrice
UnitPrice

Base item:
(previous)
(next)
Jan
Feb
Mar
Apr
May
Jun
Jul

Number Format | OK | Cancel

Figure 6-50: Configure the second Sum of Sales Amount field to show month-over-month variance.

As you can see, after the settings are applied, the pivot table gives you a nice view of raw sales dollars and the variance over last month. You can obviously change the field names (see the section, "Customizing field names," earlier in this chapter) to reflect the appropriate labels for each column.

In the sample data for this chapter, you don't see Months and Years. You have to create them by grouping the SalesDate field. Feel free to review the section, "Creating views by month, quarter, and year," earlier in this chapter to find out how.

To create the view in Figure 6-50, take these actions:

1. **Right-click any value within the target field.**

   In this case, the target field is the second Sum of Sales Amount field.

2. **Select Value Field Settings.**

   The Value Field Settings dialog box appears.

3. **Click the Show Values As tab.**

4. **Select % Difference From from the drop-down list.**

5. **In the Base Field list, select the field that you want the running totals to be calculated against.**

   In most cases, this is a time series like, in this example, the SalesDate field.

6. **In the Base Item list, select the item you want to compare against when calculating the percent variance.**

   In this example, you want to calculate each month's variance to the previous month. Therefore, select the (Previous) item.

Part III

Building Advanced Dashboard Components

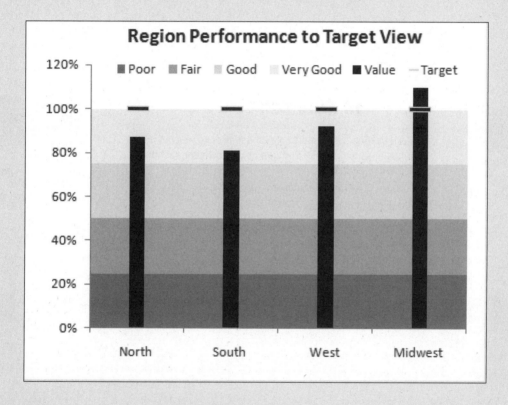

Check out the advanced trick at www.dummies.com/extras/
exceldashboardsandreports, which enables you to add an
extra dynamic layer of analysis to your charts.

In this part . . .

- ✔ Go beyond basic charting with a look at some advanced business techniques that can help make your dashboards more meaningful.

- ✔ Find out how to represent trending across multiple series and distinct time periods.

- ✔ Explore how best to use charts to group data into meaningful views.

- ✔ Uncover techniques that can help you display and measure performance against a target.

Chapter 7

Charts That Show Trending

• •

• •

*N*o matter what business you're in, you can't escape the tendency to trend. In fact, one of the most common concepts used in dashboards and reports is the concept of *trending*. A *trend* is a measure of variance over some defined interval — typically time periods such as days, months, or years.

The reason trending is so popular is that trending provides a rational expectation of what might happen in the future. If I know this book has sold 10,000 copies a month over the last 12 months (I wish), I have reasonable expectation to believe sales next month will be around 10,000 copies. In short, trending tells you where you've been and where you might be going.

In this chapter, you explore basic trending concepts and some of the advanced techniques you can use to take your trending components beyond simple line charts.

Trending Dos and Don'ts

Building trending components for your dashboards has some dos and don'ts. This section helps you avoid some common trending faux pas.

Using chart types appropriate for trending

It would be nice if you could definitively say which chart type you should use when building trending components. But, the truth is, no chart type is the silver bullet for all situations. For effective trending, you want to understand which chart types are most effective in different trending scenarios.

Using line charts

Line charts are the kings of trending. In business presentations, a line chart almost always indicates movement across time. Even in areas not related to business, the concept of lines is used to indicate time — consider timelines, family lines, bloodlines, and so on. The benefit of using a line chart for trending is that it's instantly recognized as a trending component, avoiding any delay in information processing.

Line charts are especially effective in presenting trends with many data points — as the top chart in Figure 7-1 shows. You can also use a line chart to present trends for more than one time period, as shown in the bottom chart in Figure 7-1.

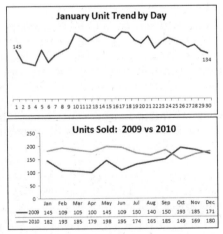

Figure 7-1:
Line charts are the chart of choice when you need to show trending over time.

Using area charts

An area chart is essentially a line chart that's been filled in. So, technically, area charts are appropriate for trending. They're particularly good at highlighting trends over a large time span. For example, the chart in Figure 7-2 spans over 120 days of data.

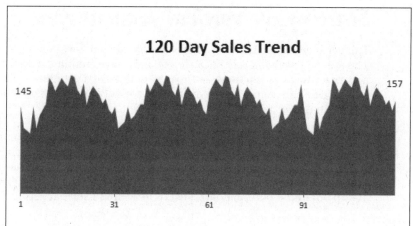

Figure 7-2:
Area charts
can be used
to trend
over a large
time span.

Using column charts

If you're trending one series of time, a line chart is absolutely the way to go. However, if you're comparing two or more time periods on the same chart, columns may best bring out the comparisons.

Figure 7-3 demonstrates how a combination chart can instantly call attention to the exact months when 2010 sales fell below 2009 sales. A combination of line and column charts is an extremely effective way to show the difference in units sold between two time periods. You see how to create this type of chart later in this chapter.

Figure 7-3:
Using
columns
and lines
emphasizes
the trending
differences
between
two time
periods.

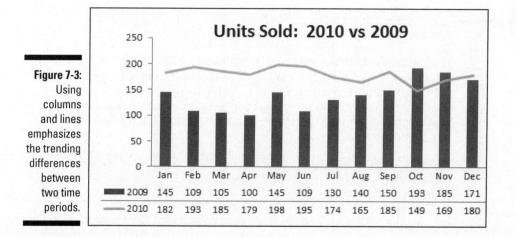

	Jan	Feb	Mar	Apr	May	Jun	Jul	Aug	Sep	Oct	Nov	Dec
2009	145	109	105	100	145	109	130	140	150	193	185	171
2010	182	193	185	179	198	195	174	165	185	149	169	180

Starting the vertical scale at zero

The vertical axis on trending charts should almost always start at zero. The reason I say *almost* is because you may have trending data that contains negative values or fractions. In those situations, it's generally best to keep Excel's default scaling. However, if you have only non-negative integers, ensure that your vertical axis starts at zero.

This is because the vertical scale of a chart can have a significant impact on the representation of a trend. For instance, compare the two charts shown in Figure 7-4. Both charts contain the same data. The only difference is that in the top chart, I did nothing to fix the vertical scale assigned by Excel (it starts at 96), but in the bottom chart, I fixed the scale to start at zero.

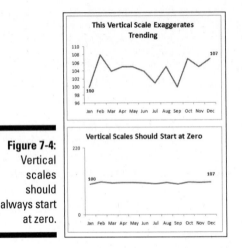

Figure 7-4: Vertical scales should always start at zero.

Now, you may think the top chart is more accurate because it shows the ups and downs of the trend. However, if you look at the numbers closely, you see that the units represented went from 100 to 107 in 12 months. That's not exactly a material change, and it certainly doesn't warrant such a dramatic chart. In truth, the trend is relatively flat, yet the top chart makes it look as though the trend is way up.

The bottom chart more accurately reflects the true nature of the trend. I achieved this effect by locking the Minimum value on the vertical axis to zero.

To adjust the scale of your vertical axis, follow these simple steps:

1. **Right-click the vertical axis and choose Format Axis.**

   The Format Axis dialog box appears; see Figure 7-5.

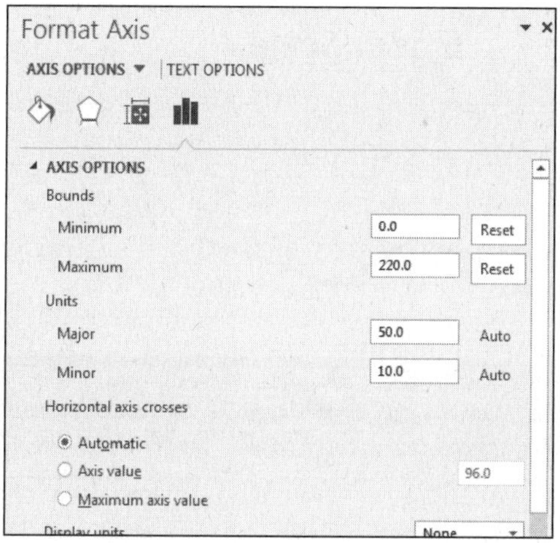

Figure 7-5: Always set the Minimum value of your vertical axis to zero.

[Format Axis dialog box showing:]

Format Axis ▾ ✕

AXIS OPTIONS ▾ | TEXT OPTIONS

◢ AXIS OPTIONS

Bounds
- Minimum: 0.0 — Reset
- Maximum: 220.0 — Reset

Units
- Major: 50.0 — Auto
- Minor: 10.0 — Auto

Horizontal axis crosses
- ⦿ Automatic
- ◯ Axis value: 96.0
- ◯ Maximum axis value

Display units: None

2. **In the Format Axis dialog box, expand the Axis Options section and set the Minimum value to 0.**

3. **(Optional) Set the Major Unit value to twice the Maximum value in your data.**

   Setting this value ensures that your trend line gets placed in the middle of your chart.

4. **Click Close to apply your changes.**

Many would argue that the bottom chart shown in Figure 7-4 hides the small-scale trending that may be important. That is, a seven unit difference may be very significant in some businesses. Well, if that's true, why use a chart at all? If each unit has such an impact on the analysis, why use a broad-sweep representation like a chart? A table with conditional formatting would do a better job at highlighting small-scale changes than any chart ever could.

Leveraging Excel's logarithmic scale

In some situations, your trending may start with very small numbers and end with very large numbers. In these cases, you end up with charts that don't accurately represent the true trend. Take Figure 7-6, for instance. In this figure, you see the unit trending for both 2009 and 2010. As you can see in the source data, 2009 started with a modest 50 units. As the months progressed, the monthly unit count increased to 11,100 units through December 2010. Because the two years are on such different scales, it's difficult to discern a comparative trending for the two years together.

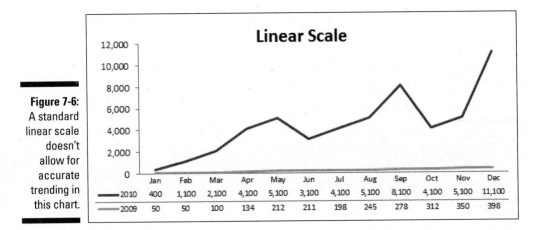

Figure 7-6:
A standard linear scale doesn't allow for accurate trending in this chart.

The solution is to use a logarithmic scale instead of a standard linear scale.

Without going into high school math, a logarithmic scale allows your axis to jump from 1 to 10; to 100 to 1,000; and so on without changing the spacing between axis points. In other words, the distance between 1 and 10 is the same as the distance between 100 and 1,000.

Figure 7-7 shows the same chart as that in Figure 7-6, but in a logarithmic scale. Notice that the trending for both years is now clear and accurately represented.

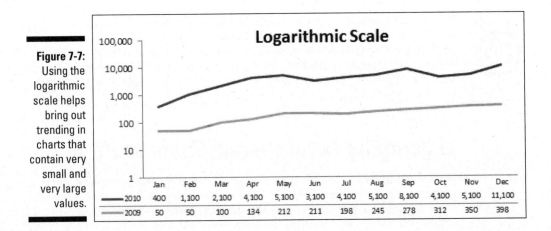

Figure 7-7:
Using the logarithmic scale helps bring out trending in charts that contain very small and very large values.

To change the vertical axis of a chart to logarithmic scaling, follow these steps:

1. **Right-click the vertical axis and choose Format Axis.**

   The Format Axis dialog box appears.

2. **Expand the Axis Options section and select the Logarithmic Scale check box as shown in Figure 7-8.**

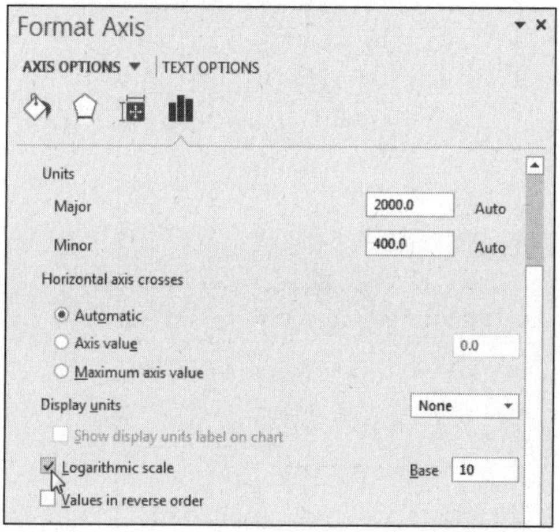

Figure 7-8:
Setting the vertical axis to logarithmic scale.

Format Axis

AXIS OPTIONS ▼ | TEXT OPTIONS

Units
Major   2000.0   Auto
Minor   400.0   Auto

Horizontal axis crosses
● Automatic
○ Axis value   0.0
○ Maximum axis value

Display units   None ▼
☐ Show display units label on chart

☑ Logarithmic scale   Base 10
☐ Values in reverse order

Logarithmic scales work only with positive numbers.

Applying creative label management

As trivial as it may sound, labeling can be one of the sticking points to creating effective trending components. Trending charts tend to hold lots of data points, whose category axis labels take up lots of room. Inundating users with a gaggle of data labels can definitely distract from the main message of the chart. In this section, you find a few tips to help manage the labels in your trending components.

Abbreviating instead of changing alignment

Month names look and feel very long when you place them in a chart — especially when that chart has to fit on a dashboard. However, the solution isn't to change their alignment, as shown in Figure 7-9. Words placed on their sides inherently cause a reader to stop for a moment and read the labels. This isn't ideal when you want them to think about your data and not spend time reading with their heads tilted.

Although it's not always possible, the first option is always to keep your labels normally aligned. So instead of jumping right to the alignment option to squeeze them in, try abbreviating the month names. As you can see in Figure 7-9, even using the first letter of the month name is appropriate.

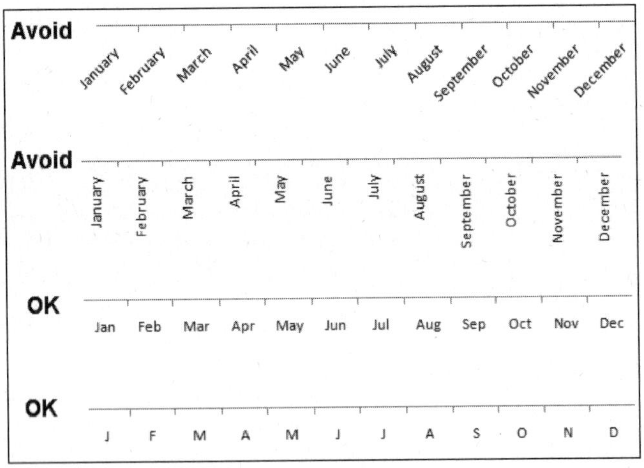

Figure 7-9: Choose to abbreviate category names instead of changing alignment.

Implying labels to reduce clutter

When you're listing the same months over the course of multiple years, you may be able to imply the labels for months instead of labeling each and every one of them.

Take Figure 7-10, for example. The chart in this figure shows trending through two years. There are so many data points that the labels are forced to be vertically aligned. To reduce clutter, as you can see, only certain months are explicitly labeled. The others are implied by a dot. To achieve this effect, you can simply replace the label in the original source data with a dot (or whatever character you like).

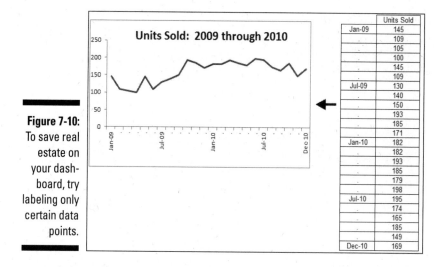

	Units Sold
Jan-09	145
	109
	105
	100
	145
	109
Jul-09	130
	140
	150
	193
	185
	171
Jan-10	182
	182
	193
	185
	179
	198
Jul-10	195
	174
	165
	185
	149
Dec-10	169

Units Sold: 2009 through 2010

Figure 7-10: To save real estate on your dashboard, try labeling only certain data points.

Going vertical when you have too many data points for horizontal

Trending data by day is common, but it does prove to be painful if the trending extends to 30 days or more. In these scenarios, it becomes difficult to keep the chart to a reasonable size and even more difficult to effectively label it.

One solution is to show the trending vertically using a bar chart. See Figure 7-11 for an example. With a bar chart, you have room to label the data points and keep the chart to a reasonable size. This isn't something to aspire to, however. Trending vertically isn't as intuitive and may not convey your information in a very readable form. Nevertheless, this solution can be just the work-around you need when the horizontal view is impractical.

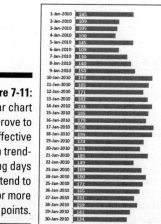

Figure 7-11: A bar chart can prove to be effective when trending days extend to 30 or more data points.

Nesting labels for clarity

Often, the data you're trying to chart has multiple time dimensions. In these cases, you can call out these dimensions by nesting your labels. Figure 7-12 demonstrates how including a year column next to the month labels clearly partitions each year's data. You would simply include the year column when identifying the data source for your chart.

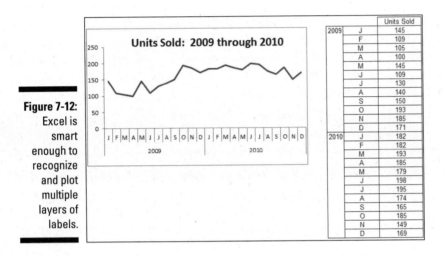

Figure 7-12: Excel is smart enough to recognize and plot multiple layers of labels.

Comparative Trending

Although the name is fancy, comparative trending is a simple concept. You chart two or more data series on the same chart so that the trends from those series can be visually compared. In this section, you walk through a few techniques that allow you to build components that present comparative trending.

Creating side-by-side time comparisons

Figure 7-13 shows a chart that presents a side-by-side time comparison of three time periods. With this technique, you can show different time periods in different colors without breaking the continuity of the overall trending. Here's how to create this type of chart:

1. **Structure your source data similar to the structure shown in Figure 7-14.**

   Note that instead of placing all the data into one column, you're staggering the data into respective years. This tells the chart to create three separate lines, allowing for the three colors.

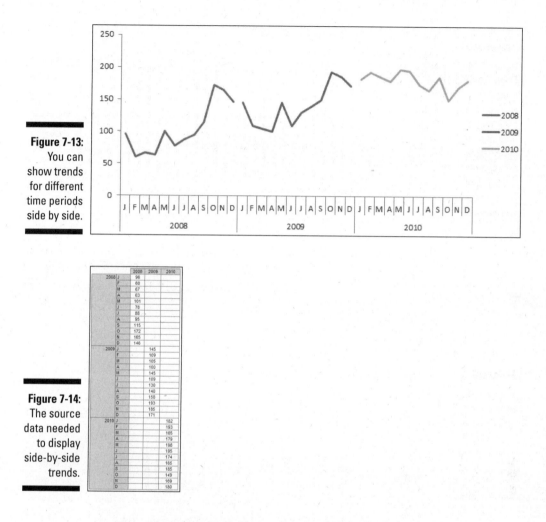

Figure 7-13:
You can show trends for different time periods side by side.

Figure 7-14:
The source data needed to display side-by-side trends.

		2008	2009	2010
2008	J	96		
	F	60		
	M	67		
	A	63		
	M	101		
	J	78		
	J	88		
	A	95		
	S	115		
	O	172		
	N	165		
	D	146		
2009	J		145	
	F		109	
	M		105	
	A		100	
	M		145	
	J		109	
	J		130	
	A		140	
	S		150	
	O		193	
	N		185	
	D		171	
2010	J			182
	F			193
	M			165
	A			179
	M			198
	J			195
	J			174
	A			165
	S			185
	O			149
	N			169
	D			180

2. **Select the entire table and create a line chart.**

   This creates the chart shown in Figure 7-13.

3. **If you want to get a bit fancy, click the chart to select it, then right-click and select Change Chart Type from the context menu that opens.**

4. **When the Change Chart Type dialog box opens, select Stacked Column Chart.**

   As you can see in Figure 7-15, your chart now shows the trending for each year in columns.

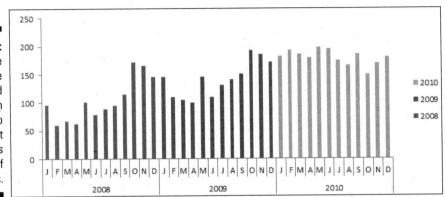

Figure 7-15: Change the chart type to Stacked Column Chart to present columns instead of lines.

Would you like a space between the years? Adding a space in the source data (between each 12 month sequence) adds a space in the chart, as shown in Figure 7-16.

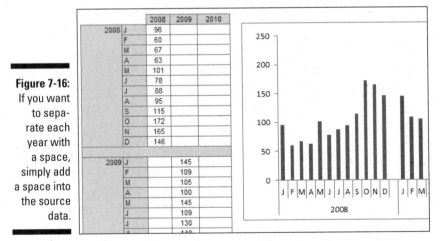

Figure 7-16: If you want to separate each year with a space, simply add a space into the source data.

Creating stacked time comparisons

The stacked time comparison places two series on top of each other instead of side by side. Although this removes the benefit of having an unbroken overall trending, it replaces it with the benefit of an at-a-glance comparison within a compact space. Figure 7-17 illustrates a common stacked time comparison.

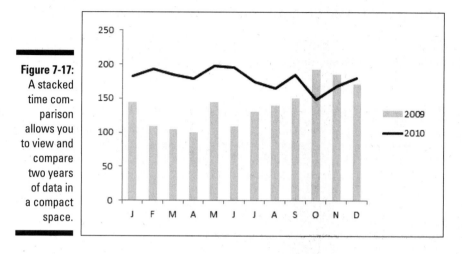

Figure 7-17:
A stacked
time com-
parison
allows you
to view and
compare
two years
of data in
a compact
space.

To create a stacked time comparison, follow these steps:

1. **Create a new structure and add data to it like the one shown in Figure 7-18.**

⊿	A	B	C
1		2009	2010
2	J	145	182
3	F	109	193
4	M	105	185
5	A	100	179
6	M	145	198
7	J	109	195
8	J	130	174
9	A	140	165
10	S	150	185
11	O	193	149
12	N	185	169
13	D	171	180

Figure 7-18:
Start with
a structure
containing
the data for
two time
periods.

2. **Highlight the entire structure and create a column chart.**

3. **Select and right-click any of the bars for the 2010 data series and then choose Change Series Chart Type.**

   The Change Chart Type dialog box appears.

4. **In the Change Chart Type dialog box, select the line type in the Line section.**

TIP

This technique works well with two time series. You generally want to avoid stacking any more than that. Stacking more than two series often muddies the view and causes users to constantly reference the legend to keep track of the series they're evaluating.

Trending with a secondary axis

In some trending components, you have series that trend two very different units of measure. For instance, the table in Figure 7-19 shows a trend for People Count and a trend for % of Labor Cost.

Figure 7-19:
You often need to trend two very different units of measure, such as counts and percentages.

	A	B	C
1		People Count	% Labor Cost
2	J	145	20%
3	F	109	21%
4	M	105	23%
5	A	100	23%
6	M	145	24%
7	J	109	25%
8	J	130	24%
9	A	140	25%
10	S	150	24%
11	O	193	26%
12	N	185	28%
13	D	171	29%

These are two very different units of measure that, when charted, produce the unimpressive chart you see in Figure 7-20. Because Excel builds the vertical axis to accommodate the largest number, the percentage of labor cost trending gets lost at the bottom of the chart. Even a logarithmic scale doesn't help in this scenario.

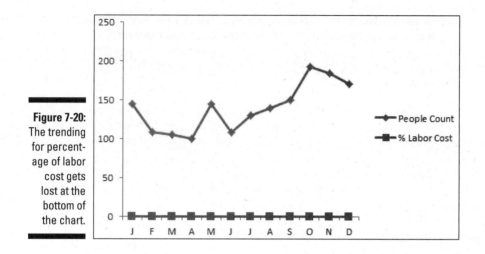

Figure 7-20:
The trending for percentage of labor cost gets lost at the bottom of the chart.

Because the default vertical axis (or primary axis) doesn't work for both series, the solution is to create another axis to accommodate the series that doesn't fit into the primary axis. This other axis is the secondary axis.

To place a data series on the secondary axis, follow these steps:

1. **Right-click the data series and select Format Data Series.**

   The Format Data Series dialog box appears, as shown in Figure 7-21.

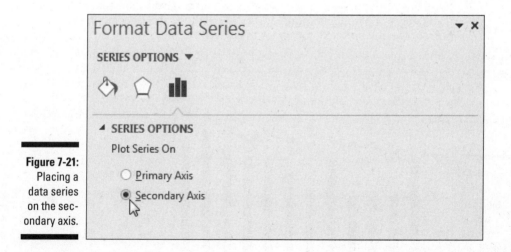

Figure 7-21:
Placing a data series on the secondary axis.

2. **In the Format Data Series dialog box, expand the Series Options section and then click the Secondary Axis radio button.**

Figure 7-22 illustrates the newly added axis to the right of the chart. Any data series on the secondary axis has its vertical axis labels shown on the right.

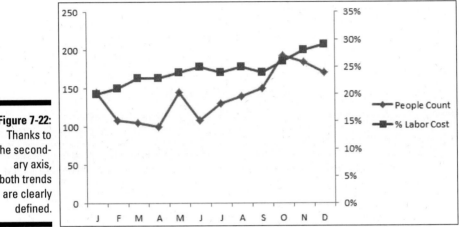

Figure 7-22:
Thanks to the secondary axis, both trends are clearly defined.

Again, changing the chart type of any one of the data series can help in comparing the two trends. In Figure 7-23, the chart type for the People Count trend has been changed to a column. Now you can easily see that although the number of people has gone down in November and December, the percentage of labor cost continues to rise.

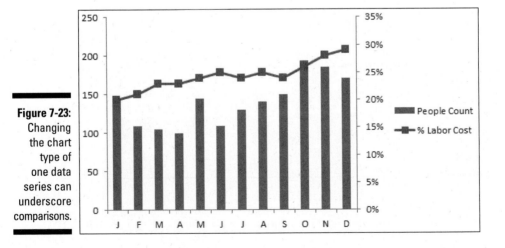

Figure 7-23:
Changing the chart type of one data series can underscore comparisons.

Technically, it doesn't matter which data series you place on the secondary axis. A general rule is to place the problem data series on the secondary axis. In this scenario, because the data series for percentage of labor cost seems to be the problem, I place that series on the secondary axis.

Emphasizing Periods of Time

Some of your trending components may contain certain periods in which a special event occurred, causing an anomaly in the trending pattern. For instance, you may have an unusually large spike or dip in the trend caused by some occurrence in your organization. Or maybe you need to mix actual data with forecasts in your charting component. In such cases, it could be helpful to emphasize specific periods in your trending with special formatting.

Formatting specific periods

Imagine you just created the chart component illustrated in Figure 7-24 and you want to explain the spike in October. You could, of course, use a footnote somewhere, but that would force your audience to look for an explanation elsewhere on your dashboard. Calling attention to an anomaly directly on the chart helps give your audience context without the need to look away from the chart.

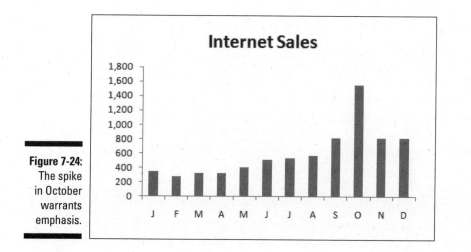

Figure 7-24: The spike in October warrants emphasis.

A simple solution is to format the data point for October to appear in a different color and then add a simple text box that explains the spike.

To format a single data point:

1. **Click the data point once.**

   This places dots on all the data points in the series.

2. **Click the data point again to ensure Excel knows you're formatting only that one data point.**

   The dots disappear from all but the target data point.

3. **Right-click and select Format Data Point.**

   This opens the Format Data Point dialog box shown in Figure 7-25. The idea is to adjust the formatting properties of the data point as you see fit.

   The dialog box shown in Figure 7-25 is for a column chart. Different chart types have different options in the Format Data Point dialog box. Nevertheless, the idea remains the same in that you can adjust the properties in the Format Data Point dialog to change the formatting of a single data point.

   After changing the fill color of the October data point and adding a text box with some context, the chart nicely explains the spike, as shown in Figure 7-26.

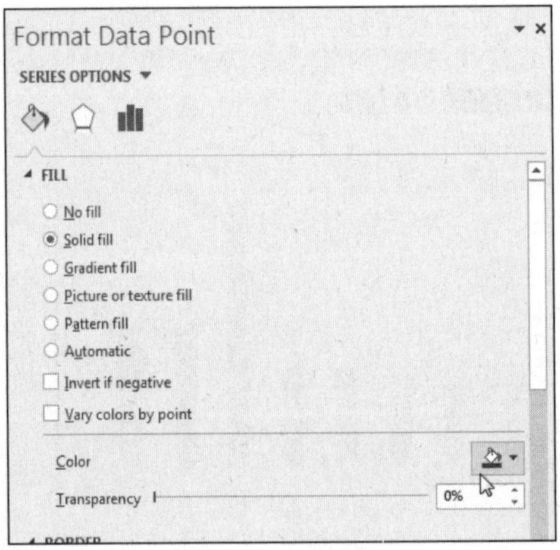

Figure 7-25: The Format Data Point dialog box gives you formatting options for a single data point.

Format Data Point ▾ ×

SERIES OPTIONS ▾

◢ FILL
- ○ No fill
- ● Solid fill
- ○ Gradient fill
- ○ Picture or texture fill
- ○ Pattern fill
- ○ Automatic
- ☐ Invert if negative
- ☐ Vary colors by point

Color

Transparency ⎸―――――――――― 0%

◢ BORDER

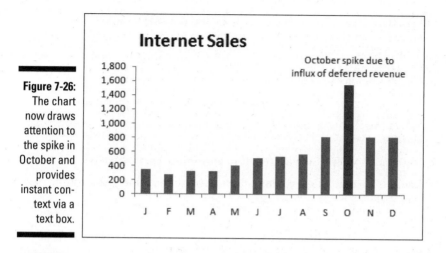

Figure 7-26:
The chart
now draws
attention to
the spike in
October and
provides
instant con-
text via a
text box.

To add a text box to a chart, click the Insert tab on the Ribbon and select the Text Box icon. Then click inside the chart to create an empty text box, which you can fill with your words.

Using dividers to mark significant events

Every now and then a particular event shifts the entire paradigm of your data permanently. A good example is a price increase. The trend shown in Figure 7-27 has been permanently affected by a price increase implemented in October. As you can see, a dividing line (along with some labeling) provides a distinct marker for the price increase, effectively separating the old trend from the new.

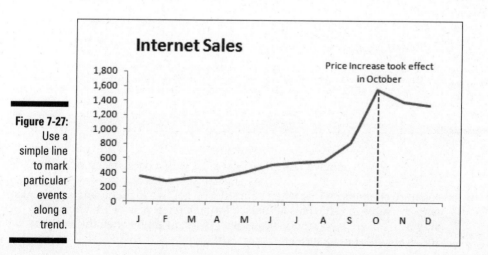

Figure 7-27:
Use a
simple line
to mark
particular
events
along a
trend.

Although there are lots of fancy ways to create this effect, you'll rarely need to get any fancier than manually drawing a line yourself. To draw a dividing line inside a chart, take the following steps:

1. **Click the chart to select it.**

2. **Click the Insert tab on the Ribbon and click the Shapes button.**

3. **Select the line shape, go to your chart, and draw the line where you want it.**

4. **Right-click your newly drawn line and select Format Shape.**

5. **Use the Format Shape dialog box to format your line's color, thickness, and style.**

Representing forecasts in your trending components

It's common to be asked to show both actual data and forecast data as a single trending component. When you do show the two together, you want to ensure that your audience can clearly distinguish where actual data ends and where forecasting begins. Take a look at Figure 7-28.

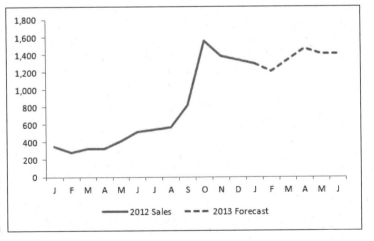

Figure 7-28: You can easily see where sales trending ends and forecast trending begins.

The best way to achieve this effect is to start with a data structure similar to the one shown in Figure 7-29. As you can see, sales and forecasts are in separate columns so that when charted, you get two distinct data series. Also note the value in cell B14 is actually a formula referencing C14. This value serves to ensure a continuous trend line (with no gaps) when the two data series are charted together.

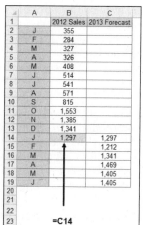

Figure 7-29:
Start with
a table that
places your
actual data
and your
forecasts
in separate
columns.

	A	B	C
1		2012 Sales	2013 Forecast
2	J	355	
3	F	284	
4	M	327	
5	A	326	
6	M	408	
7	J	514	
8	J	541	
9	A	571	
10	S	815	
11	O	1,553	
12	N	1,385	
13	D	1,341	
14	J	1,297	1,297
15	F		1,212
16	M		1,341
17	A		1,469
18	M		1,405
19	J		1,405
20			
21			
22			
23		=C14	

When you have the appropriately structured dataset, you can create a line chart. At this point, you can apply special formatting to the 2013 Forecast data series. Follow these steps:

1. **Click the data series that represents 2013 Forecast.**

   This places dots on all the data points in the series.

2. **Right-click and select Format Data Series.**

   This opens the Format Data Series dialog box.

3. **In this dialog box, you can adjust the properties to format the series color, thickness, and style.**

Other Trending Techniques

In this section, you explore a few techniques that go beyond the basic concepts covered so far.

Avoiding overload with directional trending

Do you work with a manager that's crazy for data? Are you getting headaches from trying to squeeze three years of monthly data into a single chart? Although it's understandable to want to see a three-year trend, placing too much information on a single chart can make for a convoluted trending component that tells you almost nothing.

When you're faced with the need to display impossible amounts of data, step back and think about the true purpose of the analysis. When your manager asks for a three-year sales trend by month, what's he really looking for? It could be that he's really asking whether current monthly sales are declining versus history. Do you really need to show each and every month or can you show the directional trend?

A *directional trend* is one that uses simple analysis to imply a relative direction of performance. The key attribute of a directional trend is that the data used is often a set of calculated values as opposed to actual data values. For instance, instead of charting each month's sales for a single year, you could chart the average sales for Q1, Q2, Q3, and Q4. With such a chart, you'd get a directional idea of monthly sales, without the need to look into detailed data.

Take a look at Figure 7-30, which shows two charts. The bottom chart trends each year's monthly data in a single chart. You can see how difficult it is to discern much from this chart. It looks like monthly sales are dropping in all three years. The top chart shows the same data in a directional trend, showing average sales for key time periods. The trend really jumps at you, showing that sales have flattened out after healthy growth in 2011 and 2012.

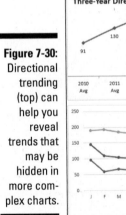

Figure 7-30: Directional trending (top) can help you reveal trends that may be hidden in more complex charts.

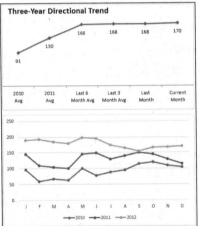

Smoothing data

Certain lines of business lend themselves to wide fluctuations in data from month to month. For instance, a consulting practice may go months without a steady revenue stream before a big contract comes along and spikes the sales figures for a few months. Some call these ups and downs *seasonality* or *business cycles*.

Whatever you call them, wild fluctuations in data can prevent you from effectively analyzing and presenting trends. Figure 7-31 demonstrates how highly volatile data can conceal underlying trends.

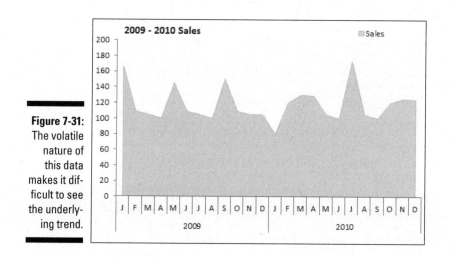

Figure 7-31: The volatile nature of this data makes it difficult to see the underlying trend.

This is where the concept of smoothing comes in. *Smoothing* does just what it sounds like — it forces the range between the highest and lowest values in a dataset to smooth to a predictable range without disturbing the proportions of the dataset.

Now, you can use lots of different techniques to smooth a dataset. Take a moment to walk through two of the easier ways to apply smoothing.

Smoothing with Excel's moving average functionality

Excel has a built-in smoothing mechanism in the form of a moving average trend line. That is, a trend line that calculates and plots the moving average at each data point. A *moving average* is a statistical operation used to track daily, weekly, or monthly patterns. A typical moving average starts calculating the average of a fixed number of data points, then with each new day's (or week's or month's) numbers, the oldest number is dropped, and the newest number is included in the average. This calculation is repeated over the entire dataset, creating a trend that represents the average at specific points in time.

Figure 7-32 illustrates how Excel's moving average trend line can help smooth volatile data, highlighting a predictable range.

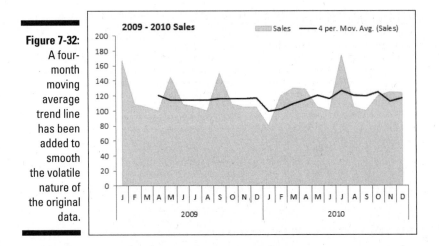

Figure 7-32:
A four-
month
moving
average
trend line
has been
added to
smooth
the volatile
nature of
the original
data.

In this example, a four-month moving average has been applied.

To add a moving average trend line, follow these steps:

1. **Right-click the data series that represents the volatile data, and then select Add Trendline.**

   The Format Trendline dialog box appears, shown in Figure 7-33.

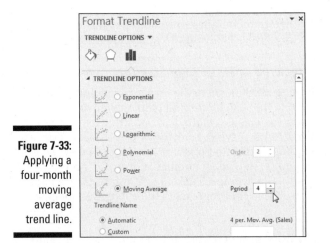

Figure 7-33:
Applying a
four-month
moving
average
trend line.

2. **In the Format Trendline dialog box, select Moving Average, and then specify the number of periods.**

   In this case, Excel will average a four-month moving trend line.

Creating your own smoothing calculation

As an alternative to Excel's built-in trend lines, you can create your own smoothing calculation and simply include it as a data series in your chart. In Figure 7-34, a calculated column (appropriately called Smoothing) provides the data points needed to create a smoothed data series.

	A	B	C	D	E
1				Sales	Smoothing
2		2009	J	167	
3			F	109	=AVERAGE($D$2:D3)
4			M	105	127
5			A	100	120
6			M	145	125
7			J	109	123
8			J	105	120
9			A	100	118
10			S	150	121
11			O	109	120
12			N	105	119
13			D	105	117
14		2010	J	80	115

Figure 7-34: A calculated smoothing column feeds a new series to your chart.

In this example, the second row of the smoothing column contains a simple average formula that averages the first data point and the second data point. Note that the reference to the first data point (cell D2) is locked as an absolute value with dollar ($) signs. This ensures that when this formula is copied down, the range grows to include all previous data points.

After the formula is copied down to fill the entire smoothing column, it can simply be included in the data source for the chart. Figure 7-35 illustrates the smoothed data plotted as a line chart.

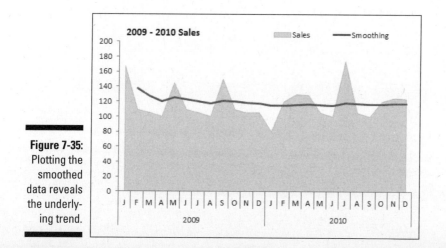

Figure 7-35: Plotting the smoothed data reveals the underlying trend.

Chapter 8

Grouping and Bucketing Data

· ·

In This Chapter

▶ Making top and bottom displays

▶ Using histograms to track groups

▶ Creating histograms with pivot tables

▶ Highlighting top and bottom values in charts

· ·

*I*t's often helpful to organize your analyses into logical groups of data. Grouping allows you to focus on manageable sets that have key attributes. For example, instead of looking at all customers in one giant view, you can analyze customers who buy only one product. This allows you to focus attention and resources on those customers who have the potential of buying more products.

The benefit of grouping data is that it allows you to more easily pick out groups that fall outside the norm for your business.

In this chapter, you explore some of the techniques you can use to create components that group and bucket data.

Creating Top and Bottom Displays

When you look at the list of Fortune 500 companies, you often look for the top 20 companies. Then perhaps you look at who eeked out at the bottom 20 slots. It's unlikely that you would check to see which company came in at number 251. It's not necessarily because you don't care about number 251; it's just that you can't spend the time or energy to process all 500 companies. So you process the top and bottom of the list.

This is the same concept behind creating top and bottom displays. Your audience has only a certain amount of time and resources to dedicate to solving any issues you can emphasize on your dashboard. Showing them the top and bottom values in your data can help them pinpoint where and how they can have the most impact with the time and resources they do have.

Incorporating top and bottom displays into dashboards

The top and bottom displays you create can be as simple as source data that you incorporate into your dashboard. Typically placed to the right of a dashboard, this data can emphasize details a manager may use to take action on a metric. For example, the simple dashboard shown in Figure 8-1 shows sales information with top and bottom sales reps.

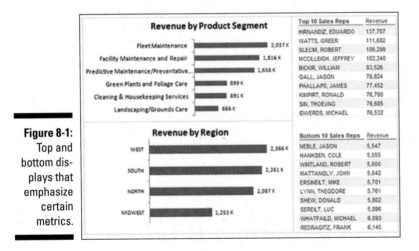

Figure 8-1:
Top and bottom displays that emphasize certain metrics.

To get a little fancier, you can supplement your top and bottom displays with some ranking information, some in-cell bar charts, or some conditional formatting; see Figure 8-2.

Top 10 Sales Reps	Sales		Rank	Last Month	vs Last Month
HIRNANDIZ, EDUARDO	$137,707		1	1	⇨ 0
WATTS, GREER	$111,682		2	3	⇧ 1
SLECIM, ROBERT	$106,299		3	5	⇧ 2
MCCILLEIGH, JEFFREY	$102,240		4	2	⇩ -2
BICKIR, WILLIAM	$83,526		5	3	⇩ -2
GALL, JASON	$78,824		6	12	⇧ 6
PHALLAPS, JAMES	$77,452		7	7	⇨ 0
KIMPIRT, RONALD	$76,790		8	9	⇧ 1
SIN, THOEUNG	$76,685		9	8	⇩ -1
DWERDS, MICHAEL	$76,532		10	4	⇩ -6

Bottom 10 Sales Reps	Sales		Rank	Last Month	vs Last Month
NEBLE, JASON	$5,547		244	244	⇨ 0
CELIMAN, WILLIAM	$9,779		243	241	⇩ -2
KRIZILL, ADAM	$11,454		242	235	⇩ -7
MIDANA, FRANK	$15,044		241	221	⇩ -20
GRANGIR, DAVID	$16,129		240	240	⇨ 0
DALLEARE, ANDRE	$16,265		239	239	⇨ 0
HICKLIBIRRY, JERRY	$16,670		238	225	⇩ -13
VAN HUILE, KENNETH	$18,821		237	242	⇧ 5
RACHERDSEN, KENNETH	$19,675		236	237	⇧ 1
STIGALL, DAVID	$20,092		235	243	⇧ 8

Figure 8-2: You can use some conditional formatting to add visual components to your top and bottom displays.

You can create the in-cell bar charts with the Data Bars conditional formatting function, covered in Chapter 5. The arrows are also simple conditional formatting rules that are evaluated against the variance in current and last months' ranks.

Using pivot tables to get top and bottom views

If you've read Chapter 6, you know that a pivot table is an amazing tool that can help create interactive reporting. Take a moment now to look over an example of how pivot tables can help you build interactive top and bottom displays.

Open the Chapter 8 Samples file, found on this book's companion website to follow along.

Follow these steps to display a Top and a Bottom filter with a pivot table:

1. **Start with a pivot table that shows the data you want to display with your top and bottom views.**

   In this case, the pivot table shows Sales Rep and Sales_Amount; see Figure 8-3.

2. **Right-click the field you want to use to determine the top values. In this example, use the Sales Rep field. Choose Filter⇨Top 10, shown in Figure 8-4.**

   The Top 10 Filter (Sales Rep) dialog box appears, shown in Figure 8-5.

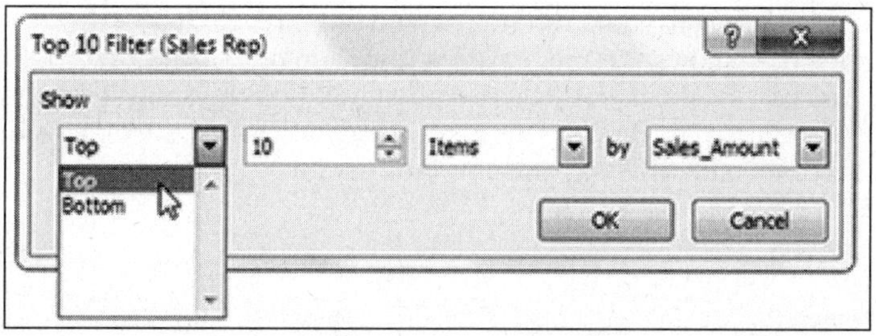

Figure 8-5: Specify the filter you want to apply.

3. **In the Top 10 Filter (Sales Rep) dialog box, define the view you're looking for. In this example, you want the Top 10 Items (Sales Reps) as defined by the Sales_Amount field.**
4. **Click OK to apply the filter.**

   At this point, your pivot table is filtered to show the top ten sales reps for the selected region and market. You can change the Market filter to Charlotte and get the top ten sales reps for Charlotte only; see Figure 8-6.

	A	B
1	Region	(All)
2	Market	CHARLOTTE
3		
4	Sales Rep	Sales_Amount
5	MCCILLEIGH, JEFFREY	$98,090
6	CERDWILL, TIMOTHY	$54,883
7	BRADFERD, JAMES	$49,435
8	DIDLIY, CHARLES	$47,220
9	SWANGIR, ADAM	$46,608
10	SKILTEN, JAMES	$43,569
11	PIORSEN, HEYWARD	$41,005
12	CRIOMIR, TIMOTHY	$34,169
13	PERSENS, GREGORY	$33,026
14	BIOCH, RONALD	$30,168
15	Grand Total	$478,172

Figure 8-6: You can interactively filter your pivot table report to instantly show the top ten sales reps for any region and market.

5. **To view the bottom ten Sales Rep list, copy the entire pivot table and paste it next to the existing one.**
6. **Repeat Steps 2 through 4 in the newly copied pivot table — except this time, choose to filter the bottom ten items as defined by the Sales_Amount field.**

If all goes well, you now have two pivot tables similar to those in Figure 8-7: one that shows the top ten sales reps, and one that shows the bottom ten. You can link back to these two pivot tables in the analysis layer of your data model using formulas. This way, when you update the data, your top and bottom values display the new information.

	A	B	C	D	E
1	Region	(All) ▼		Region	(All) ▼
2	Market	CHARLOTTE ⊤		Market	CHARLOTTE ⊤
3					
4	Sales Rep	⊺ Sales_Amount		Sales Rep	⊺ Sales_Amount
5	MCCILLEIGH, JEFFREY	$98,090		MEERE, TERRY	$27,149
6	CERDWILL, TIMOTHY	$54,883		BRAGHT, THOMAS	$25,005
7	BRADFERD, JAMES	$49,435		CRAVIY, ANTHONY	$22,761
8	DIDLIY, CHARLES	$47,220		WALLAEMS, SHAUN	$15,477
9	SWANGIR, ADAM	$46,608		HERVIY, CHRISTOPHER	$15,260
10	SKILTEN, JAMES	$43,569		HELT, CHRISTOPHER	$15,147
11	PIORSEN, HEYWARD	$41,005		REBIRTS, ADAMS	$13,237
12	CRIOMIR, TIMOTHY	$34,169		BECKMAN, ADRIAN	$9,236
13	PERSENS, GREGORY	$33,026		GERRUIS, ROBERT	$7,786
14	BIOCH, RONALD	$30,168		MEERE, RUSSELL	$6,635
15	Grand Total	$478,172		Grand Total	$157,693

Figure 8-7:
You now have two pivot tables that show top and bottom displays.

If there's a tie for any rank in the top or bottom values, Excel shows you all the tied records. This means you may get more than the number you filtered for. If you filtered for the top 10 sales reps and there's a tie for the number 5 rank, Excel shows you 11 sales reps (both reps ranked at number 5 will be shown).

Using Histograms to Track Relationships and Frequency

A *histogram* is a graph that plots frequency distribution. A *frequency distribution* shows how often an event or category of data occurs. With a histogram, you can visually see the general distribution of a certain attribute.

Take a look at the histogram shown in Figure 8-8. This histogram represents the distribution of units sold in one month among your sales reps. As you can see, most reps sell somewhere between 5 and 25 units a month. As a manager, you want the hump in the chart to move to the right — more people selling a higher number of units per month. So you set a goal for a majority of your sales reps to sell between 15 and 25 units within the next three months. With this histogram, you can visually track the progress toward that goal.

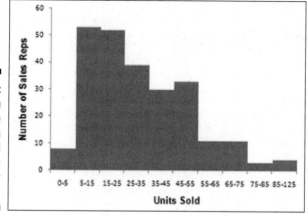

Figure 8-8:
A histogram showing the distribution of units sold per month among your sales force.

This section discusses how to create a histogram using formulas and pivot tables. The techniques covered here fit nicely in data models in which you separate data, analysis, and presentation information. In addition, these techniques allow for a level of automation and interactivity, which comes in handy when updating dashboards each month.

See how to develop a data model in Chapter 2.

Adding formulas to group data

Follow these steps to create a formula-driven histogram:

1. **Before you create your histogram, you need a table that contains your raw data, and you need to create a bin table; see Figure 8-9.**

   The raw data should ideally consist of records that represent unique counts for the data you want to group. For instance, the raw data table in Figure 8-9 contains unique sales reps and the number of units each has sold.

   The bin table dictates the grouping parameters used to break your raw data into the frequency groups. The bin table tells Excel to cluster all sales reps selling fewer than 5 units into the first frequency group, any sales reps selling 5 to 14 units in the second frequency group, and so on.

   You can freely set your own grouping parameters when you build your bin table. However, it's generally a good idea to keep your parameters as equally spaced as possible. You typically want to end your bin tables with the largest number in the dataset. This allows you to have clean groupings that end in a finite number — not in an open-ended greater-than designation.

Figure 8-9:
Start with
your raw
data table
and a bin
table.

2. **Create a new column in the bin table to hold the FREQUENCY formulas. Name the new column Frequency Formulas, as shown in Figure 8-10.**

Excel's FREQUENCY function counts how often values occur within the ranges you specify in a bin table.

Figure 8-10:
Type the
FRE-
QUENCY
formula you
see here,
and then be
sure to hold
down the
Ctrl+Shift+
Enter keys
on your
keyboard.

3. **Select the cells in the newly created column.**

4. **Type the FREQUENCY formula you see in Figure 8-10 and then press Ctrl+Shift+Enter on your keyboard.**

The FREQUENCY function has a quirk that often confuses first-time users. The FREQUENCY function is an array formula — a formula that returns many values at one time. In order for this formula to work properly, you have to press Ctrl+Shift+Enter on your keyboard after typing the formula. If you just press the Enter key, you won't get the results you need.

At this point, you should have a table that shows the number of sales reps that fall into each of your bins. You could chart this table, but the data labels would come out wonky. For the best results, you should build a simple chart feeder table that creates appropriate labels for each bin. You do this in the next step.

5. **Create a new table that feeds the charts a bit more cleanly; see Figure 8-11. Use a simple formula that concatenates bins into appropriate labels. Use another formula to bring in the results of your FREQUENCY calculations.**

   In Figure 8-11, the formulas in the first record of the chart feeder table are visible. These formulas are essentially copied down to create a table appropriate for charting.

Figure 8-11: Build a simple chart feeder table that creates appropriate labels for each bin.

	C	D	E	F	G	H
1					Chart Feeder	
2		Bins	Frequency Formulas		Units Sold	Count of Sales Reps
3		0	0		=D3& "-" &D4	=E4
4		5	8		5-15	53
5		15	53		15-25	52
6		25	52		25-35	39
7		35	39		35-45	30
8		45	30		45-55	33
9		55	33		55-65	11
10		65	11		65-75	11
11		75	11		75-85	3
12		85	3		85-125	4
13		125	4			

6. **Use your newly created chart feeder table to plot the data into a column chart.**

   Figure 8-12 illustrates the resulting chart. You can very well use the initial column chart as your histogram.

   If you like your histograms to have spaces between the data points, you're done. If you like the continuous, blocked look you get with no gaps between the data points, follow the next few steps.

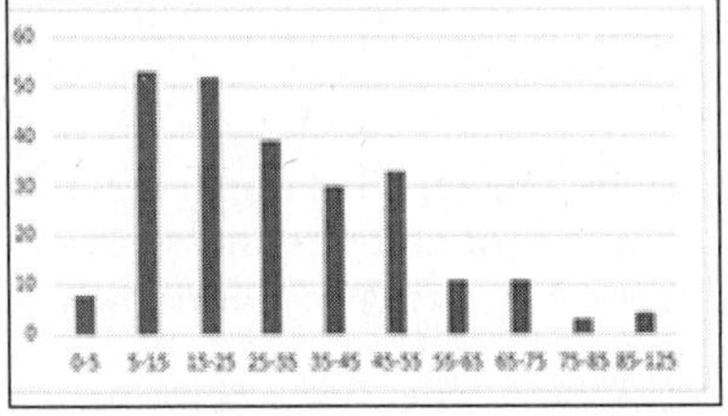

Figure 8-12:
Plot your
histogram
data into
a column
chart.

7. **Right-click any of the columns in the chart and choose Format Data Series.**

   The Format Data Series dialog box appears.

8. **Adjust the Gap Width property to 0%, as shown in Figure 8-13.**

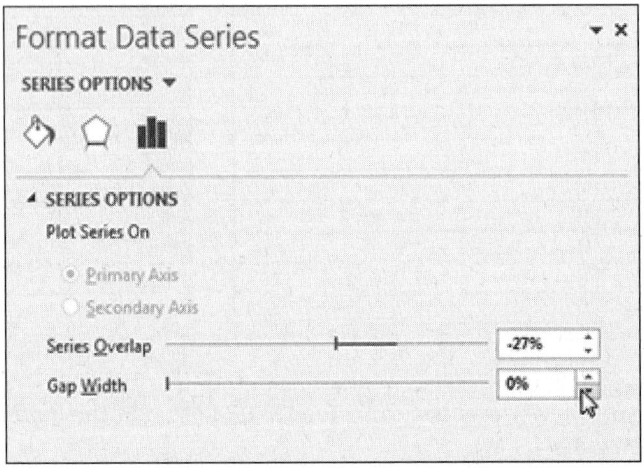

Figure 8-13:
To eliminate
the spaces
between
columns,
set the Gap
Width to 0%.

Adding a cumulative percent

A nice feature to add to your histograms is a cumulative percent series. With a cumulative percent series, you can show the percent distribution of the data points to the left of the point of interest.

Figure 8-14 shows an example of a cumulative percent series. At each data point in the histogram, the cumulative percent series tells you the percent of the population that fills all the bins up to that point. For instance, you can see that 25% of the sales reps represented sold 15 units or less. In other words, 75% of the sales reps sold more than 15 units.

Figure 8-14: The cumulative percent series shows the percent of the population that fills all the bins up to each point in the histogram.

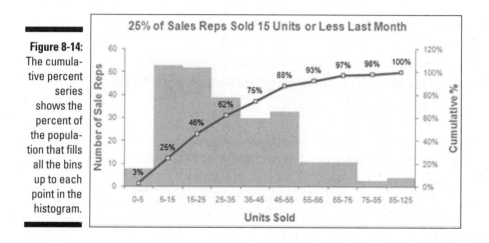

Take another look at the chart in Figure 8-14 and find the point where you see 75% on the cumulative series. At 75%, look at the label for that bin range (you see 35–45). The 75% mark tells you that 75% of sales reps sold between 0 and 45 units. This means that only 25% of sales reps sold more than 45 units.

To create a cumulative percent series for your histogram, follow these steps:

1. **Perform Steps 1 through 5 of creating a histogram (in the "Adding formulas to group data" section), then add a column to your chart feeder table that calculates the percent of total sales reps for the first bin; see Figure 8-15.**

   Note the dollar symbols ($) used in the formula to lock the references while you copy the formula down.

Chart Feeder

Units Sold	Count of Sales Reps	Cumulative %
0-5	8	=SUM($H$3:H3)/SUM($H$3:$H$12)
5-15	53	
15-25	52	
25-35	39	
35-45	30	
45-55	33	
55-65	11	
65-75	11	
75-85	3	
85-125	4	

Figure 8-15:
In a new column, create a formula that calculates the percent of total sales reps for the first bin.

2. **Copy the formula down for all the bins in the table.**

3. **Use the chart feeder table to plot the data into a line chart.**

   As you can see in Figure 8-16, the resulting chart needs some additional formatting.

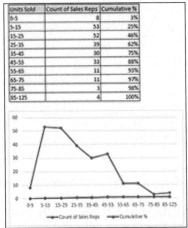

Figure 8-16:
Your initial chart will need some formatting to make it look like a histogram.

4. **Right-click the series that makes up your histogram (Count of Sales Reps), select Change Chart Type, and then change the chart type to a column chart.**

5. **Right-click any of the columns in the chart and choose Format Data Series.**

6. **Adjust the Gap Width property to 0%, as demonstrated in Figure 8-13.**

7. **Right-click Cumulative % series in the chart and choose Format Data Series.**

8. **In the Format Data Series dialog box, change the Plot Series On option to Secondary Axis.**

9. **Right-click Cumulative % series in the chart and choose Add Data Labels.**

At this point, your base chart is complete. It should look similar to the one shown at the beginning of this section in Figure 8-14. When you get to this point, you can adjust the colors, labels, and other formatting.

Using a pivot table to create a histogram

Did you know you can use a pivot table as the source for a histogram? That's right. With a little-known trick, you can create a histogram that's as interactive as a pivot table!

As in the formula-driven histogram, the first step in creating a histogram with a pivot table is to create a frequency distribution. Just follow these steps:

1. **Create a pivot table and plot the data values in the row area (not the data area). As you can see in Figure 8-17, the SumOfSales_Amount field is placed in the ROWS drop zone. Place the Sales Rep field in the VALUES dropzone.**

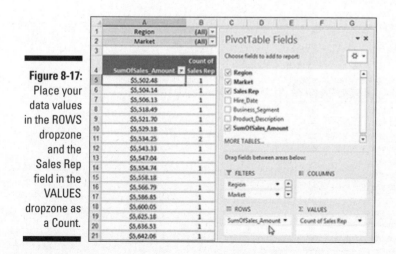

Figure 8-17: Place your data values in the ROWS dropzone and the Sales Rep field in the VALUES dropzone as a Count.

2. **Right-click any value in the ROWS area and choose Group.**

   The Grouping dialog box appears, as shown in Figure 8-18.

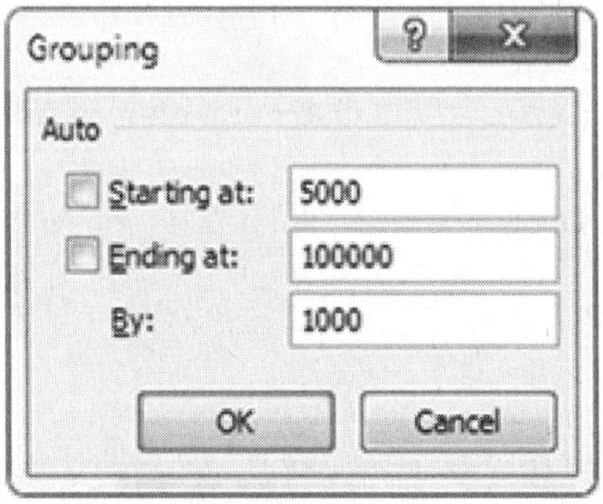

Figure 8-18: The Grouping dialog box.

3. **In this dialog box, set the Starting At and Ending At values and then set the interval.**

   This creates your frequency distribution. In Figure 8-18, the distribution is set to start at 5,000 and to create groups in increments of 1,000 until it ends at 100,000.

4. **Click OK to confirm your settings.**

   The pivot table calculates the number of sales reps for each defined increment, just as in a frequency distribution; see Figure 8-19. You can now leverage this result to create a histogram!

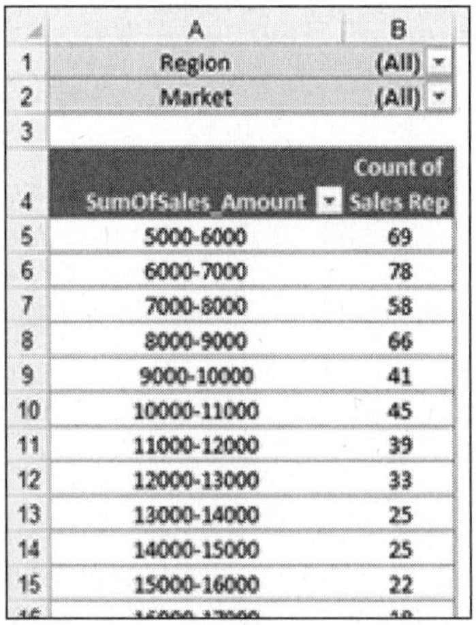

	A	B
1	Region	(All)
2	Market	(All)
3		
4	SumOfSales_Amount	Count of Sales Rep
5	5000-6000	69
6	6000-7000	78
7	7000-8000	58
8	8000-9000	66
9	9000-10000	41
10	10000-11000	45
11	11000-12000	39
12	12000-13000	33
13	13000-14000	25
14	14000-15000	25
15	15000-16000	22

Figure 8-19: The result of grouping the values in the row area is a frequency distribution that can be charted into a histogram.

The obvious benefit to this technique is that after you have a frequency distribution and a histogram, you can interactively filter the data based on other dimensions, like region and market. For instance, you can see the histogram for the Canada market and then quickly switch to see the histogram for the California market.

Note that you can't add cumulative percentages to a histogram based on a pivot table.

Emphasizing Top Values in Charts

Sometimes a chart is indeed the best way to display a set of data, but you still would like to call attention to the top values in that chart. In these cases, you can use a technique that actually highlights the top values in your charts. That is to say, you can use Excel to figure out which values in your data series are in the top *n*th value and then apply special formatting to them. Figure 8-20 illustrates an example in which the top five quarters are highlighted and given a label.

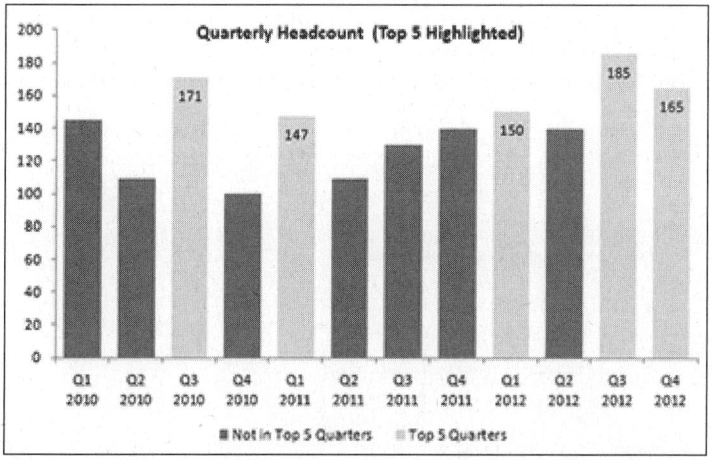

Figure 8-20:
This chart highlights the top five quarters with different font and labeling.

The secret to this technique is Excel's obscure LARGE function. The LARGE function returns the *n*th largest number from a dataset. In other words, you tell it where to look and the number rank you want.

To find the largest number in the dataset, you enter the formula LARGE(Data_ Range, 1). To find the fifth largest number in the dataset, use LARGE(Data_ Range, 5). Figure 8-21 illustrates how the LARGE function works.

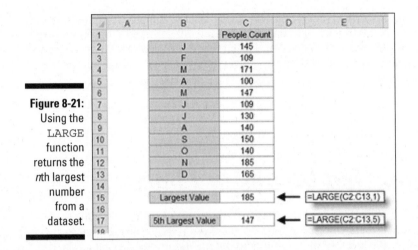

Figure 8-21:
Using the
LARGE
function
returns the
*n*th largest
number
from a
dataset.

The idea is fairly simple. In order to identify the top five values in a dataset, you first need to identify the fifth largest number (LARGE function to the rescue) and then test each value in the dataset to see if it's bigger than the fifth largest number. Here's what you do:

1. **Build a chart feeder that consists of formulas that link back to your raw data. The feeder should have two columns: one to hold data that isn't in the top five and one to hold data that is in the top five; see Figure 8-22.**

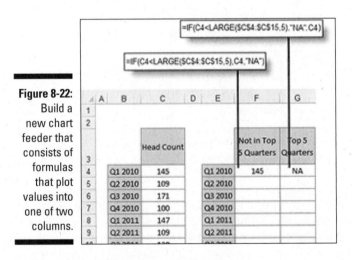

Figure 8-22:
Build a
new chart
feeder that
consists of
formulas
that plot
values into
one of two
columns.

2. **In the first row of the chart feeder, enter the formulas shown in Figure 8-22.**

   The formula for the first column (F4) checks to see if the value in cell C4 is less than the number returned by the LARGE formula (the fifth largest value). If it is, the value in cell C4 is returned. Otherwise, NA is used. The formula for the second column works in the same way, except the IF statement is reversed: If the value in cell C4 is greater than or equal to the number returned by the LARGE formula, then the value is returned; otherwise, NA is used.

3. **Copy the formulas down to fill the table.**

4. **Use the chart feeder table to plot the data into a stacked column chart.**

   You immediately see a chart that displays two data series: one for data points not in the top five, and one for data points in the top five; see Figure 8-23.

   Notice that the chart in Figure 8-23 shows some rogue zeros. You can fix the chart so that the zeros don't appear by performing the next few steps.

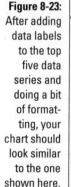

Figure 8-23:
After adding data labels to the top five data series and doing a bit of formatting, your chart should look similar to the one shown here.

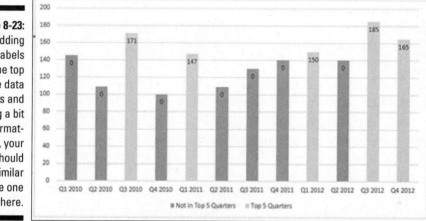

5. **Right-click any of the data labels for the "not in top 5" series and choose Format Data Labels.**

   The Format Data Labels dialog box appears.

6. **In this dialog box, expand the Numbers section and select Custom in the Category list.**

7. **Enter #,##0;; as the custom number format, as shown in Figure 8-24.**

8. **Click Add and then click Close.**

When you go back to your chart, you see that the rogue zeros are now hidden and your chart is ready for colors, labels, and other formatting you want to apply.

You can apply the same technique to highlight the bottom five values in your dataset. The only difference is that instead of using the LARGE function, you use the SMALL function. Whereas the LARGE function returns the largest *n*th value from a range, the SMALL function returns the smallest *n*th value.

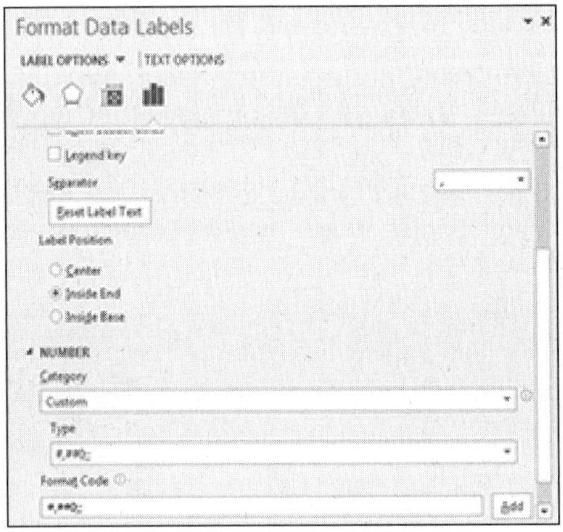

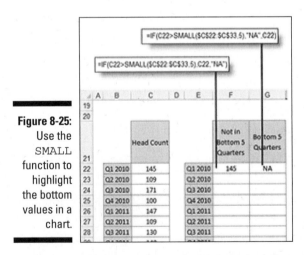

Figure 8-24:
Entering
#,##0;; as
the custom
format for a
data label
hides all
zeroes in
that data
series.

Figure 8-25 illustrates the formulas you use to apply the same technique outlined here for the bottom five values.

Figure 8-25:
Use the
SMALL
function to
highlight
the bottom
values in a
chart.

The formula for the first column (F22) checks to see if the value in cell C22 is greater than the number returned by the SMALL formula (the fifth smallest value). If it is, the value in cell C22 is returned. Otherwise, NA is used. The formula for the second column works in the same way except the IF statement is reversed: If the value in cell C22 is greater than the number returned by the SMALL formula, then NA is used; otherwise the value is returned.

Chapter 9

Displaying Performance against a Target

*H*opefully, this is an easy one to grasp. Someone sets a target, and someone else tries to reach that target. The target could be anything from a certain amount of revenue to a number of boxes shipped or to phone calls made. The business world is full of targets and goals. Your job is to find effective ways to represent performance against those targets.

What do I mean by performance against a target? Imagine your goal is to break the land speed record, which is currently 763 miles per hour. That makes your target 764 miles per hour, which will break the record. After you jump into your car and go as fast as you can, you will have a final speed. That number is your performance against the target.

In this chapter, I explore some new and interesting ways to create components that show performance against a target.

Showing Performance with Variances

The standard way of displaying performance against a target is to plot the target and then plot the performance. This is usually done with a line chart or a combination chart, such as the one shown in Figure 9-1.

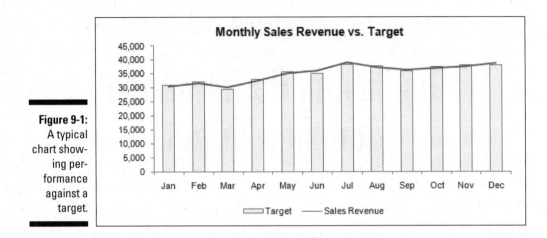

Although this chart allows you to visually pick the points where performance exceeded or fell below targets, it gives you a rather one-dimensional view and provides minimal information. Even if this chart offered labels that showed the actual percent of sales revenue versus target, you'd still get only a mildly informative view.

A more effective and informative way to display performance against a target is to plot the variances between the target and the performance. Figure 9-2 shows the same performance data you see in Figure 9-1, but includes the variances (sales revenue minus target) under the month label. This way, you see not only where performance exceeded or fell below targets, but you also get an extra layer of information showing the dollar impact of each rise and fall.

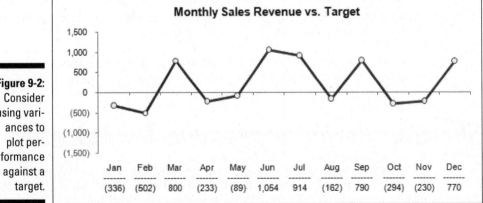

Showing Performance against Organizational Trends

The target you use to measure performance doesn't necessarily have to be set by management or organizational policy. In fact, some of the things you measure may never have a formal target or goal set for them. In situations in which you don't have a target to measure against, it's often helpful to measure performance against some organizational statistic.

For example, the component in Figure 9-3 measures the sales performance for each division against the median sales for all the divisions. You can see that divisions 1, 3, and 6 fall well below the median for the group.

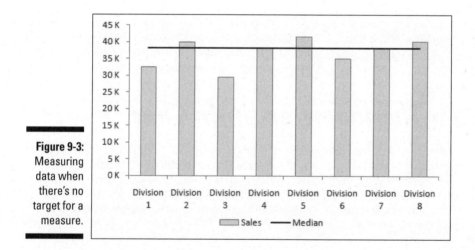

Figure 9-3: Measuring data when there's no target for a measure.

Here's how you'd create a median line similar to the one you see in Figure 9-3:

1. **Start a new column next to your data and type the simple MEDIAN formula, as shown in Figure 9-4.**

   Note that this formula can be any mathematical or statistical operation that works for the data you're representing. Just make sure that the values returned are the same for the entire column. This gives you a straight line.

2. **Copy the formula down to fill the table.**

   Again, all the numbers in the newly created column should be the same.

3. **Plot the table into a column chart.**

4. **Right-click the Median data series and choose Change Series Chart Type.**

5. **Change the chart type to a line chart.**

	A	B	C
1		Sales	Median
2	Division 1	32,526	=MEDIAN($B$2:$B$9)
3	Division 2	39,939	
4	Division 3	29,542	
5	Division 4	38,312	
6	Division 5	41,595	
7	Division 6	35,089	
8	Division 7	38,270	
9	Division 8	40,022	
10			

Figure 9-4: Start a new column and enter a formula.

Using a Thermometer-Style Chart

A thermometer-style chart offers a unique way to view performance against a goal. As the name implies, the data points shown in this type of chart resemble a thermometer. Each performance value and its corresponding target are stacked on top of one another, giving an appearance similar to that of mercury rising in a thermometer. In Figure 9-5, you see an example of a thermometer-style chart.

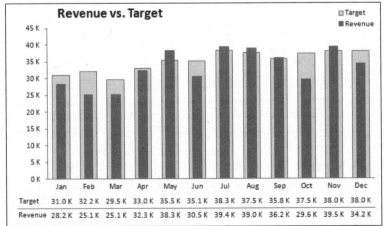

Figure 9-5: Thermometer-style charts offer a unique way to show performance against a goal.

Revenue vs. Target

	Jan	Feb	Mar	Apr	May	Jun	Jul	Aug	Sep	Oct	Nov	Dec
Target	31.0 K	32.2 K	29.5 K	33.0 K	35.5 K	35.1 K	38.3 K	37.5 K	35.8 K	37.5 K	38.0 K	38.0 K
Revenue	28.2 K	25.1 K	25.1 K	32.3 K	38.3 K	30.5 K	39.4 K	39.0 K	36.2 K	29.6 K	39.5 K	34.2 K

To create this type of chart, follow these steps:

1. **Starting with a table that contains revenue and target data, plot the data into a new column chart.**

2. **Right-click the Revenue data series and choose Format Data Series.**

3. **In the Format Data Series dialog box, select Secondary Axis.**

4. **Go back to your chart and delete the new vertical axis that was added; it's the vertical axis to the right of the chart.**

5. **Right-click the Target series and choose Format Data Series.**

6. **In the dialog box, adjust the Gap Width property so that the Target series is slightly wider than the Revenue series — between 45% and 55% is typically fine.**

Using a Bullet Graph

A *bullet graph* is a type of column/bar graph developed by visualization expert Stephen Few to serve as a replacement for dashboard gauges and meters. He developed bullet graphs to allow you to clearly display multiple layers of information without occupying a lot of space on a dashboard. A bullet graph, as seen in Figure 9-6, contains a single performance measure (such as YTD [year-to-date] revenue), compares that measure with a target, and displays it in the context of qualitative ranges, such as Poor, Fair, Good, and Very Good.

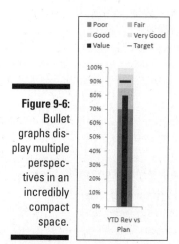

Figure 9-6:
Bullet graphs display multiple perspectives in an incredibly compact space.

Figure 9-7 breaks down the three main parts of a bullet graph. The single bar represents the performance measure. The horizontal marker represents the comparative measure. And the background color banding represents the qualitative ranges.

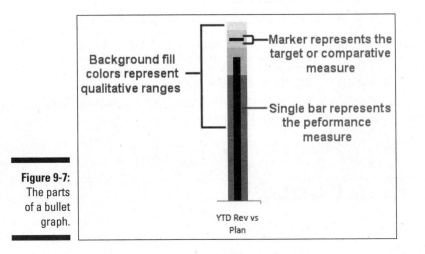

Figure 9-7:
The parts
of a bullet
graph.

Creating a bullet graph

Creating a bullet graph in Excel involves quite a few steps, but the process isn't necessarily difficult. Follow these steps to create your first bullet graph:

1. **Start with a data table that gives you all the data points you need to create the three main parts of the bullet graph.**

   Figure 9-8 illustrates what that data table looks like. The first four values in the dataset (Poor, Fair, Good, and Very Good) make up the qualitative range. You don't have to have four values — you can have as many or as few as you need. In this scenario, we want our qualitative range to span from 0 to 100%. Therefore, the percentages (70%, 15%, 10%, and 5%) must add up to 100%. Again, this can be adjusted to suit your needs. The fifth value in Figure 9-8 (Value) creates the performance bar. The sixth value (Target) makes the target marker.

2. **Select the entire table and plot the data on a stacked column chart.**

   The chart that's created is initially plotted in the wrong direction.

3. **To fix the direction, click the chart and select the Switch Row/Column button, as shown in Figure 9-9.**

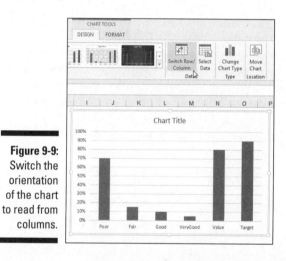

Figure 9-8:
Start with
data that
contains the
main data
points of the
bullet graph.

	A	B
1		YTD Rev vs Plan
2	Poor	70%
3	Fair	15%
4	Good	10%
5	VeryGood	5%
6	Value	80%
7	Target	90%
8		

Figure 9-9:
Switch the
orientation
of the chart
to read from
columns.

4. **Right-click the Target series and choose Change Series Chart Type.**
   Use the Change Chart Type dialog box to change the Target series to a
   Line with Markers and to place it on the secondary axis; see Figure 9-10.
   After confirming your change, the Target series appears on the chart
   as a single dot.

5. **Right-click the Target series again and choose Format Data Series to**
   open that dialog box. Click the Marker option, and adjust the marker
   to look like a dash, as shown in Figure 9-11.

6. **Still in the Format Data Series dialog box, expand the Fill section and**
   in the Solid Fill property, set the color of the marker to a noticeable
   color such as red.

7. **Still in the Format Data Series dialog box, expand the Border section**
   and set the Border to No Line.

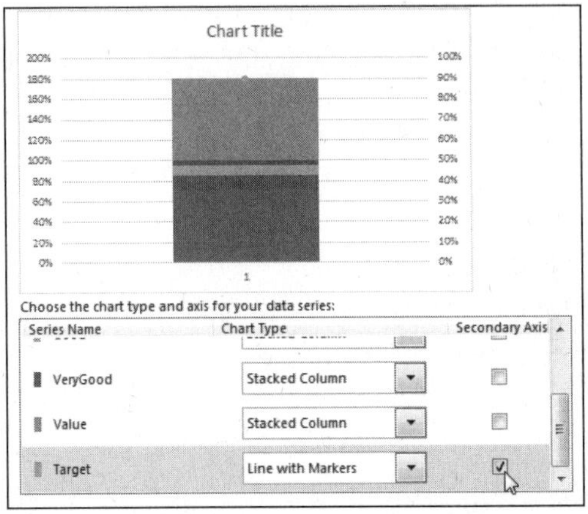

Figure 9-10:
Use the
Change
Chart Type
dialog box
to change
the Target
series to a
Line with
Markers
and place
it on the
secondary
axis.

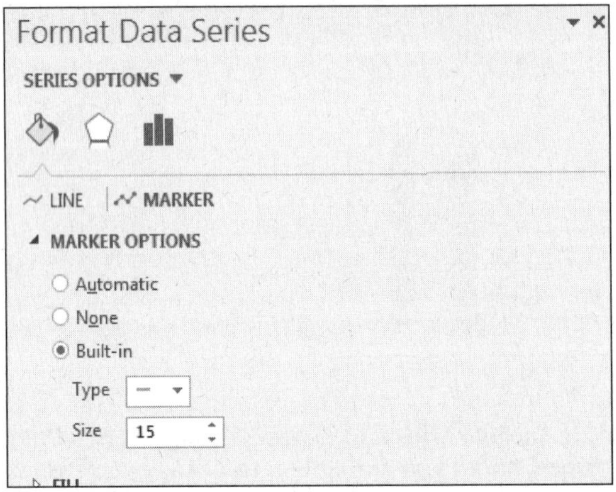

Choose the chart type and axis for your data series:

Series Name	Chart Type	Secondary Axis
VeryGood	Stacked Column	☐
Value	Stacked Column	☐
Target	Line with Markers	☑

Format Data Series

SERIES OPTIONS ▼

∿ LINE | ⫨ MARKER

◢ MARKER OPTIONS

○ Automatic
○ None
◉ Built-in

Type [— ▼]

Size [15]

Figure 9-11:
Adjust the
marker to a
dash.

8. **Go back to your chart and delete the new secondary axis that was added to the right of your chart; see Figure 9-12.**

   This is an important step to ensure the scale of the chart is correct for all data points.

9. **Right-click the Value series and choose Format Data Series.**

10. **In the Format Data Series dialog box, click Secondary Axis.**

11. **Still in the Format Data Series dialog box, under Series Options, adjust the Gap Width property so that the Value series is slightly narrower than the other columns in the chart — between 205% and 225% is typically okay.**

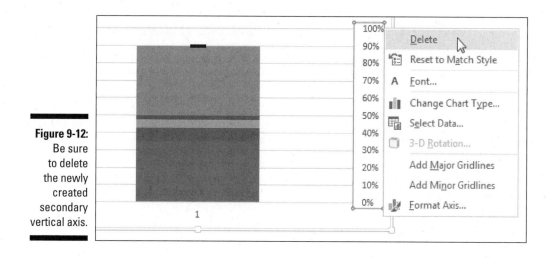

Figure 9-12: Be sure to delete the newly created secondary vertical axis.

12. **Still in the Format Data Series dialog box, click the Fill icon (the paint bucket), expand the Fill section, and then select the Solid Fill option to set the color of the Value series to black.**

13. **All that's left to do is change the color for each qualitative range to incrementally lighter hues.**

    At this point, your bullet graph is essentially done! You can apply whatever minor formatting adjustments to size and shape of the chart to make it look the way you want. Figure 9-13 shows our newly created bullet graph formatted with a legend and horizontal labels.

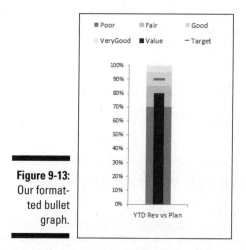

Figure 9-13: Our formatted bullet graph.

Adding data to your bullet graph

After you've built your chart for the first performance measure, you can use the same chart for any additional measures. Take a look at Figure 9-14.

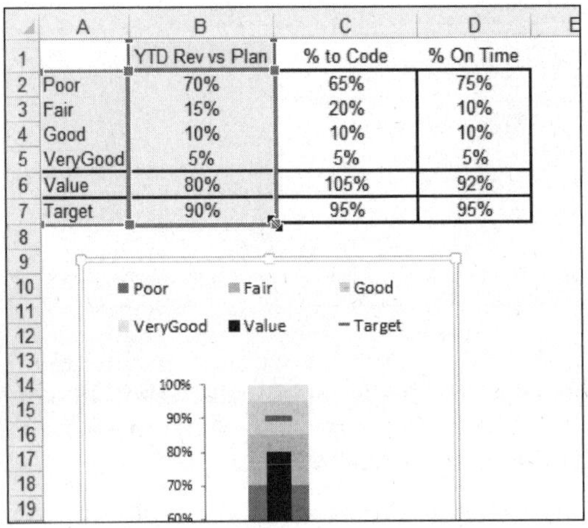

Figure 9-14:
To add more
data to your
chart, man-
ually expand
the chart's
data source
range.

	A	B	C	D	E
1		YTD Rev vs Plan	% to Code	% On Time	
2	Poor	70%	65%	75%	
3	Fair	15%	20%	10%	
4	Good	10%	10%	10%	
5	VeryGood	5%	5%	5%	
6	Value	80%	105%	92%	
7	Target	90%	95%	95%	

Legend: ■ Poor ■ Fair ■ Good ■ VeryGood ■ Value — Target

As you can see in Figure 9-14, you've already created this bullet graph with the first performance measure. Imagine that you add two more measures and want to graph those. Here's how to do it:

1. **Click the chart so that the blue outline appears around the original source data.**

2. **Hover your mouse pointer over the blue dot in the lower-right corner of the blue box.**

   Your cursor turns into an arrow, as seen in Figure 9-14.

3. **Click and drag the blue dot to the last column in your expanded dataset.**

   Figure 9-15 illustrates how the new data points are added without one ounce of extra work!

Final thoughts on formatting bullet graphs

Before wrapping up this introduction to bullet graphs, I discuss two final thoughts on formatting:

✔ Creating qualitative bands

✔ Creating horizontal bullet graphs

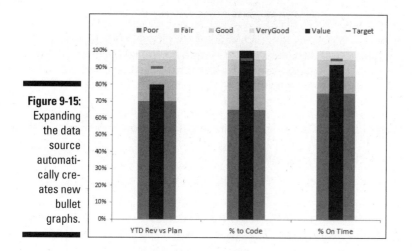

Figure 9-15:
Expanding
the data
source
automatically creates new
bullet
graphs.

Creating qualitative bands

First, if the qualitative ranges are the same for all the performance measures
in your bullet graphs, you can format the qualitative range series to have no
gaps between them. For instance, Figure 9-16 shows a set of bullet graphs in
which the qualitative ranges have been set to 0% Gap Width. This creates the
clever effect of qualitative bands. Here's how to do it:

1. **Right-click any one of the qualitative series and choose Format Data
   Series.**

2. **In the Format Series dialog box, adjust the Gap Width property to 0%.**

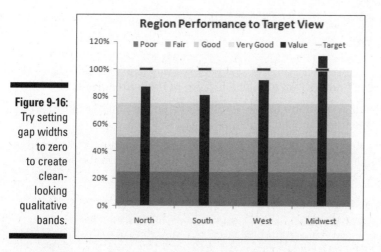

Figure 9-16:
Try setting
gap widths
to zero
to create
clean-
looking
qualitative
bands.

Creating horizontal bullet graphs

For those of you waiting on the section about horizontal bullet graphs, there's good and bad news. The bad news is that creating a horizontal bullet graph from scratch in Excel is a much more complex endeavor than creating a vertical bullet graph — one that doesn't warrant the time and effort it takes to create them.

The good news is that there is a clever way to get a horizontal bullet graph from a vertical one — and in three steps, no less. Here's how you do it:

1. **Create a vertical bullet graph.**

   For how to do this, see the "Creating a bullet graph" section earlier in this chapter.

2. **Change the alignment for the axis and other labels on the bullet graph so that they're rotated 270 degrees; see Figure 9-17.**

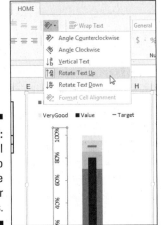

Figure 9-17: Rotate all labels so that they're on their sides.

3. **Use Excel's Camera tool to take a picture of the bullet graph.**

   After you have a picture, you can rotate it to be horizontal. Figure 9-18 illustrates a horizontal bullet graph.

   The nifty thing about this trick is that because the picture is taken with the Camera tool, the picture automatically updates when the source table changes.

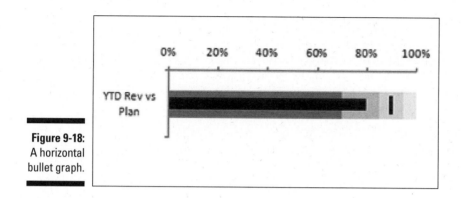

Figure 9-18:
A horizontal
bullet graph.

Showing Performance against a Target Range

In some businesses, a target isn't one value — it's a range of values. That is to say, the goal is to stay within a defined target range. Imagine you manage a small business selling boxes of meat. Part of your job is to keep your inventory stocked between 25 and 35 boxes in a month. If you have too many boxes of meat, the meat will go bad. If you have too few boxes, you'll lose money.

To track how well you do at keeping your inventory of meat between 25 and 35 boxes, you need a performance component that displays on-hand boxes against a target range. Figure 9-19 illustrates a component you can build to track performance against a target range. The gray band represents the target range you must stay within each month. The line represents the trend of on-hand meat.

Obviously, the trick to this type of component is to set up the band that represents the target range. Here's how you do it:

1. **Set up a limit table in which you can define and adjust the upper and lower limits of your target range.**

   Cells B2 and B3 in Figure 9-20 serve as the place to define the limits for the range.

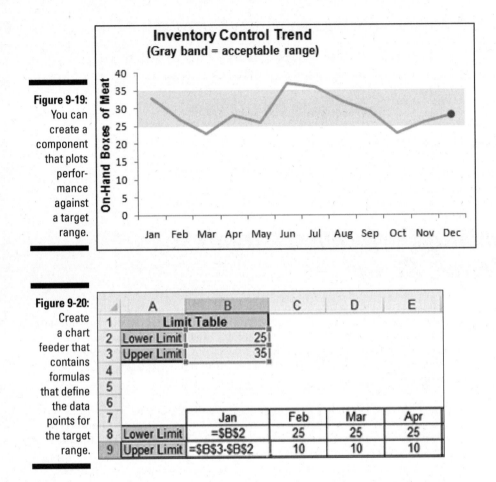

Figure 9-19: You can create a component that plots performance against a target range.

	A	B	C	D	E
1	Limit Table				
2	Lower Limit	25			
3	Upper Limit	35			
4					
5					
6					
7		Jan	Feb	Mar	Apr
8	Lower Limit	=$B$2	25	25	25
9	Upper Limit	=$B$3-$B$2	10	10	10

Figure 9-20: Create a chart feeder that contains formulas that define the data points for the target range.

2. **Build a chart feeder that's used to plot the data points for the target range.**

   This feeder consists of the formulas revealed in cells B8 and B9 in Figure 9-20. The idea is to copy these formulas across all the data. The values you see for Feb, Mar, and Apr are the results of these formulas.

3. **Add a row for the actual performance values, as shown in Figure 9-21.**

   These data points create the performance trend line.

4. **Select the entire chart feeder table and plot the data on a stacked area chart.**

5. **Right-click the Values series and choose Change Series Chart Type. Use the Change Chart Type dialog box to change the Values series to a Line and to place it on the secondary axis, as shown in Figure 9-22. After confirming your change, the Values series appears on the chart as a line.**

	A	B	C	D	E	F
1	Limit Table					
2	Lower Limit	25				
3	Upper Limit	35				
4						
5						
6						
7		Jan	Feb	Mar	Apr	May
8	Lower Limit	25	25	25	25	25
9	Upper Limit	10	10	10	10	10
10	Values	33	27	23	28	26

Figure 9-21: Add a row for the performance values.

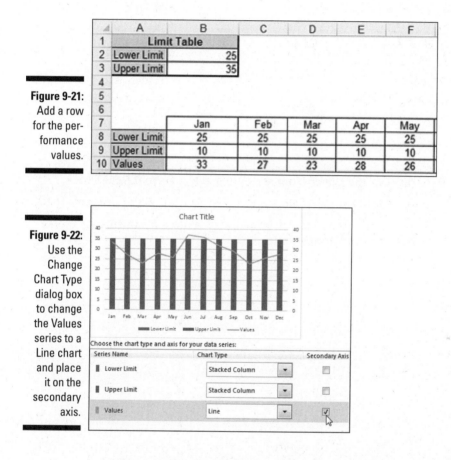

Figure 9-22: Use the Change Chart Type dialog box to change the Values series to a Line chart and place it on the secondary axis.

6. **Go back to your chart and delete the new vertical axis that was added; it's the vertical axis to the right of the chart.**
7. **Right-click the Lower Limit data series and choose Format Data Series.**
8. **In the Format Data Series dialog, click the Fill icon. Choose the No Fill option under Fill, and the No Line option under Border; see Figure 9-23.**

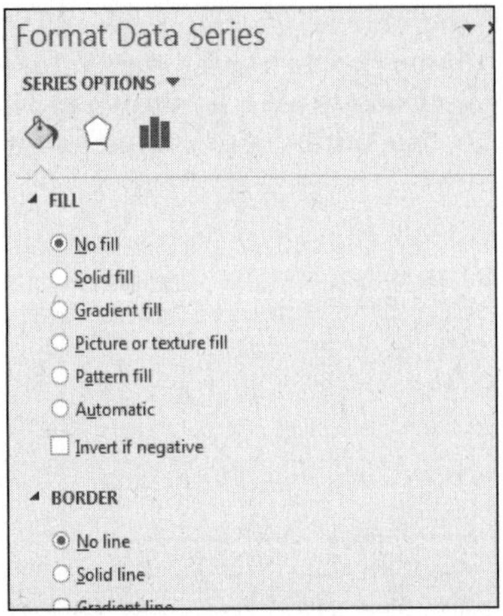

Figure 9-23:
Format
the Lower
Limit series
so that it's
hidden.

9. **Right-click the Upper Limit series and select Format Data Series.**

10. **In the Format Series dialog box, adjust the Gap Width property to 0%.**

That's it. All that's left to do is apply the minor adjustments to colors, labels, and other formatting.

Part IV
Advanced Reporting Techniques

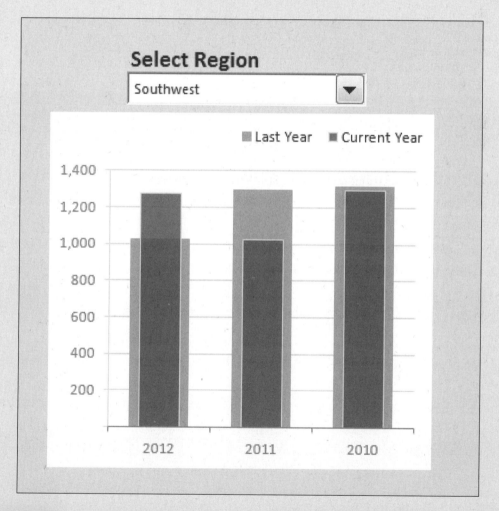

In this part . . .

✔ Take an in-depth look at some of the key dashboarding concepts you can leverage to create cutting-edge presentations.

✔ Gain a clear understanding of how you can leverage macros to automate your reporting systems.

✔ Discover how interactive controls can provide your clients with simple interfaces, allowing them to easily navigate through and interact with your dashboard or report.

✔ Explore pivot slicers and see how to use them to add interactive filtering capabilities to your pivot reporting.

Chapter 10

Macro-Charged Dashboarding

• •

In This Chapter

▶ Introducing macros

▶ Recording macros

▶ Setting up trusted locations for your macros

▶ Adding macros to your dashboards and reports

• •

A macro is essentially a set of instructions or code that you create to tell Excel to execute any number of actions. In Excel, macros can be written or recorded. The key word here is *recorded.*

Recording a macro is like programming a phone number into your cell phone. You first manually dial and save a number. Then when you want, you can redial those numbers with the touch of a button. Just as on a cell phone, you can record your actions in Excel while you perform them. While you record, Excel gets busy in the background, translating your keystrokes and mouse clicks to written code, also known as Visual Basic for Applications (VBA). After you record a macro, you can play back those actions anytime you want.

In this chapter, you explore macros and learn how you can use them to automate your recurring processes to simplify your life.

Why Use a Macro?

The first step in using macros is admitting you have a problem. Actually, you may have several problems:

Problem 1: *Repetitive tasks.* As each new month rolls around, you have to make the donuts — that is, crank out those reports. You have to import that data. You have to update those pivot tables. You have to delete those columns, and so on. Wouldn't it be nice if you could fire up a macro and have those more redundant parts of your dashboard processes done automatically?

Problem 2: *You're making mistakes.* When you go hand-to-hand combat with Excel, you're bound to make mistakes. When you're repeatedly applying formulas, sorting, and moving things around manually, there's always that risk of catastrophe. Add to that the looming deadlines and constant change requests, and your error rate goes up. Why not calmly record a macro, ensure that everything is running correctly, and then forget it? The macro is sure to perform every action the same way every time you run it, reducing the chance of errors.

Problem 3: *Awkward navigation.* Remember that you're creating these dashboards and reports for an audience that probably has a limited knowledge of Excel. If your reports are a bit too difficult to use and navigate, you'll find that you'll slowly lose support for your cause. It's always helpful to make your dashboard more user-friendly.

Here are some ideas for macros that make things easier for everyone:

- ✔ A macro that formats and prints a worksheet or range of worksheets at the touch of a button
- ✔ Macros that navigate a multisheet worksheet with a navigation page or with a go-to button for each sheet in your workbook
- ✔ A macro that saves the open document in a specified location and then closes the application at the touch of a button

Obviously, you can perform each of the preceding examples in Excel without the aid of a macro. However, your audience will appreciate these little touches that help make perusal of your dashboard a bit more pleasant.

Recording Your First Macro

If you're a beginner to dashboard automation, it's unlikely that you'll be able to write the VBA code by hand. Without full knowledge of Excel's object model and syntax, writing the needed code would be impossible for most beginning users. This is where recording a macro comes in handy. The idea is that you record the desired action, and then run the macro each time you want that action performed.

To get started in creating your first macro, open the Chapter 10 Samples file found on this book's companion website. After the file is open, go to the Recording your First Macro tab.

To begin, you first need to unhide the Developer tab. You can find the full macro toolset in Excel 2013 on the Developer tab, which is initially hidden. You have to explicitly tell Excel to make it visible. To enable the Developer tab, follow these steps:

1. **Go to the Ribbon and click the File button.**

2. **To open the Excel Options dialog box, click the Options button.**

3. Click the Customize Ribbon button.

In the list box on the right, you see all the available tabs.

4. Select the Developer tab, as shown in Figure 10-1.

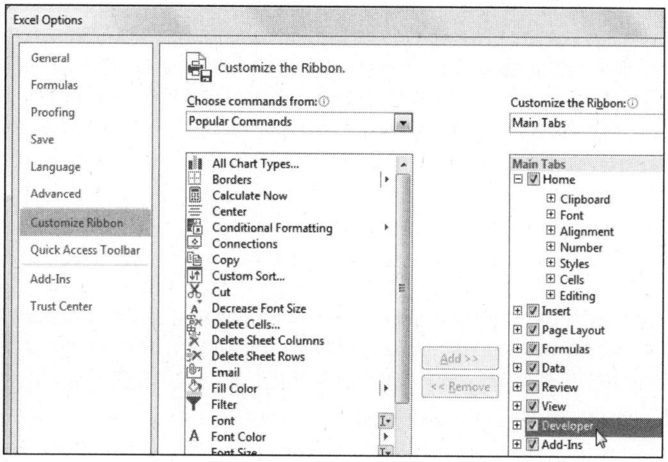

Figure 10-1: Enabling the Developer tab.

5. Click OK.

Now that you have the Developer tab, select it and click the Record Macro command. This opens the Record Macro dialog box, as shown in Figure 10-2.

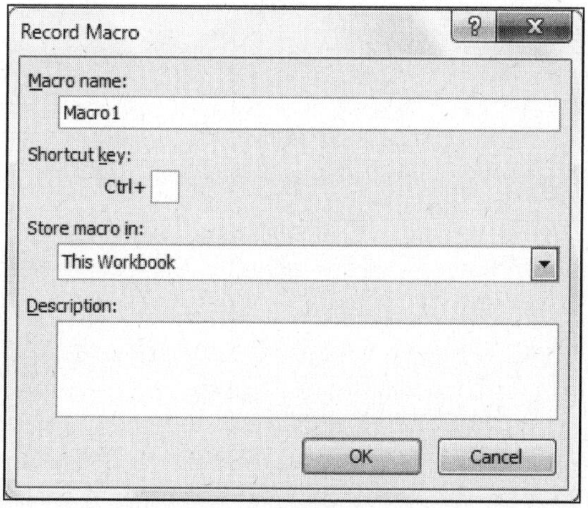

Figure 10-2: The Record Macro dialog box.

Here are the four fields in the Record Macro dialog box:

- ✔ **Macro Name:** Excel gives a default name to your macro, such as Macro1, but it's best practice to give your macro a name more descriptive of what it actually does. For example, you might name a macro that formats a generic table as AddDataBars.

- ✔ **Shortcut Key:** This field is optional. Every macro needs an event, or something to happen, for it to run. This event can be a button press, a workbook opening, or in this case, a keystroke combination. When you assign a shortcut key to your macro, entering that combination of keys triggers your macro to run. You need not enter a shortcut key to run your macro.

- ✔ **Store Macro In:** This Workbook is the default option. Storing your macro in This Workbook simply means that the macro is stored along with the active Excel file. The next time you open that particular workbook, the macro will be available to run. Similarly, if you send the workbook to another user, that user can run the macro as well, provided the macro security is properly set by your user — but more on that later.

- ✔ **Description:** This field is optional, but it's useful if you have numerous macros in a spreadsheet or if you need to give a user a more detailed description about what the macro does.

In this first example, enter AddDataBars into the Macro Name field and select This Workbook from the Store Macro In drop-down menu; see Figure 10-3. Press OK.

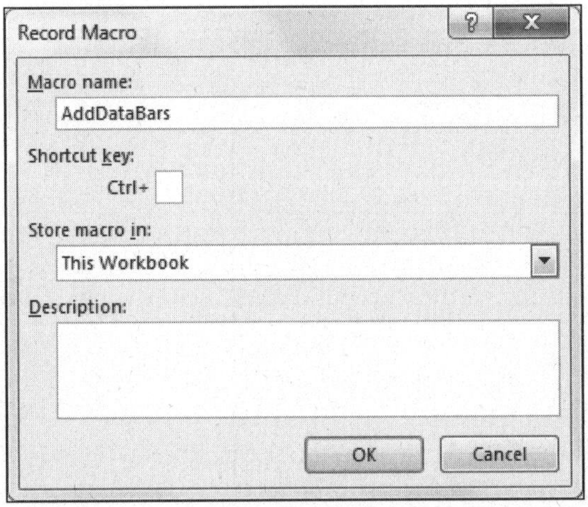

Figure 10-3:
Start recording a new Macro called AddData-Bars.

Excel is now recording your actions. While Excel is recording, you can perform any actions you'd like. In this scenario, you record a macro to add Data Bars to a column of numbers.

Follow along using these steps:

1. **Highlight cells C1:C21.**

2. **Go to the Home tab and select Conditional Formatting⇨New Rule.**

3. **In the New Formatting Rule dialog box, go to the Format Style drop-down menu and select Data Bar.**

4. **Another dialog box appears. Here, select the Show Bar Only check box.**

5. **Press OK to apply your change.**

6. **Go to the Developer tab and click the Stop Recording command.**

   At this point, Excel stops recording. You now have a macro that replaces the data in C1:C21 with Data Bars. Now, let's record a new macro to remove the Data Bars.

7. **Go to the Developer tab and click the Record Macro command.**

8. **Enter RemoveDataBars into the Macro Name field and select the This Workbook from the Store Macro In drop-down menu; see Figure 10-4. Press OK.**

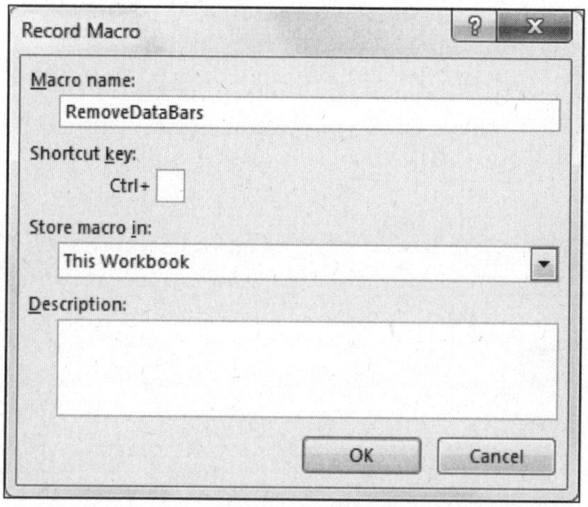

Figure 10-4: Start recording a new Macro called Remove-DataBars.

9. **Highlight cells C1:C21.**

10. **Go to the Home tab and select Conditional Formatting⇨Clear Rules⇨Clear Rules from Selected Cells.**

11. **Go to the Developer tab and click the Stop Recording command.**

    Again, Excel stops recording. You now have a new macro that removes conditional formatting rules from cells C1:C21.

Running Your Macros

To see your macros in action, select the Macros command from the Developer tab. The dialog box in Figure 10-5 appears, allowing you to select the macro you want to run. Select the AddDataBars macro and click the Run button.

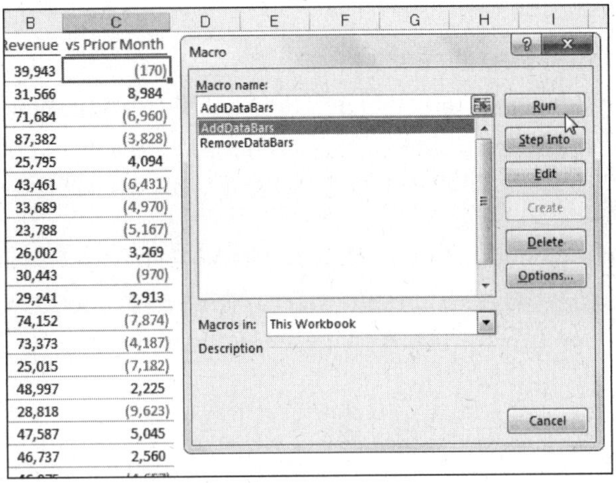

Figure 10-5: Use the Macro dialog box to select a macro and run it.

If all goes well, the macro plays back your actions to a T and applies the Data Bars as designed; see Figure 10-6.

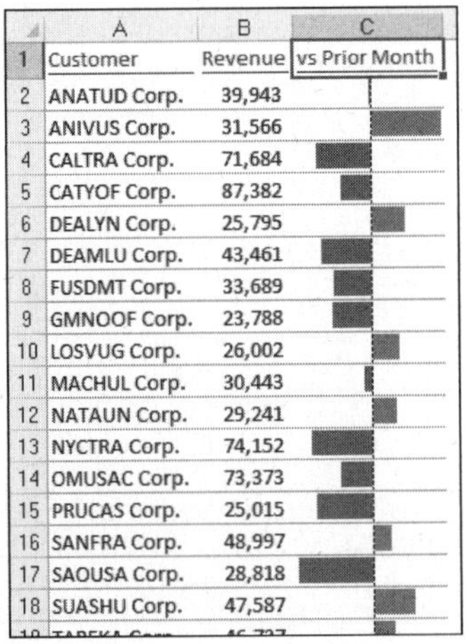

Figure 10-6: Your macro applies Data Bars automatically!

You can now call up the Macro dialog box again and test the RemoveDataBars macro shown in Figure 10-7.

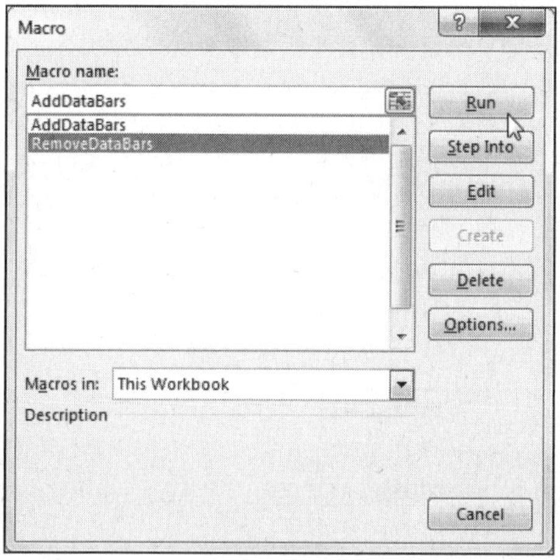

Figure 10-7:
The
Remove-
DataBars
macro
removes the
applied Data
Bars.

When you create macros, you want to give your audience a clear and easy way to run each macro. A button, used directly on the dashboard or report, can provide a simple but effective user interface.

Excel Form controls enable you to create user interfaces directly on your worksheets, simplifying work for your users. Form controls range from buttons (the most commonly used control) to scroll bars and check boxes.

For a macro, you can place a Form control in a worksheet and then assign that macro to it — that is, a macro you've already recorded. When a macro is assigned to the control, that macro is executed, or played, each time the control is clicked.

Take a moment to create buttons for the two macros (AddDataBars and RemoveDataBars) you create earlier in this chapter. Here's how:

1. **Click the Insert drop-down list under the Developer tab.**

2. **Select the Button Form control, as shown in Figure 10-8.**

3. **Click the location you want to place your button.**

   When you drop the Button control into your worksheet, the Assign Macro dialog box, as shown in Figure 10-9, opens and asks you to assign a macro to this button.

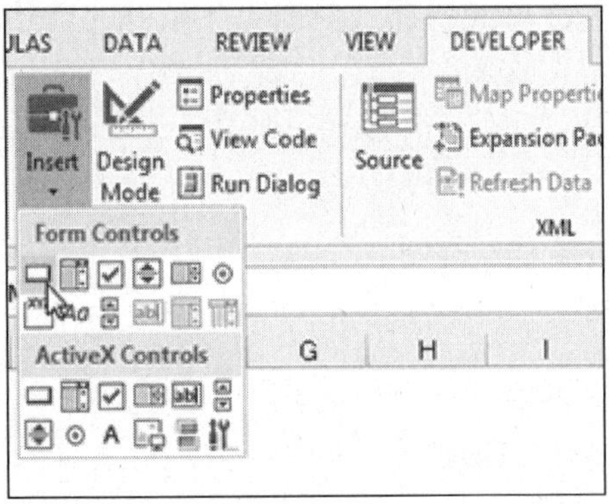

Figure 10-8:
You can find
the Form
Controls
menu on the
Developer
tab.

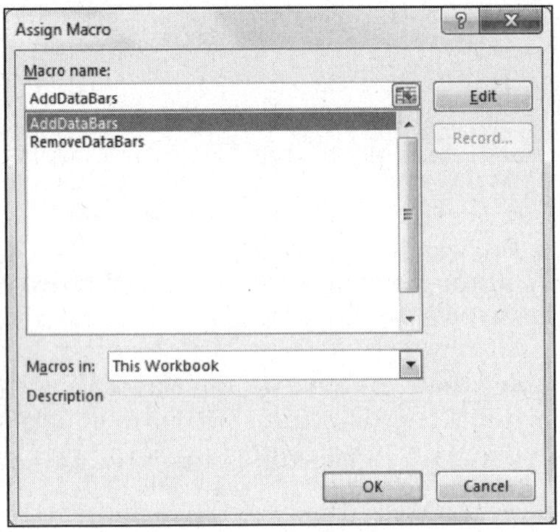

Figure 10-9:
Assign a
macro to
the newly
added
button.

4. **Select the macro that you want to assign. In this case, select the AddDataBars macro and click OK.**

5. **Repeat Steps 1 through 4 for the RemoveDataBars macro.**

The buttons you create come with a default name, such as Button3. To rename your button, right-click the button and then click the existing name. Then you can delete the existing name and replace it with a name of your choosing.

Keep in mind that all the controls in the Form Controls menu work in the same way as the command button, in that you assign a macro to run when the control is selected.

Notice the Form Controls and ActiveX Controls in Figure 10-8. Although they look similar, they're quite different. Form controls are designed specifically for use on a worksheet, and ActiveX controls are typically used on Excel UserForms. As a general rule, you always want to use Form controls when working on a worksheet. Why? Form controls need less overhead, so they perform better, and configuring Form controls is far easier than configuring their ActiveX counterparts.

Enabling and Trusting Macros

With the release of Office 2007, Microsoft introduced significant changes to its Office security model. One of the most significant changes is the concept of trusted documents. Without getting into the technical minutia, a *trusted document* is essentially a workbook you have deemed safe by enabling macros.

Macro-enabled file extensions

It's important to note that Microsoft has created a separate file extension for workbooks that contain macros.

Excel 2007, 2010, and 2013 workbooks have the standard file extension .xlsx. Files with the xlsx extension cannot contain macros. If your workbook contains macros and you then save that workbook as an .xlsx file, your macros are removed automatically. Of course, Excel warns you that macro content will be disabled when saving a workbook with macros as an .xlsx file.

If you want to retain the macros, you must save your file as an Excel Macro-Enabled Workbook. This gives your file an .xlsm extension. All workbooks with an .xlsx file extension are automatically known to be safe, whereas you can recognize .xlsm files as a potential threat.

Enabling macro content

If you open a workbook that contains macros in Excel 2013, you'll get a message in the form of a yellow bar under the Ribbon stating that Macros (active content) have in effect, been disabled.

If you click Enable, it automatically becomes a trusted document. This means you will no longer be prompted to enable the content as long as you open that file on your computer. If you told Excel that you trust a particular workbook by enabling macros, it's highly likely that you will enable macros each time you open it. Thus, Excel remembers that you've enabled macros before and inhibits any further messages about macros for that workbook.

This is great news for you and your clients. After enabling your macros just one time, they won't be annoyed at the constant messages about macros, and you won't have to worry that your macro-enabled dashboard will fall flat because macros have been disabled.

Setting up trusted locations

If the thought of any macro message coming up (even one time) unnerves you, you can set up a trusted location for your files. A trusted location is a directory deemed a safe zone where only trusted workbooks are placed. A trusted location allows you and your clients to run a macro-enabled workbook with no security restrictions as long as the workbook is in that location.

To set up a trusted location, follow these steps:

1. **Select the Macro Security button on the Developer tab.**

2. **Click the Trusted Locations button.**

    This opens the Trusted Locations menu shown in Figure 10-10. Here you see all the directories that Excel considers trusted.

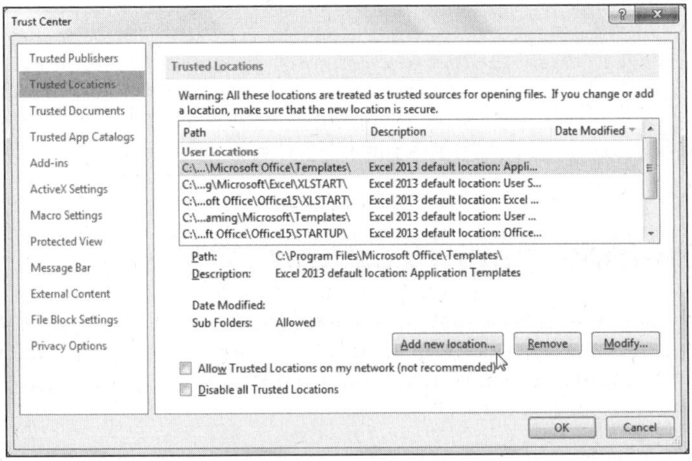

Figure 10-10: The Trusted Locations menu allows you to add directories that are considered trusted.

3. **Click the Add New Location button.**

4. **Click Browse to find and specify the directory that will be considered a trusted location.**

   After you specify a trusted location, any Excel file that's opened from this location will have macros automatically enabled. Have your clients specify a trusted location and use your Excel files from there.

Excel Macro Examples

Covering the fundamentals of building and using macros is one thing. Coming up with good ways to incorporate them into your reporting processes is another. Take a moment to review a few examples of how you can implement macros in your dashboards and reports.

Open the `Chapter 10 Samples.xlsm` file found on this book's companion website to follow along in the next section.

Building navigation buttons

The most common use of macros is navigation. Workbooks that have many worksheets or tabs can be frustrating to navigate. To help your audience, you can create some sort of a switchboard, like the one shown in Figure 10-11. When users click the `Example 1` button, they're taken to the Example 1 sheet.

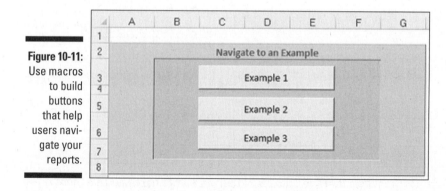

Figure 10-11: Use macros to build buttons that help users navigate your reports.

Creating a macro to navigate to a sheet is quite simple:

1. **Start at the sheet that will become your switchboard or starting point.**

2. **Start recording a macro.**

3. **While recording, click the destination sheet — the sheet this macro will navigate to.**

4. **After you click in the destination sheet, stop recording the macro.**

5. **Assign the macro to a button.**

It's useful to know that Excel has a built-in hyperlink feature, allowing you to convert the contents of a cell into a hyperlink that links to another location. That location can be a separate Excel workbook, a website, or even another tab in the current workbook. Although using a hyperlink may be easier than setting up a macro, you can't apply a hyperlink to Form controls (like buttons). Instead of a button, you use text to let users know where they'll go when they click the link.

Dynamically rearranging pivot table data

In the example illustrated in Figure 10-12, macros allow a user to change the perspective of the chart simply by selecting any one of the buttons shown.

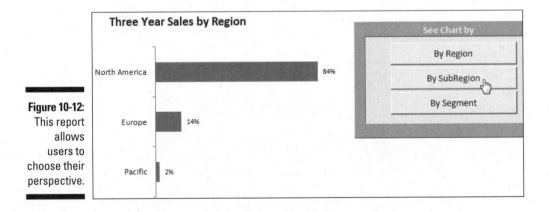

Figure 10-12: This report allows users to choose their perspective.

Figure 10-13 reveals that the chart is actually a pivot chart tied to a pivot table. The recorded macros assigned to each button are doing nothing more than rearranging the pivot table to slice the data using various pivot fields.

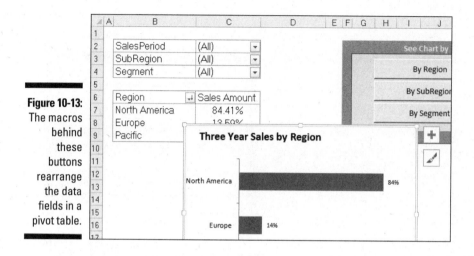

Figure 10-13:
The macros behind these buttons rearrange the data fields in a pivot table.

Here are the high-level steps needed to create this type of setup:

1. **Create your pivot table add a pivot chart by clicking inside the pivot table and then selecting Insert⇨Charts⇨Bar.**

2. **Start recording a macro.**

3. **While recording, move a pivot field from one area of the pivot table to the other. When you're done, stop recording the macro.**

4. **Record another macro to move the data field back to its original position.**

5. **After both macros are set up, assign each one to a separate button.**

You can fire your new macros in turn to see your pivot field dynamically move back and forth.

Offering one-touch reporting options

The last two examples demonstrate that you can record any action that you find of value. That is, if you think users would appreciate a certain feature being automated for them, why not record a macro to do so?

In Figure 10-14, notice that you can filter the pivot table for top or bottom 20 customers. Because the steps to filter a pivot table for the top and bottom 20 have been recorded, anyone can get the benefit of this functionality without knowing how to do it themselves. Also, recording specific actions allows you to manage risk a bit. That is to say, you'll know that your users will interact with your reports in a method that has been developed and tested by you.

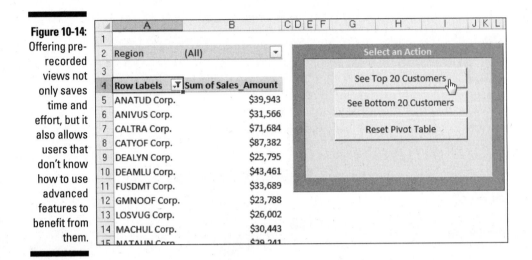

Figure 10-14:
Offering pre-recorded views not only saves time and effort, but it also allows users that don't know how to use advanced features to benefit from them.

This not only saves them time and effort, but it also allows users that don't know how to take these actions to benefit from them.

Figure 10-15 demonstrates how you can give your audience a quick and easy way to see the same data on different charts. Don't laugh too quickly at the uselessness of this example. It's not uncommon to be asked to see the same data different ways. Instead of taking up real estate, just record a macro that changes the chart type. Your clients can switch views to their hearts' content.

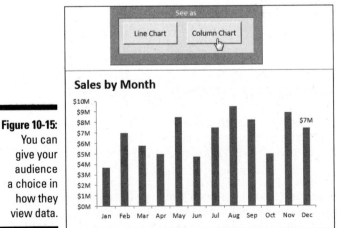

Figure 10-15:
You can give your audience a choice in how they view data.

Chapter 11

Giving Users an Interactive Interface

*T*oday, business professionals increasingly want to be empowered to switch from one view of data to another with a simple list of choices. For those who build dashboards and reports, this empowerment comes with a whole new set of issues. The overarching question is — how do you handle a user who wants to see multiple views for multiple regions or markets?

Fortunately, Excel offers a handful of tools that enable you to add interactivity into your presentations. With these tools and a bit of creative data modeling, you can accomplish these goals with relative ease. In this chapter, you discover how to incorporate various controls, such as buttons, check boxes, and scroll bars, into your dashboards and reports. Also, I present you with several solutions that you can implement.

Getting Started with Form Controls

Excel offers a set of controls called Form controls, designed specifically for adding user interface elements directly onto a worksheet. After you place a Form control on a worksheet, you can then configure it to perform a specific task. Later in the chapter, I demonstrate how to apply the most useful controls to a presentation.

Finding Form controls

You can find Excel's Form controls on the Developer tab, which is initially hidden in Excel 2013. To enable the Developer tab, follow these steps:

1. **Go to the Ribbon and click the File button.**

2. **To open the Excel Options dialog box, click the Options button.**

3. **Click the Customize Ribbon button.**

   In the list box on the right, you see all the available tabs.

4. **Select the check box next to the Developer tab; see Figure 11-1.**

5. **Click OK.**

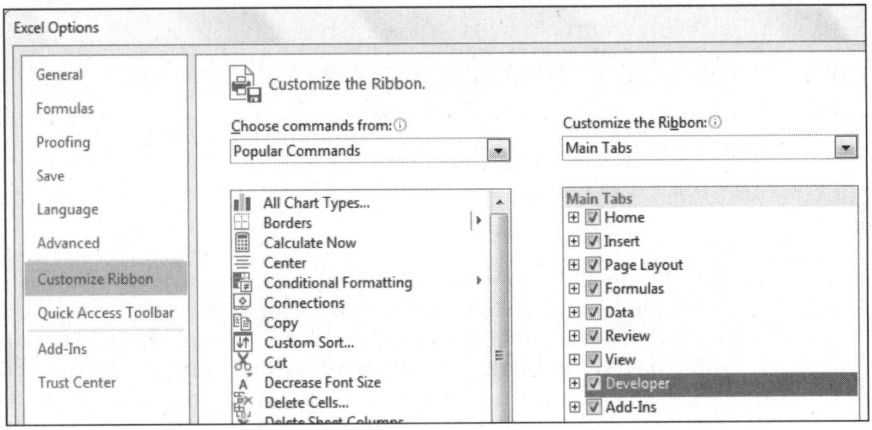

Figure 11-1: Enabling the Developer tab.

Now, click the Developer tab and choose the Insert command, as shown in Figure 11-2. Here you find two sets of controls: Form controls and ActiveX controls. Form controls are designed specifically for use on a spreadsheet, whereas ActiveX controls are typically used on Excel UserForms. Because Form controls need less overhead and can be configured far easier than their ActiveX counterparts, you generally want to use Form controls.

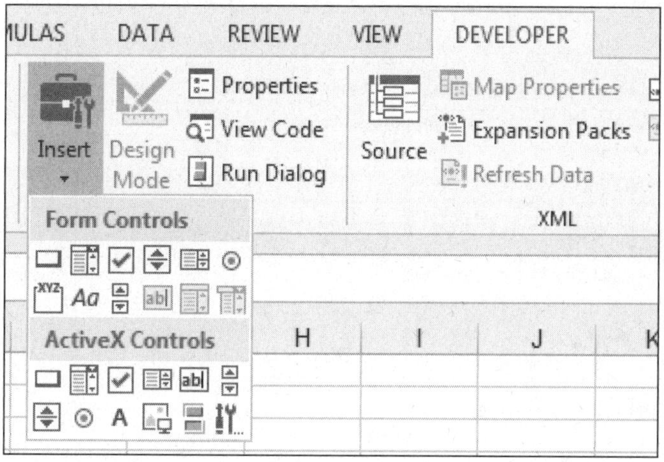

Figure 11-2:
Form
controls and
ActiveX
controls.

Here are the nine Form controls that you can add directly to a worksheet. Shown in Figure 11-3, they are as follows:

- ✔ **Button:** Executes an assigned macro when a user clicks the button.

- ✔ **Combo Box:** Gives a user an expandable list of options from which to choose.

- ✔ **Check Box:** Provides a mechanism for a select/deselect scenario. When selected, it returns a value of `True`. Otherwise, it returns `False`.

- ✔ **Spin Button:** Enables a user to easily increase or decrease a value by clicking the up and down arrows.

- ✔ **List Box:** Gives a user a list of options from which to choose.

- ✔ **Option Button:** Enables a user to toggle through two or more options one at a time. Selecting one option automatically deselects the others.

- ✔ **Scroll Bar:** Enables a user to scroll to a value or position using a sliding scale that can be moved by clicking and dragging the mouse.

- ✔ **Label:** Allows you to add text labels to your worksheet. You can also assign a macro to the label, effectively using it as a button of sorts.

- ✔ **Group Box:** Typically used for cosmetic purposes, this control serves as a container for groups of other controls.

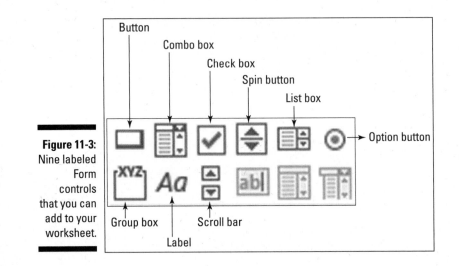

Figure 11-3:
Nine labeled
Form
controls
that you can
add to your
worksheet.

Button

Combo box

Check box

Spin button

List box

Option button

Group box

Label

Scroll bar

Adding a control to a worksheet

To add a control to a worksheet, simply click the control that you require and click the approximate location that you want to place the control. You can easily move and resize the control later just as you would a chart or shape.

After you add a control, you want to configure it to define its look, behavior, and utility. Each control has its own set of configuration options that allow you to customize it for your purposes. To get to these options, right-click the control and select Format Control. This opens the Format Control dialog box, illustrated in Figure 11-4, with all the configuration options for that control.

Figure 11-4:
Right-click
and select
Format
Control
to open a
dialog box
with the
configuration
options.

Format Control

| Size | Protection | Properties | Alt Text | Control |

Size and rotate

Height: 1"   Width: 1"

Rotation: 0°

Scale

Height: 100 %   Width: 100 %

☐ Lock aspect ratio

☐ Relative to original picture size

Original size

Height: Width:

Reset

OK   Cancel

Each control has its own set of tabs that allow you to customize everything from formatting to security to configuration arguments. You see different tabs based on which control you're using, but most Form controls have the Control tab, where the meat of the configuration lies. Here, you find the variables and settings that need to be defined for the control to function.

The Button and Label controls don't have the Control tab. They have no need for one. The button simply fires whichever macro you assign it. As for the label, it's not designed to run macro events.

Throughout the rest of the chapter, you walk through a few exercises that demonstrate how to use the most useful controls in a reporting environment. At the end of this chapter, you'll have a solid understanding of Form controls and how they can enhance your dashboards and reports.

Using the Button Control

The Button control gives your audience a clear and easy way to execute the macros you've recorded. To insert and configure a Button control, follow these steps:

1. **Click the Insert drop-down list under the Developer tab.**

2. **Select the Button Form control.**

3. **Click the location in your spreadsheet where you want to place your button.**

   The Assign Macro dialog box appears and asks you to assign a macro to this button, as shown in Figure 11-5.

4. **Edit the text shown on the button by right-clicking the button, high-lighting the existing text, and then overwriting it with your own.**

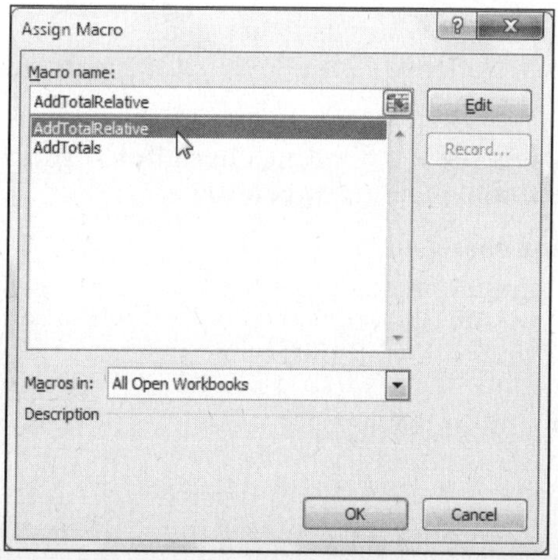

Figure 11-5:
Assign a macro to the newly added button.

Assign Macro	? X
Macro name:	
AddTotalRelative	Edit
AddTotalRelative	
AddTotals	Record...
Macros in: All Open Workbooks	
Description	
OK	Cancel

To assign a different macro to the button, simply right-click and select Assign Macro to reactivate the Assign Macro dialog box, as shown in Figure 11-5.

When you add macros to a workbook, you'll have to save that workbook as an .xlsm file in order to share your macros with others. If you save the workbook as a standard .xlsx file, Excel will strip your macros out of the workbook.

Using the Check Box Control

The Check Box control provides a mechanism for selecting/deselecting options. When a check box is selected, it returns a value of True. When it isn't selected, False is returned. To add and configure a Check Box control, follow these steps:

1. **Click the Insert drop-down list under the Developer tab.**

2. **Select the Check Box Form control.**

3. **Click the location in your spreadsheet where you want to place your check box.**

4. **After you drop the Check Box control onto your spreadsheet, right-click the control and select Format Control.**

5. **Click the Control tab to see the configuration options shown in Figure 11-6.**

6. **Select the state in which the check box should open.**

   The default selection (Unchecked) typically works for most scenarios, so it's rare that you'd have to change this selection.

7. **In the Cell Link box, enter the cell to which you want the check box to output its value.**

   By default, a Check Box control outputs either True or False, depending on whether it's checked. Notice in Figure 11-6 that this particular check box outputs to cell A5.

8. **(Optional) You can select the 3-D Shading check box if you want the control to have a three-dimensional appearance.**

9. **Click OK to apply your changes.**

To rename the Check Box control, right-click the control, select Edit Text, and then overwrite the existing text with your own.

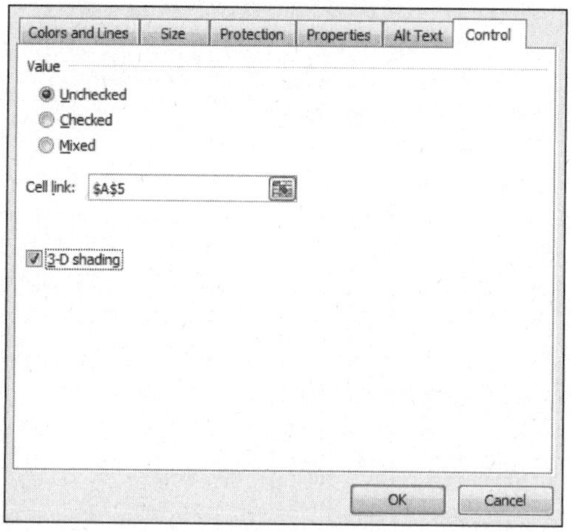

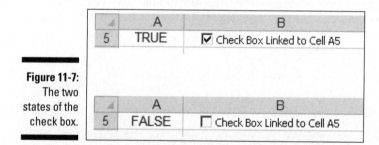

Figure 11-6:
Formatting
the Check
Box control.

As Figure 11-7 illustrates, the check box outputs its value to the specified cell. If the check box is selected, a value of True is output. If the check box isn't selected, a value of False is output.

	A	B
5	TRUE	☑ Check Box Linked to Cell A5

	A	B
5	FALSE	☐ Check Box Linked to Cell A5

Figure 11-7:
The two
states of the
check box.

If you're having a hard time figuring out how this could be useful, take a stab at this next exercise, which illustrates how you can use a check box to toggle a chart series on and off.

Check box example: Toggling a chart series on and off

Figure 11-8 shows the same chart twice. Notice that the top chart contains only one series, with a check box offering to show 2011 trend data. The bottom chart shows the same chart with the check box selected. The on/off nature of the Check Box control is ideal for interactivity that calls for a visible/not visible state.

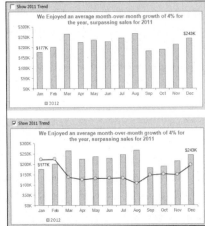

Figure 11-8:
A check box can help create the disappearing data series effect.

To download the `Chapter 11 Samples.xlsx` file, go to this book's companion website.

You start with the raw data (in `Chapter 11 Samples.xlsx`) that contains both 2011 and 2012 data; see Figure 11-9. The first column has a cell in which the Check Box control will output its value (cell A12, in this example). This cell will contain either `True` or `False`.

Figure 11-9:
Start with raw data and a cell in which a Check Box control can output its value.

	A	B	C	D	E	F	G
10			Raw Data				
11	Toggle for 2011 Data		Jan	Feb	Mar	Apr	May
12	TRUE	2011	$222,389	$224,524	$136,104	$125,260	$130,791
13		2012	$176,648	$201,000	$265,720	$225,461	$235,494
14							

Next, create the analysis layer (staging table) that consists of all formulas, as shown in Figure 11-10. The chart actually reads from this data, not the raw data. This way, you can control what the chart sees.

As you can see in Figure 11-10, the formulas for the 2012 row simply reference the cells in the raw data for each respective month. You do that because you want the 2012 data to appear at all times.

Figure 11-10:
Create a
staging table
that will feed
the chart.
The values of
this data are
all formulas.

◢	A	B	C	D	E	
4						
5			Jan	Feb	Mar	
6		2011	=IF($A12=TRUE,C12,NA())	=IF($A12=TRUE,D12,NA())	=IF($A12=TRUE,E12,NA())	=I
7		2012	=C13	=D13	=E13	=F
8						
9						
10			Raw Data			
11	Toggle for 2011 Data		Jan	Feb	Mar	
12	TRUE	2011	$222,389	$224,524	$136,104	$1
13		2012	$176,648	$201,000	$265,720	$2
14						

For the 2011 row, test the value of cell A12 (the cell that contains the output from the check box). If A12 reads True, you reference the respective 2011 cell in the raw data. If A12 doesn't read True, the formula uses Excel's NA() function to return an #N/A error. Excel charts can't read a cell with the #N/A error. Therefore, they simply don't show the data series for any cell that contains #N/A. This is ideal when you don't want a data series to be shown at all.

TIP

Notice that the formula shown in Figure 11-10 uses an absolute reference with cell A12 — that is, the reference to cell A12 in the formula is prefixed with a $ sign ($A12). This ensures that the column references in the formulas don't shift when they're copied across.

Figure 11-11 illustrates the two scenarios in action in the staging tables. In the scenario shown at the bottom of Figure 11-11, cell A12 is True, so the staging table actually brings in 2011 data. In the scenario shown at the top of Figure 11-11, cell A12 is False, so the staging table returns #N/A for 2011.

Figure 11-11:
When cell
A12 reads
True, 2011
data is
displayed;
when it reads
False, the
2011 row
shows only
#N/A errors.

◢	A	B	C	D	E	F	G
4							
5			Jan	Feb	Mar	Apr	May
6		2011	#N/A	#N/A	#N/A	#N/A	#N/A
7		2012	$176,648	$201,000	$265,720	$225,461	$235,494
8							
9							
10			Raw Data				
11	Toggle for 2011 Data		Jan	Feb	Mar	Apr	May
12	FALSE	2011	$222,389	$224,524	$136,104	$125,260	$130,791
13		2012	$176,648	$201,000	$265,720	$225,461	$235,494
14							

◢	A	B	C	D	E	F	G
4							
5			Jan	Feb	Mar	Apr	May
6		2011	$222,389	$224,524	$136,104	$125,260	$130,791
7		2012	$176,648	$201,000	$265,720	$225,461	$235,494
8							
9							
10			Raw Data				
11	Toggle for 2011 Data		Jan	Feb	Mar	Apr	May
12	TRUE	2011	$222,389	$224,524	$136,104	$125,260	$130,791
13		2012	$176,648	$201,000	$265,720	$225,461	$235,494
14							

Finally, create the chart that you saw earlier in this section (refer to Figure 11-8) using the staging table. Keep in mind that you can scale this to as many series as you like.

Figure 11-12 illustrates a chart that has multiple series whose visibility is controlled by Check Box controls. This allows you to make all but two series invisible so you can compare those two series unhindered. Then you can make another two visible, comparing those.

Figure 11-12:
You can use check boxes to control how much data is shown in your chart at one time.

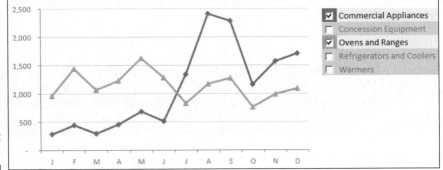

Using the Option Button Control

Option buttons allow users to toggle through several options one at a time. The idea is to have two or more option buttons in a group. Then selecting one option button automatically deselects the others. To add option buttons to your worksheet, follow these steps:

1. **Click the Insert drop-down list under the Developer tab.**

2. **Select the Option Button Form control.**

3. **Click the location in your spreadsheet where you want to place your option button.**

4. **After you drop the control onto your spreadsheet, right-click the control and select Format Control.**

5. **Click the Control tab to see the configuration options shown in Figure 11-13.**

6. **First, select the state in which the option button should open.**

   The default selection (Unchecked) typically works for most scenarios, so it's rare that you'd have to change this selection.

7. **In the Cell Link box, enter the cell to which you want the option button to output its value.**

   By default, an Option Button control outputs a number that corresponds to the order it was put onto the worksheet. For instance, the first option button you place on your worksheet outputs a number 1, the second outputs a number 2, the third outputs a number 3, and so on. Notice in Figure 11-13 that this particular control outputs to cell A1.

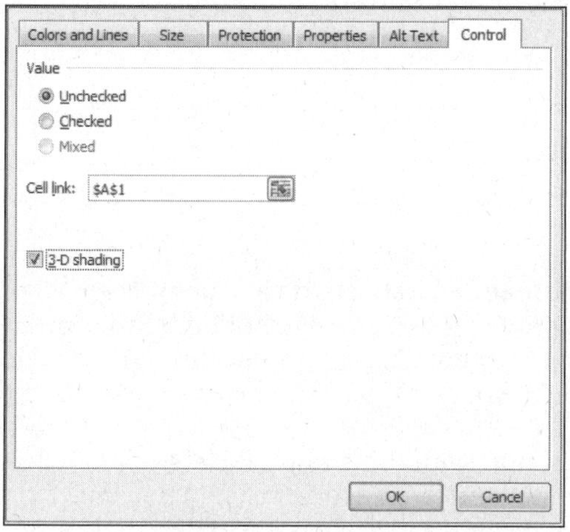

Figure 11-13: Formatting the Option Button control.

8. **(Optional) You can select the 3-D Shading check box if you want the control to have a three-dimensional appearance.**

9. **Click OK to apply your changes.**

10. **To add another option button, simply copy the button you created and paste as many option buttons as you need.**

    The nice thing about copying and pasting is that all the configurations you made to the original persist in all the copies.

    To give your option button a meaningful label, right-click the control, select Edit Text, and then overwrite the existing text with your own.

Option Button Example: Showing Many Views through One Chart

One of the ways you can use option buttons is to feed a single chart with different data, based on the option selected. Figure 11-14 illustrates an example of this. When each category is selected, the single chart is updated to show the data for that selection.

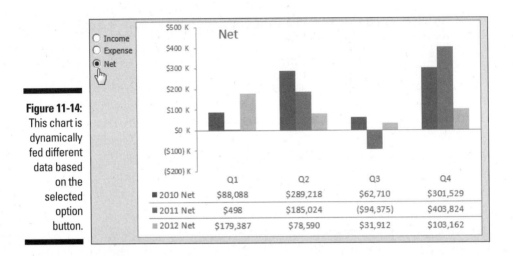

Figure 11-14:
This chart is dynamically fed different data based on the selected option button.

	Q1	Q2	Q3	Q4
■ 2010 Net	$88,088	$289,218	$62,710	$301,529
■ 2011 Net	$498	$185,024	($94,375)	$403,824
■ 2012 Net	$179,387	$78,590	$31,912	$103,162

Now, you could create three separate charts and show them all on your dashboard at the same time. However, using option buttons as an alternative saves valuable real estate by not having to show three separate charts. Plus, it's much easier to troubleshoot, format, and maintain one chart than three.

To create this example, start with three raw datasets — as shown in Figure 11-15 — that contain three categories of data; Income, Expense, and Net. Near the raw data, reserve a cell where the option buttons output their values (cell A8, in this example). This cell contains the ID of the option selected: 1, 2, or 3.

Figure 11-15:
Start with the raw datasets and a cell where the option buttons can output their values.

⊿	A	B	C	D	E	F
7	Option Button Trigger					
8	1		Q1	Q2	Q3	Q4
9		2012 Income	$399,354	$573,662	$244,661	$790,906
10		2011 Income	$219,967	$495,072	$212,749	$687,744
11		2010 Income	$159,832	$289,825	$181,961	$456,016
12						
13		2012 Expense	$219,967	$495,072	$212,749	$687,744
14		2011 Expense	$219,468	$310,048	$307,124	$283,920
15		2010 Expense	$71,744	$607	$119,251	$154,487
16						
17		2012 Net	$179,387	$78,590	$31,912	$103,162
18		2011 Net	$498	$185,024	-$94,375	$403,824
19		2010 Net	$88,088	$289,218	$62,710	$301,529

You then create the analysis layer (the staging table) that consists of all formulas, as shown in Figure 11-16. The chart reads from this staging table, allowing you to control what the chart sees. The first cell of the staging table contains the following formula:

```
=IF($A$8=1,B9,IF($A$8=2,B13,B17))
```

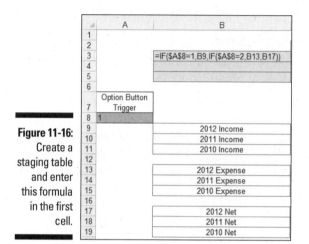

Figure 11-16:
Create a staging table and enter this formula in the first cell.

This formula tells Excel to check the value of cell A8 (the cell where the option buttons output their values). If the value of cell A8 is 1, which represents the value of the Income option, the formula returns the value in the Income dataset (cell B9). If the value of cell A8 is 2, which represents the value of the Expense option, the formula returns the value in the Expense dataset (cell B13). If the value of cell A8 is not 1 or 2, the value in cell B17 is returned.

Notice that the formula shown in Figure 11-16 uses absolute references with cell A8. That is, the reference to cell A8 in the formula is prefixed with $ signs ($A$8). This ensures that the cell references in the formulas don't shift when they're copied down and across.

To test that the formula is working fine, you could change the value of cell A8 manually, from 1 to 3. When the formula works, you simply copy the formula across and down to fill the rest of the staging table.

When the setup is created, all that's left to do is create the chart using the staging table. Again, the two major benefits you get from this type of setup are that you can make any formatting changes to one chart and it's easy to add another dataset by adding another option button and you can edit your formulas easily.

Using the Combo Box Control

The Combo Box control allows users to select from a drop-down list of predefined options. When an item from the Combo Box control is selected, some action is taken with that selection. To add a combo box to your worksheet, follow these steps:

1. **Click the Insert drop-down list under the Developer tab.**

2. **Select the Combo Box Form control.**

3. **Click the location in your spreadsheet where you want to place your combo box.**

4. **After you drop the control onto your spreadsheet, right-click the control and select Format Control.**

5. **Click the Control tab to see the configuration options shown in Figure 11-17.**

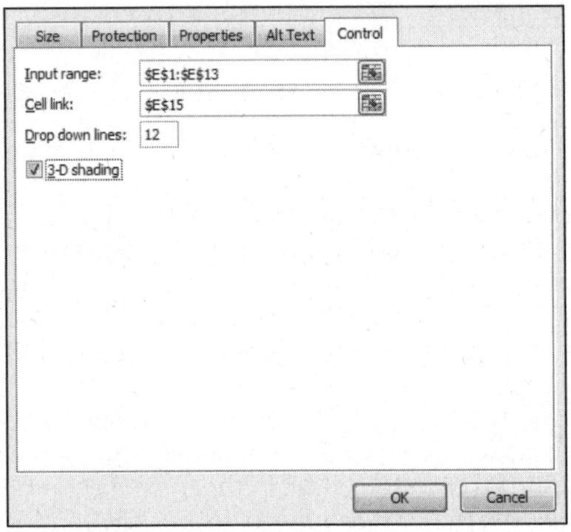

Figure 11-17:
Formatting
the Combo
Box control.

6. **In the Input Range setting, identify the range that holds the predefined items you want to present as choices in the combo box.**

7. **In the Cell Link box, enter the cell to which you want the combo box to output its value.**

   A Combo Box control outputs the index number of the selected item. This means that if the second item on the list is selected, the number 2 will be output. If the fifth item on the list is selected, the number 5 will be output. Notice in Figure 11-17 that this particular control outputs to cell E15.

8. **In the Drop Down Lines box, enter the number of items you want shown at one time.**

   You see in Figure 11-17 that this control is formatted to show 12 items at one time. This means that when users expand the combo box, they see 12 items.

9. **(Optional) You can select the 3-D Shading check box if you want the control to have a three-dimensional appearance.**

10. **Click OK to apply your changes.**

Combo Box Example: Changing Chart Data with a Drop-Down Selector

You can use Combo Box controls to give your users an intuitive way to select data via a drop-down selector. Figure 11-18 shows a thermometer chart that's controlled by the combo box above it. When a user selects the Southwest region, the chart responds by plotting the data for the selected region.

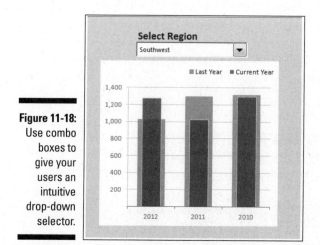

Figure 11-18: Use combo boxes to give your users an intuitive drop-down selector.

To create this example, start with the raw dataset shown in Figure 11-19. This dataset contains the data for each region. Near the raw data, reserve a cell where the combo box will output its value (cell M7, in this example). This cell will catch the index number of the combo box entry selected.

⊿	M	N	O	P	Q	R	S
5			*Raw Data*				
6	Trigger		Market	2012	2011	2010	2009
7	7		Canada	730	854	1911	1608
8			Midwest	952	1389	1113	1603
9			North	443	543	541	386
10			Northeast	1536	1760	1088	1737
11			South	1500	1600	1588	1000
12			Southeast	1257	1280	1734	1007
13			Southwest	1275	1024	1298	1312
14			West	1402	1045	1759	1075

Figure 11-19: Start with the raw dataset and a cell where the combo box can output its value.

You then create the analysis layer (the staging table) that consists of all formulas, as shown in Figure 11-20. The chart reads from this staging table, allowing you to control what the chart sees. The first cell of the staging table contains the following INDEX formula:

```
=INDEX(P7:P14,$M$7)
```

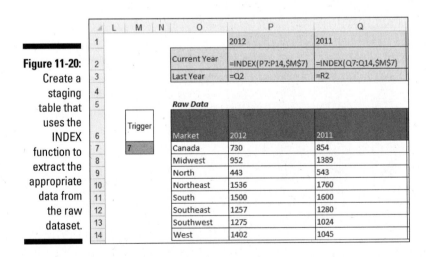

Figure 11-20: Create a staging table that uses the INDEX function to extract the appropriate data from the raw dataset.

The INDEX function converts an index number to a value that can be recognized. An INDEX function requires two arguments to work properly. The first argument is the range of the list you're working with. The second argument is the index number.

In this example, you're using the index number from the combo box (in cell M7) and extracting the value from the appropriate range (2012 data in P7:P14). Again, notice the use of the absolute $ signs. This ensures that the cell references in the formulas don't shift when they're copied down and across.

Take another look at Figure 11-20 to see what's happening. The INDEX formula in cell P2 points to the range that contains the 2012 data. It then captures the index number in cell M7 (which traps the output value of the combo box). The index number happens to be 7. So the formula in cell P2 will extract the seventh value from the 2012 data range (in this case, Southwest).

When you copy the formula across, Excel adjusts the formula to extract the seventh value from each year's data range.

After your INDEX formulas are in place, you have a clean staging table that you can use to create your chart; see Figure 11-21.

	L	M	N	O	P	Q	R	S
1					2012	2011	2010	2009
2				Current Year	1,275	1,024	1,298	1,312
3				Last Year	1,024	1,298	1,312	
4								
5				*Raw Data*				
6		Trigger		Market	2012	2011	2010	2009
7		7		Canada	730	854	1911	1608
8				Midwest	952	1389	1113	1603
9				North	443	543	541	386
10				Northeast	1536	1760	1088	1737
11				South	1500	1600	1588	1000
12				Southeast	1257	1280	1734	1007
13				Southwest	1275	1024	1298	1312
14				West	1402	1045	1759	1075

Figure 11-21: Create a chart using this clean staging table.

Using the List Box Control

The List Box control allows users to select from a list of predefined choices. When an item from the List Box control is selected, some action is taken with that selection. To add a list box to your worksheet, follow these steps:

1. **Select the Insert drop-down list under the Developer tab.**

2. **Select the List Box Form control.**

3. **Click the location in your spreadsheet where you want to place your list box.**

4. **After you drop the control onto your worksheet, right-click the control and select Format Control.**

5. **Click the Control tab to see the configuration options shown in Figure 11-22.**

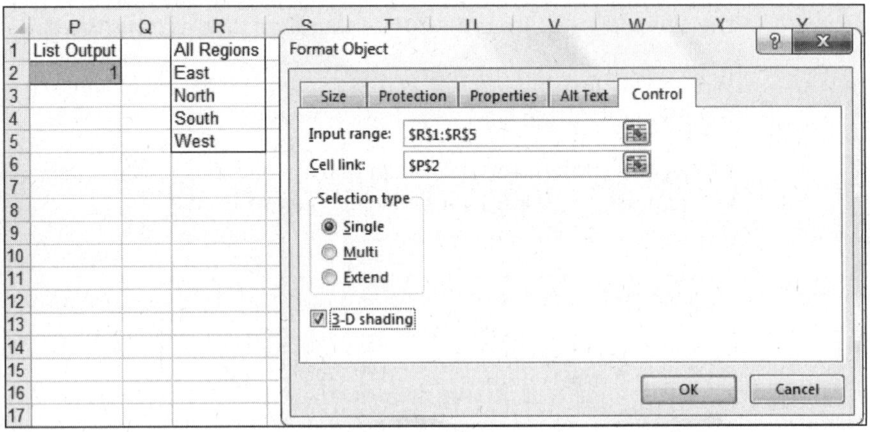

Figure 11-22:
Formatting
the List Box
control.

6. **In the Input Range setting, identify the range that holds the pre-defined items you want to present as choices in the list box.**

   As you can see in Figure 11-22, this list box is filled with region selections.

7. **In the Cell Link box, enter the cell where you want the list box to output its value.**

   By default, a List Box control outputs the index number of the selected item. This means that if the second item on the list is selected, the number 2 will be output. If the fifth item on the list is selected, the number 5 will be output. Notice in Figure 11-22 that this particular control outputs to cell P2. The Selection Type setting allows users to choose more than one selection in the list box. The choices here are Single, Multi, and Extend. Always leave this setting on Single because Multi and Extend work only in the VBA environment.

8. **(Optional) You can select the 3-D Shading check box if you want the control to have a three-dimensional appearance.**

9. **Click OK to apply your changes.**

List Box Example: Controlling Multiple Charts with One Selector

One of the more useful ways to use a list box is to control multiple charts with one selector. Figure 11-23 illustrates an example of this. As a region selection is made in the list box, all three charts are fed the data for that region, adjusting the charts to correspond with the selection made. Happily, all this is done without VBA code, just a handful of formulas and a list box.

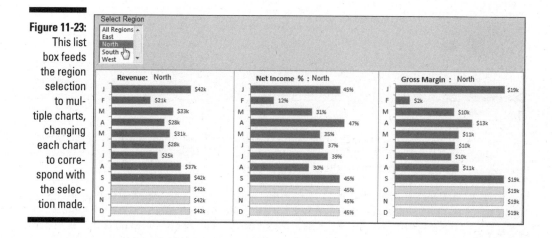

Figure 11-23: This list box feeds the region selection to multiple charts, changing each chart to correspond with the selection made.

To create this example, start with three raw datasets — as shown in Figure 11-24 — that contain three categories of data: Revenues, Net Income %, and Gross Margin. Each dataset contains a separate line for each region, including one for All Regions.

Figure 11-24: Start with the raw datasets that contain one line per region.

	A	B	C	D	E	F	G	H	I	J	K	L	M
5													
6	Revenues	Jan	Feb	Mar	Apr	May	Jun	Jul	Aug	Sep	Oct	Nov	Dec
7	All Regions	98,741	54,621	96,555	109,625	87,936	84,637	81,339	97,281	98,741	98,741	98,741	98,741
8	East	27,474	22,674	35,472	36,292	31,491	27,672	23,853	25,284	27,474	27,474	27,474	27,474
9	North	41,767	20,806	32,633	28,023	27,873	24,656	36,984	41,767	41,767	41,767	41,767	41,767
10	South	18,911	1,125	17,020	34,196	12,989	18,368	23,747	22,087	18,911	18,911	18,911	18,911
11	West	10,590	10,016	11,430	11,115	12,367	10,724	9,082	12,926	10,590	10,590	10,590	10,590
12													
13	Net Income %	Jan	Feb	Mar	Apr	May	Jun	Jul	Aug	Sep	Oct	Nov	Dec
14	All Regions	49.9%	50.6%	48.7%	47.8%	41.4%	47%	52.8%	48.7%	49.9%	49.9%	49.9%	49.9%
15	East	63.1%	53.6%	55.8%	47.4%	41.5%	42%	42.5%	31.7%	63.1%	63.1%	63.1%	63.1%
16	North	45.3%	11.8%	31.0%	47.5%	35.2%	37%	39.1%	29.8%	45.3%	45.3%	45.3%	45.3%
17	South	31.2%	61.7%	41.8%	30.9%	9.0%	33%	56.9%	71.5%	31.2%	31.2%	31.2%	31.2%
18	West	60.1%	75.4%	66.1%	65.2%	79.8%	76%	72.7%	61.9%	60.1%	60.1%	60.1%	60.1%
19													
20	Gross Margin	Jan	Feb	Mar	Apr	May	Jun	Jul	Aug	Sep	Oct	Nov	Dec
21	All Regions	48,508	22,850	44,586	48,340	35,056	37,469	39,881	42,849	48,508	48,508	48,508	48,508
22	East	17,326	12,154	19,799	17,206	13,079	11,605	10,131	8,020	17,326	17,326	17,326	17,326
23	North	18,914	2,455	10,115	13,299	10,938	10,290	9,641	11,019	18,914	18,914	18,914	18,914
24	South	5,904	694	7,115	10,582	1,171	7,339	13,506	15,803	5,904	5,904	5,904	5,904
25	West	6,364	7,547	7,557	7,253	9,867	8,235	6,604	8,005	6,364	6,364	6,364	6,364

You then add a list box that outputs the index number of the selected item to cell P2; see Figure 11-25.

▲	P	Q	R	S	T	U	V	W	X	Y
1	List Output		All Regions	Format Object						
2	1		East							
3			North		Size	Protection	Properties	Alt Text	Control	
4			South							
5			West		Input range:	$R$1:$R$5				
6					Cell link:	$P$2				
7										
8					Selection type					
9					◉ Single					
10					◯ Multi					
11					◯ Extend					
12										
13					☑ 3-D shading					
14										
15										
16								OK	Cancel	
17										

Figure 11-25: Add a list box and note the cell where the output value will be placed.

Next, create a staging table that consists of all formulas. In this staging table, you use the Excel's CHOOSE function to select the correct value from the raw data tables based on the selected region.

In Excel, the CHOOSE function returns a value from a specified list of values based on a specified position number. For instance, the formula CHOOSE(3, "Red", "Yellow", "Green", "Blue") returns Green because Green is the third item in the list of values. The formula CHOOSE(1, "Red", "Yellow", "Green", "Blue") returns Red. See Chapter 2 to get a detailed look at the CHOOSE function.

As you can see in Figure 11-26, the CHOOSE formula retrieves the target position number from cell P2 (the cell where the list box outputs the index number of the selected item) and then matches that position number to the list of cell references given. The cell references come directly from the raw data table.

Figure 11-26: Use the CHOOSE function to capture the correct data corresponding to the selected region.

▲	A	B	O	P
1		J		List Output
2	Revenues	=CHOOSE($P$2,B7,B8,B9,B10,B11)	3	
3	Net Income %			
4	Gross Margin			=INDEX(R1:R5,P2)
5				
6	Revenues	Jan		
7	All Regions	98741.4		
8	East	27473.82		
9	North	41767.27		
10	South	18910.81		
11	West	10589.5		
12				

In the example shown in Figure 11-26, the data that will be returned with this CHOOSE formula is 41767. Why? Because cell P2 contains the number 3, and the third cell reference within the CHOOSE formula is cell B9.

You enter the same type of CHOOSE formula into the Jan column and then copy it across; see Figure 11-27.

Figure 11-27:
Create simi-
lar CHOOSE
formulas for
each row/
category
of data and
then copy
the CHOOSE
formulas
across
months.

	A	B	C
1		J	F
2	Revenues	=CHOOSE($P$2,B7,B8,B9,B10,B11)	=CHOOSE($P$2,C7,C8,C9,C10,C11)
3	Net Income %	=CHOOSE($P$2,B14,B15,B16,B17,B18)	=CHOOSE($P$2,C14,C15,C16,C17,C18)
4	Gross Margin	=CHOOSE($P$2,B21,B22,B23,B24,B25)	=CHOOSE($P$2,C21,C22,C23,C24,C25)

To test that your formulas are working, change the value of cell P2 manually by entering 1, 2, 3, 4, or 5. When the formulas work, all that's left to do is create the charts using the staging table.

If Excel functions like CHOOSE or INDEX are a bit intimidating for you, don't worry. There are literally hundreds of ways to use various combinations of Form controls and Excel functions to achieve interactive reporting. The examples I give in this chapter are designed to give you a sense of how you can incorporate Form controls into your dashboards and reports. There are no set rules on which Form controls or Excel functions you need to use in your model.

Start with basic improvements to your dashboard, using controls and formulas you're comfortable with. Then gradually try to introduce some of the more complex controls and functions. With a little imagination and creativity, you can take the basics in this chapter and customize your own dynamic dashboards.

Chapter 12

Adding Interactivity with Pivot Slicers

Slicers allow you to filter your pivot table in a way that's similar to the way Filter fields filter a pivot table. The difference is that slicers offer a user-friendly interface, enabling you to better manage the filter state of your pivot table reports. Happily, Microsoft has added another dimension to slicers with the introduction of Timeline slicers. Timeline slicers are designed to work specifically with date-based filtering.

In this chapter, you explore slicers and their potential to add an attractive as well as interactive user interface to your dashboards and reports.

Understanding Slicers

If you worked your way through Chapter 6, "The Pivotal Pivot Table," you know that pivot tables allow for interactive filtering using Filter fields. Filter fields are the drop-down lists you can include at the top of your pivot table, allowing users to interactively filter for specific data items. As useful as Filter fields are, they have always had a couple of drawbacks.

First of all, Filter fields are not cascading filters — meaning, the filters don't work together to limit selections when needed. Take, for example, Figure 12-1. You can see that the Region filter is set to the North region. However, the Market filter still allows you to select markets that are clearly not in the North region (California, for example). Because the Market filter is not in any way limited based on the Region Filter field, you have the annoying possibility of selecting a market that could yield no data because it's not in the North region.

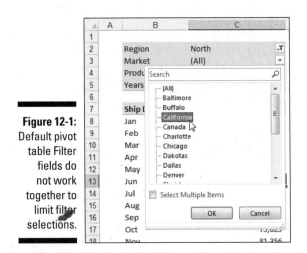

Figure 12-1:
Default pivot
table Filter
fields do
not work
together to
limit filter
selections.

Another drawback is that Filter fields don't provide an easy way to tell what exactly is being filtered when you select multiple items. In Figure 12-2, you can see an example of this. The Region filter has been limited to three regions: Midwest, North, and Northeast. However, notice that the Region filter value shows (Multiple Items). By default, Filter fields show (Multiple Items) when you select more than one item. The only way to tell what has been selected is to click the drop-down menu. You can imagine the confusion on a printed version of this report, in which you can't click down to see which data items make up the numbers on the page.

Figure 12-2:
Filter fields
show the
words
(Multiple
Items) when
multiple
selections
are made.

By contrast, slicers don't have these issues. Slicers respond to one another. As you can see in Figure 12-3, the Market slicer visibly highlights the relevant markets when the North region is selected. The rest of the markets are muted, signaling that they are not part of the North region.

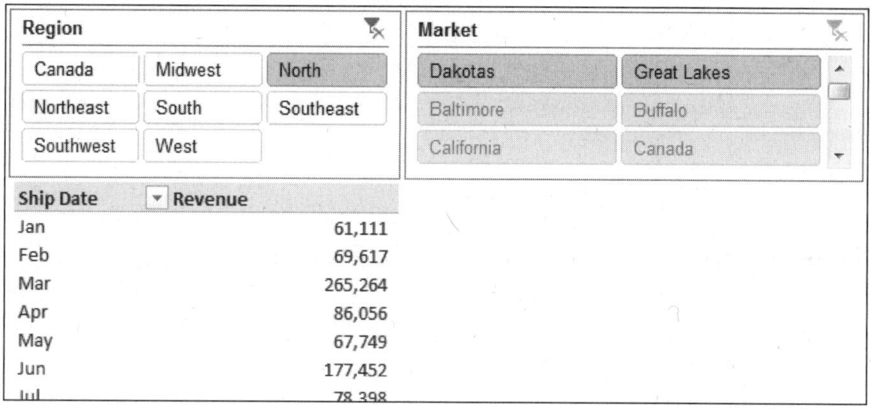

Figure 12-3:
Slicers work together to show you relevant data items based on your selection.

When selecting multiple items in a slicer, you can easily see that multiple items have been chosen. In Figure 12-4, you can see that the pivot table is being filtered by the Midwest, North, and Northeast regions. No more (Multiple Items).

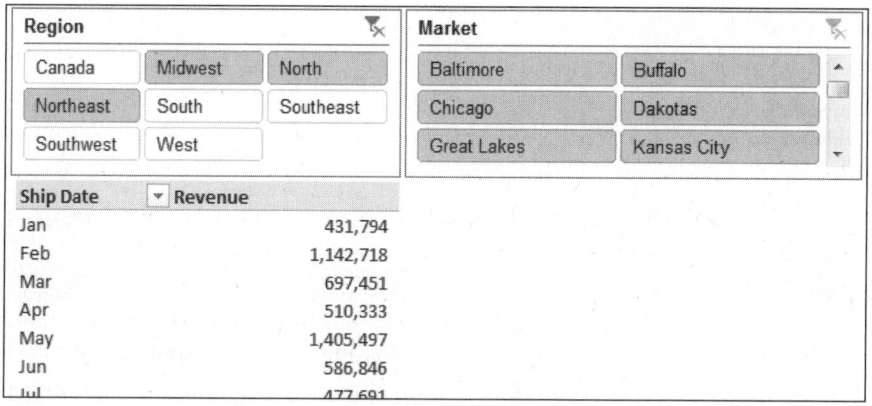

Figure 12-4:
Slicers do a better job at displaying multiple item selections.

Creating a Standard Slicer

Enough talk. It's time to create your first slicer. Just follow these steps:

1. **Place your cursor anywhere inside your pivot table, then go up to the Ribbon and click the Analyze tab. There, click the Insert Slicer icon shown in Figure 12-5.**

   This activates the Insert Slicers dialog box shown in Figure 12-6. Select the dimensions you want to filter. In this example, the Region and Market slicers are created.

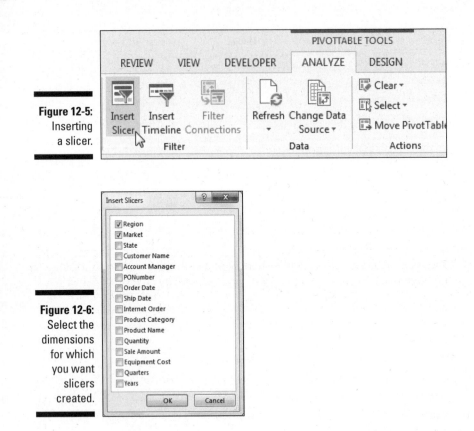

Figure 12-5:
Inserting
a slicer.

Figure 12-6:
Select the
dimensions
for which
you want
slicers
created.

2. **After the slicers are created, simply click the filter values to filter your pivot table.**

   As you can see in Figure 12-7, clicking Midwest in the Region slicer not only filters your pivot table, but the Market slicer also responds by highlighting the markets that belong to the Midwest region.

   You can also select multiple values by holding down the Ctrl key on your keyboard while selecting the needed filters. In Figure 12-8, I held down the Ctrl key while selecting Baltimore, California, Charlotte, and Chicago. This not only highlights the selected markets in the Market slicer, but it also highlights their associated regions in the Region slicer.

   To clear the filtering on a slicer, simply click the Clear Filter icon on the target slicer, as shown in Figure 12-9.

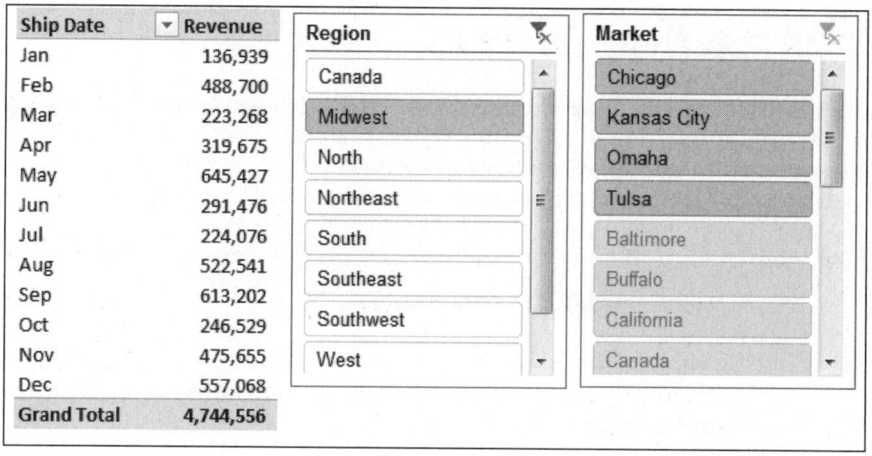

Ship Date	Revenue
Jan	136,939
Feb	488,700
Mar	223,268
Apr	319,675
May	645,427
Jun	291,476
Jul	224,076
Aug	522,541
Sep	613,202
Oct	246,529
Nov	475,655
Dec	557,068
Grand Total	**4,744,556**

Region
- Canada
- Midwest
- North
- Northeast
- South
- Southeast
- Southwest
- West

Market
- Chicago
- Kansas City
- Omaha
- Tulsa
- Baltimore
- Buffalo
- California
- Canada

Figure 12-7: Select the dimensions you want filtered using slicers.

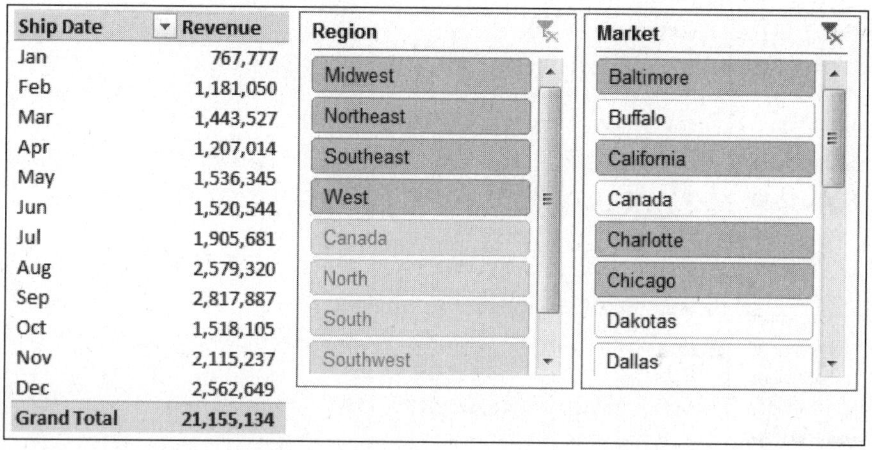

Ship Date	Revenue
Jan	767,777
Feb	1,181,050
Mar	1,443,527
Apr	1,207,014
May	1,536,345
Jun	1,520,544
Jul	1,905,681
Aug	2,579,320
Sep	2,817,887
Oct	1,518,105
Nov	2,115,237
Dec	2,562,649
Grand Total	**21,155,134**

Region
- Midwest
- Northeast
- Southeast
- West
- Canada
- North
- South
- Southwest

Market
- Baltimore
- Buffalo
- California
- Canada
- Charlotte
- Chicago
- Dakotas
- Dallas

Figure 12-8: The fact that you can see the current filter state gives slicers a unique advantage over Filter fields.

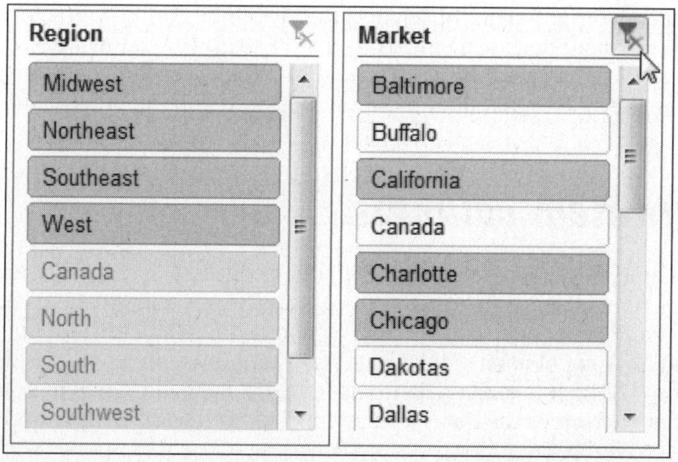

Region
- Midwest
- Northeast
- Southeast
- West
- Canada
- North
- South
- Southwest

Market
- Baltimore
- Buffalo
- California
- Canada
- Charlotte
- Chicago
- Dakotas
- Dallas

Figure 12-9: Clearing the filters on a slicer.

Formatting Slicers

If you're going to use slicers on a dashboard, you should do a bit of formatting to have your slicers match the theme and layout of your dashboard. The following sections cover a few common formatting adjustments you can make to your slicers.

Size and placement

A slicer behaves like a standard Excel shape object in that you can move it around and adjust its size by clicking it and dragging its position points; see Figure 12-10.

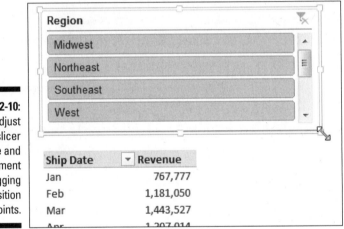

Figure 12-10: Adjust the slicer size and placement by dragging its position points.

You can also right-click the slicer and select Size and Properties. This brings up the Format Slicer pane illustrated in Figure 12-11, allowing you to adjust the size of the slicer, how the slicer should behave when cells are shifted, and whether the slicer should appear on a printed copy of your dashboard.

Data item columns

By default, all slicers are created with one column of data items. You can change this by right-clicking the slicer and selecting Size and Properties. This brings up the Format Slicer pane. Under the Position and Layout section, you can specify the number of columns in the slicer. Adjusting the number to 2, as demonstrated in Figure 12-12, forces the data items to be displayed in 2 columns, adjusting the number to 3 forces the data items to be displayed in 3 columns, and so on.

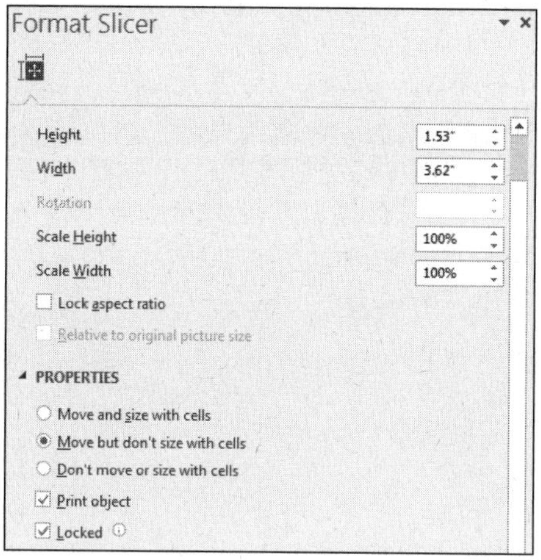

Figure 12-11:
The Format
Slicer pane
offers more
control
over how
the slicer
behaves
in relation
to the
worksheet
it's on.

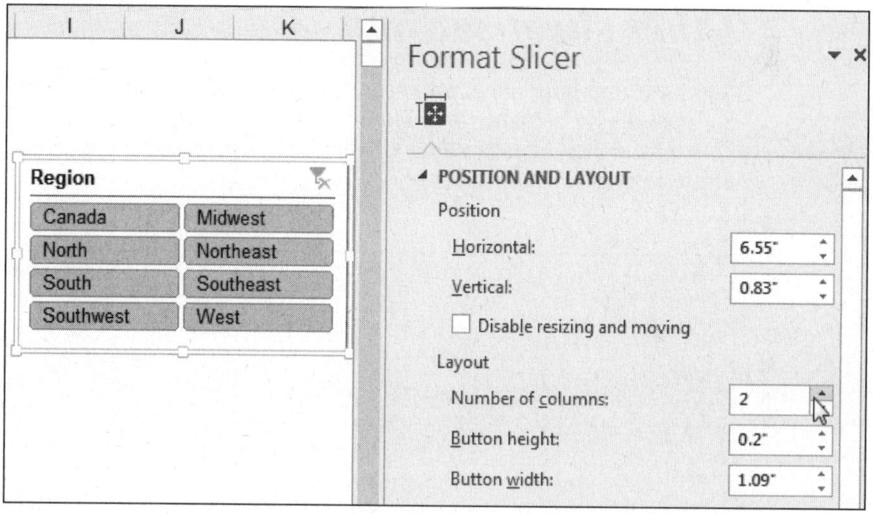

Figure 12-12:
Adjust the
Number of
Columns
property to
display the
slicer data
items in
more than
one column.

Slicer color and style

To change the color and style of your slicer, click it and select a style from the Slicer Style gallery on the Slicer Tools Options tab shown in Figure 12-13. The default styles available suit a majority of your dashboards, but if you want more control over the color and style of your slicer, click the New Slicer Style button in the lower-left corner of the Slicer Style gallery, as shown in Figure 12-13. This activates a dialog box that enables you to format each component part of the slicer.

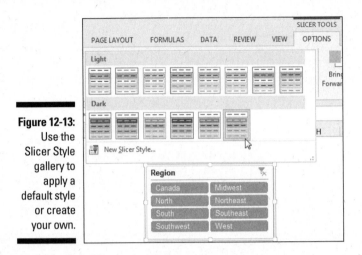

Figure 12-13:
Use the
Slicer Style
gallery to
apply a
default style
or create
your own.

Other slicer settings

Right-clicking your slicer and selecting Slicer Settings activates the Slicer
Settings dialog box shown in Figure 12-14. With this dialog box, you can
control the look of your slicer's header, how your slicer is sorted, and how
filtered items are handled.

Figure 12-14:
The Slicer
Settings
dialog box.

With minimal effort, your slicers can be integrated nicely into your dashboard
layout. Figure 12-15 illustrates two slicers and a pivot chart working together
as a cohesive dashboard component.

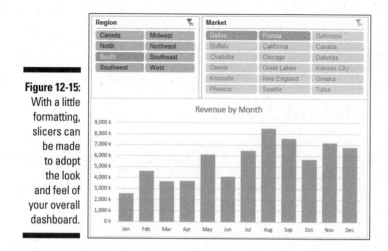

Figure 12-15:
With a little
formatting,
slicers can
be made
to adopt
the look
and feel of
your overall
dashboard.

Controlling Multiple Pivot Tables with One Slicer

Another advantage you gain with slicers is that each slicer can be tied to more than one pivot table; that is to say, any filter you apply to your slicer can be applied to multiple pivot tables.

To connect your slicer to more than one pivot table, simply right-click the slicer and select Report Connections. This activates the Report Connections dialog box shown in Figure 12-16. Place a check next to any pivot table that you want to filter using the current slicer.

Figure 12-16:
Choose the
pivot tables
that will be
filtered by
this slicer.

Report Connections (Market)

Select PivotTable and PivotChart reports to connect to this filter

		Name	Sheet
✓		PivotTable6	Filtering Multiple PivotTables
✓		PivotTable7	Filtering Multiple PivotTables
✓		PivotTable2	Slicer Basics

OK   Cancel

At this point, any filter you apply to your slicer will be applied to all the connected pivot tables. Controlling the filter state of multiple pivot tables is a powerful feature, especially in dashboards that run on multiple pivot tables.

Creating a Timeline Slicer

New in Excel 2013 is the Timeline slicer. The Timeline slicer works in the same way a standard slicer does, in that it lets you filter a pivot table using a visual selection mechanism instead of the old Filter fields. The difference is the Timeline slicer is designed to work exclusively with date fields, providing an excellent visual method to filter and group the dates in your pivot table.

To create a Timeline slicer, your pivot table must contain a field where *all* the data is formatted as a date. It's not enough to have a column of data that contains a few dates. All the values in your date field must be a valid date and formatted as such.

To create a Timeline slicer, follow these steps:

1. **Place your cursor anywhere inside your pivot table, and then click the Analyze tab on the Ribbon. There, click the Insert Timeline command shown in Figure 12-17.**

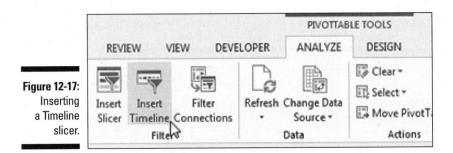

Figure 12-17: Inserting a Timeline slicer.

The Insert Timelines dialog box shown in Figure 12-18 appears, showing you all the available date fields in the chosen pivot table.

2. **In the Insert Timelines dialog box, select the date fields for which you want to create the timeline.**

After your Timeline slicer is created, you can filter the data in your pivot table and pivot chart, using this dynamic data selection mechanism. Figure 12-19 demonstrates how selecting Mar, Apr, and May in the Timeline slicer automatically filters the pivot chart.

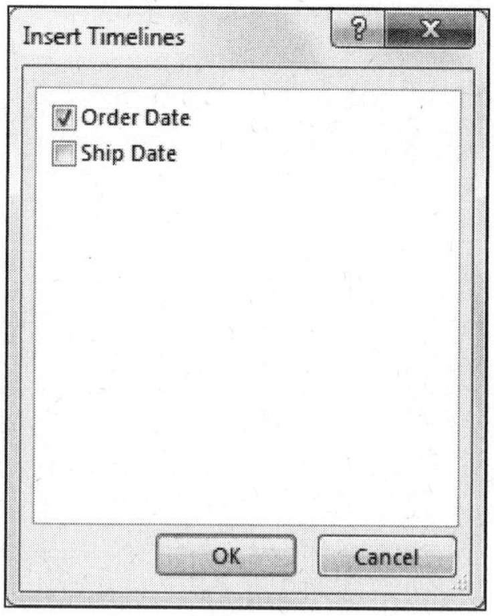

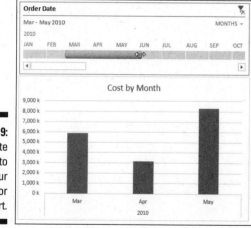

Figure 12-18:
Select the
date fields
for which
you want
slicers
created.

Figure 12-19:
Click a date
selection to
filter your
pivot table or
pivot chart.

Figure 12-20 illustrates how you can expand the slicer range with the mouse to include a wider range of dates in your filtered numbers.

Want to quickly filter your pivot table by quarters? Well, that's easy with a Timeline slicer. Simply click the time period drop-down menu and select Quarters. As you can see in Figure 12-21, you can also switch to Years or Days, if needed.

Timeline slicers are not *backward compatible;* meaning they are usable only in Excel 2013. If you open a workbook with Timeline slicers in Excel 2010 or previous versions, the Timeline slicers will be disabled.

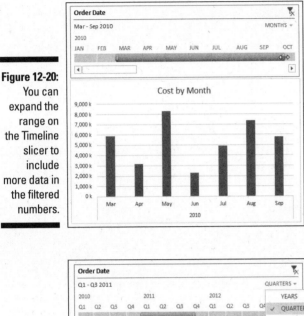

Figure 12-20:
You can expand the range on the Timeline slicer to include more data in the filtered numbers.

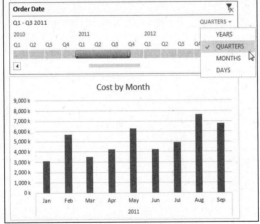

Figure 12-21:
Quickly switch among Quarters, Years, Months, and Days.

Using Slicers as Form Controls

In Chapter 11, "Giving Users an Interactive Interface," you see how to add interactivity to a dashboard using data modeling techniques and Form controls. Although the techniques in that chapter are powerful, the one drawback is that Excel Form controls are starting to look a bit dated, especially when paired with the modern-looking charts that come with Excel 2013.

One clever way to alleviate this problem is to hijack the slicer feature for use as a proxy Form control of sorts. Figure 12-22 demonstrates this with a chart that responds to the slicer on the left. When you click the Income selection, the chart fills with income data. When you click Expense, the chart fills with expense data. Keep in mind that the chart itself is in no way connected to a pivot table.

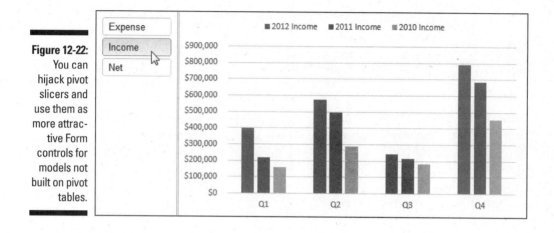

Figure 12-22:
You can hijack pivot slicers and use them as more attractive Form controls for models not built on pivot tables.

To build this basic model, follow these steps:

1. **Create a simple table that holds the names you'd like for your controls, along with some index numbering.**

   In this case, the table should contain three rows under a field called Metric. Each row should contain a metric name and index number for each metric (Income, Expense, and Net).

2. **Create a pivot table using that simple table, illustrated in Figure 12-23.**

3. **Place your cursor anywhere inside your newly created pivot table, click the Analyze tab, and then click the Insert Slicer icon. In the Insert Slicers dialog box, create a slicer for the Metric field.**

   At this point, you have a slicer with the three metric names.

Figure 12-23:
Create a simple table that holds the names you'd like for your controls, along with some index numbering. After you have that, create a pivot table from it.

L	M	N	O
	Metric	Key	
	Income	1	
	Expense	2	
	Net	3	

Row Labels ▼	Sum of Key
Expense	2
Income	1
Net	3
Grand Total	**6**

4. **Right-click the slicer and choose Slicer Settings to activate the Slicer Settings dialog box.**

5. **In the Slicer Settings dialog box, deselect the Display Header check box shown in Figure 12-24.**

   Each time you click the Metric slicer, the associated pivot table is filtered to show only the selected metric. Figure 12-25 demonstrates that this also filters the index number for that metric. The filtered index number will always show up in the same cell (N8 in this case). So this cell can now be used as a trigger cell for: VLOOKUP formulas, index formulas, IF statements, and so on.

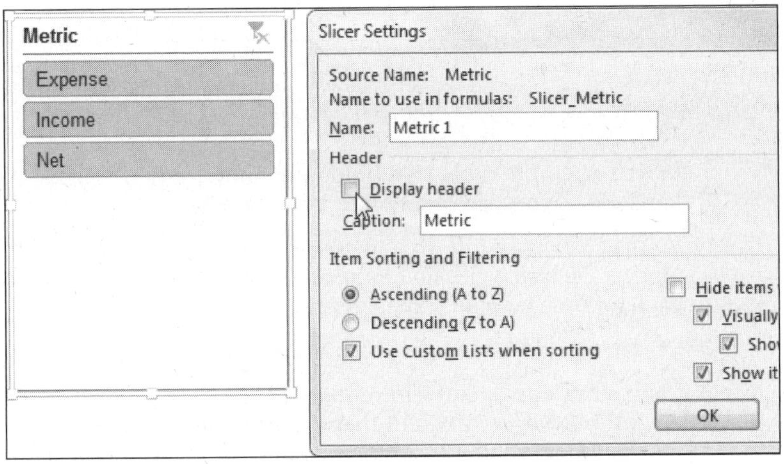

Figure 12-24:
Create a slicer for the Metric field and remove the header.

6. **Use the slicer-fed trigger cell (N8) to drive the formulas in your staging area as demonstrated in Figure 12-26.**

   This formula tells Excel to check the value of cell N8. If the value of cell N8 is 1, which represents the value of the Income option, the formula returns the value in the Income dataset (cell G9). If the value of cell N8 is 2, which

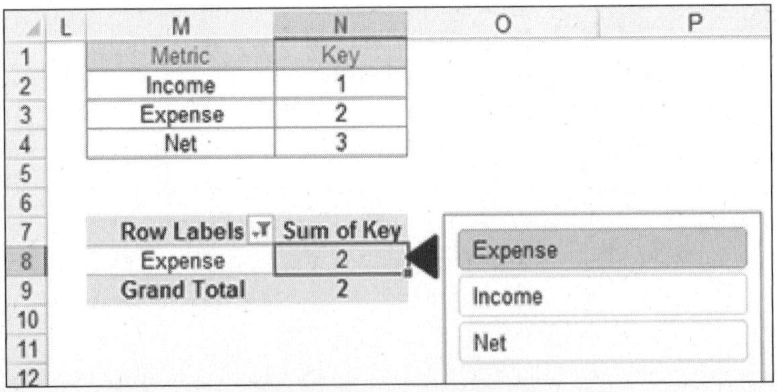

Figure 12-25:
Clicking an item in the slicer filters out the correct index number for the selected metric.

represents the value of the Expense option, the formula returns the value in the Expense dataset (cell G13). If the value of cell N8 is not 1 or 2, the value in cell G17 is returned.

7. **Copy the formula down and across to build out the full staging table; see Figure 12-27.**

8. **The final step is to simply create a chart using the staging table as the source.**

   With this simple technique, you can provide your customers with an attractive interactive menu that more effectively adheres to the look and feel of their dashboards.

	G	H	I	J	K	L	M	N
1							Metric	Key
2		Q1	Q2	Q3	Q4		Income	1
3	=IF($N$8=1,G9,IF($N$8=2,G13,G17))						Expense	2
4							Net	3
5								
6								
7							Row Labels	Sum of Key
8		Q1	Q2	Q3	Q4		Expense	2
9	2012 Income	$399,354	$573,662	$244,661	$790,906		Grand Total	2
10	2011 Income	$219,967	$495,072	$212,749	$687,744			
11	2010 Income	$159,832	$289,825	$181,961	$456,016			
12								
13	2012 Expense	$219,967	$495,072	$212,749	$687,744			
14	2011 Expense	$219,468	$310,048	$307,124	$283,920			
15	2010 Expense	$71,744	$607	$119,251	$154,487			
16								
17	2012 Net	$179,387	$78,590	$31,912	$103,162			
18	2011 Net	$498	$185,024	-$94,375	$403,824			
19	2010 Net	$88,088	$289,218	$62,710	$301,529			

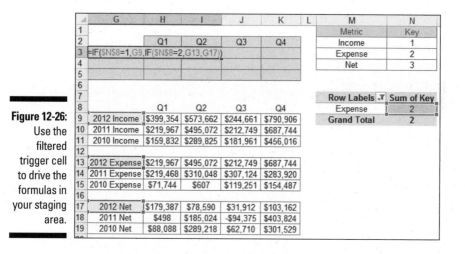

Figure 12-26: Use the filtered trigger cell to drive the formulas in your staging area.

G	H	I	J	K	L	M	N
						Metric	Key
	Q1	Q2	Q3	Q4		Income	1
2012 Income	$399,354	$573,662	$244,661	$790,906		Expense	2
2011 Income	$219,967	$495,072	$212,749	$687,744		Net	3
2010 Income	$159,832	$289,825	$181,961	$456,016			
						Row L	Sum of Key
	Q1	Q2	Q3	Q4		Income	1
2012 Income	$399,354	$573,662	$244,661	$790,906		Grand T	1
2011 Income	$219,967	$495,072	$212,749	$687,744			
2010 Income	$159,832	$289,825	$181,961	$456,016			
2012 Expense	$219,967	$495,072	$212,749	$687,744			
2011 Expense	$219,468	$310,048	$307,124	$283,920			
2010 Expense	$71,744	$607	$119,251	$154,487			
2012 Net	$179,387	$78,590	$31,912	$103,162			
2011 Net	$498	$185,024	-$94,375	$403,824			
2010 Net	$88,088	$289,218	$62,710	$301,529			

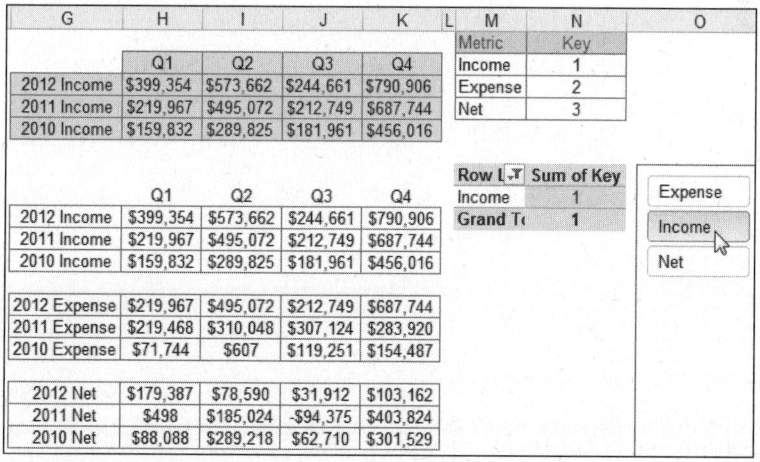

Figure 12-27: The final staging table fed via the slicer.

Part V

Working with the Outside World

See a demonstration of SkyDrive at www.dummies.com/extras/exceldashboardsandreports and find out how you can leverage Microsoft's cloud storage interface to share your reports over the web.

In this part . . .

✔ Gain an understanding of some of the ways to incorporate data that does not originate in Excel.

✔ Discover how to import data from external sources, such as Microsoft Access and SQL Server.

✔ Understand the various methods for protecting your dashboards and reports before distributing.

✔ Explore the different ways to distribute and present your work in a safe and effective way.

Chapter 13

Using External Data for Your Dashboards and Reports

*W*ouldn't it be wonderful if all the data you come across could be neatly packed into one easy-to-use Excel table? The reality is that sometimes the data you need comes from external data sources. *External data* is exactly what it sounds like: data that isn't located in the Excel workbook in which you're operating. Some examples of external data sources are text files, Access tables, SQL Server tables, and even other Excel workbooks.

This chapter explores some efficient ways to get external data into your Excel data models. Before jumping in, however, your humble author wants to throw out one disclaimer: There are numerous ways to get data into Excel. In fact, between the functionality found in the UI and the VBA/code techniques, there are too many techniques to focus on in one chapter. Instead, then, in this chapter I focus on a handful of techniques that can be implemented in most situations and don't come with a lot of pitfalls and gotchas.

Importing Data from Microsoft Access

Microsoft Access is used in many organizations to manage a series of tables that interact with each other, such as a Customers table, an Orders table, and an Invoices table. Managing data in Access provides the benefit of a relational database in which you can ensure data integrity, prevent redundancy, and easily generate datasets via queries.

Excel 2013 offers several methods for getting your Access data into your Excel data model.

The drag-and-drop method

For simplicity, you just can't beat the drag-and-drop method. You can simultaneously open an empty Excel workbook and an Access database from which you want to import a table or query. When both are open, resize each application's window so that they're both fully visible on your screen.

Hover the mouse pointer over the Access table or query you want to copy into Excel. Now click the table and drag it to the blank worksheet in Excel, illustrated in Figure 13-1.

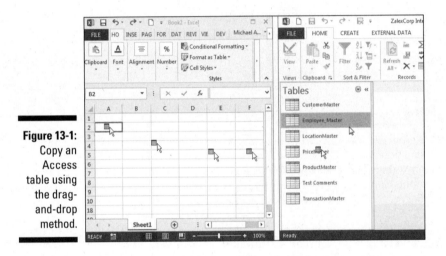

Figure 13-1:
Copy an
Access
table using
the drag-
and-drop
method.

The drag-and-drop method comes in handy when you're doing a quick one-time analysis in which you need a specific set of data in Excel. However, the method isn't so useful under the following conditions:

- ✔ You expect this step to occur routinely, as part of a repeated analysis or report.

- ✔ You expect the users of your Excel presentation to get or update the data via this method.

- ✔ It's not possible or convenient for you to simply open up Access every time you need the information.

In these scenarios, it's much better to use another technique.

The Microsoft Access Export wizard

Access has an Export wizard, and it's relatively simple to use. Just follow these steps:

1. **With your Access database open, click your target table or query to select it.**

2. **On the External Data tab on the Ribbon, select the Excel icon under the Export group.**

   The wizard that you see in Figure 13-2 opens.

   As you can see in Figure 13-2, you can specify certain options in the Excel Export wizard. You can specify the file location, the file type, and some format preservation options.

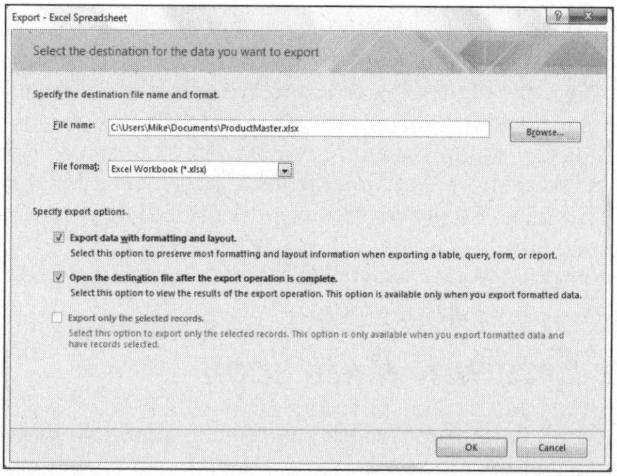

Figure 13-2:
Export
data to
Excel using
the Excel
Export
wizard.

Export - Excel Spreadsheet	
Select the destination for the data you want to export	

Specify the destination file name and format.

File name: C:\Users\Mike\Documents\ProductMaster.xlsx   Browse...

File format: Excel Workbook (*.xlsx)

Specify export options.

☑ Export data with formatting and layout.
   Select this option to preserve most formatting and layout information when exporting a table, query, form, or report.

☑ Open the destination file after the export operation is complete.
   Select this option to view the results of the export operation. This option is available only when you export formatted data.

☐ Export only the selected records.
   Select this option to export only the selected records. This option is only available when you export formatted data and have records selected.

OK   Cancel

3. **In the Excel Export wizard, select Export Data with Formatting and Layout; then select Open the Destination File After the Export Operation is Complete.**

4. **Click OK.**

   Excel opens to show you the exported data.

   In Access, the last page in the Export wizard, shown in Figure 13-3, asks if you want to save your export steps. Saving your export steps can be useful if you expect to frequently send that particular query or table to Excel. The benefit to this method is that, unlike dragging and dropping, the ability to save export steps allows you to automate your exports by using Access macros.

Save Export Steps

Finished exporting 'ProductMaster' to file 'C:\Users\Mike\Documents\ProductMaster.xlsx' successfully.

Do you want to save these export steps? This will allow you to quickly repeat the operation without using the wizard.

☑ Save export steps

Save as: Export-ProductMaster

Description:

Create an Outlook Task.

If you regularly repeat this saved operation, you can create an Outlook task that reminds you when it is time to repeat this operation. The Outlook task will include a Run Export button that runs the export operation in Access.

☐ Create Outlook Task

Hint: To create a recurring task, open the task in Outlook and click the Recurrence button on the Task tab.

Manage Data Tasks...   Save Export   Cancel

Figure 13-3: Use the Save Export Steps option if you export your data frequently.

You may export your Access table or query to an existing Excel file instead of creating a new file. But note the following: the name of the exported object is the name of the table or query in Access. Be careful if you have an Excel object with that same name in your workbook because it may be overwritten. For example, exporting an Access table named PriceMaster to an Excel worksheet that already has a worksheet named PriceMaster causes the original Excel PriceMaster worksheet to be overwritten. Also, make sure the workbook to which you're exporting is closed. If you try to export to an open workbook, you'll likely receive an error in Access.

The Get External Data icon

The option to pull data from Access has been available in Excel for many versions; it was just buried several layers deep in somewhat cryptic menu titles. This made getting Access data into Excel seem like a mysterious and tenuous proposition for many Excel analysts. With the introduction of the Ribbon in Excel 2007, Microsoft put the Get External Data group of commands right on the Ribbon under the Data tab, making it easier to import data from Access and other external data sources.

Excel allows you to establish an updatable data connection between Excel and Access. To see the power of this technique, walk through these steps:

1. **Open a new Excel workbook and click the Data tab on the Ribbon.**

2. **In the Get External Data group, select the From Access icon.**

   The Select Data Source dialog box opens, as shown in Figure 13-4. If the database from which you want to import data is local, browse to the file's location and select it. If your target Access database resides on a network drive at another location, you need the proper authorization to select it.

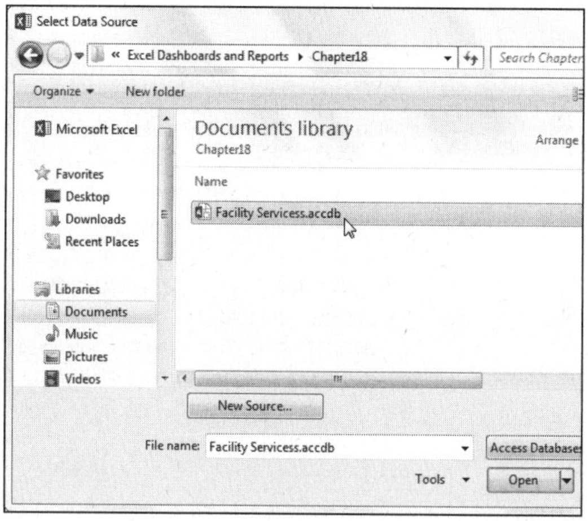

Figure 13-4:
Choose
your source
database.

3. **Navigate to your sample database and click Open.**

   In some environments, a series of Data Link Properties dialog boxes opens asking for credentials (that is, username and password). Most Access databases don't require logon credentials, but if your database does require a username and password, type them in the Data Link Properties dialog box.

4. **Click OK.**

   The Select Table dialog box shown in Figure 13-5 opens. This dialog box lists all the available tables and queries in the selected database.

   The Select Table dialog box contains a column called Type. There are two types of Access objects you can work with: views and tables. VIEW indicates that the dataset listed is an Access query, and TABLE indicates that the dataset is an Access table. In this example, Sales_By_Employee is actually an Access query. This means that you import the results of the query. This is true interaction at work; Access does all the back-end data management and aggregation, and Excel handles the analysis and presentation!

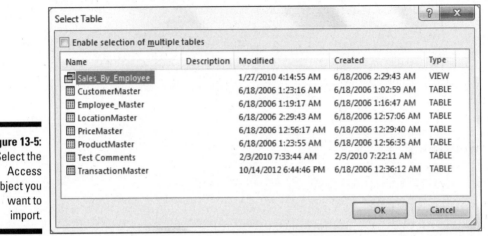

Figure 13-5:
Select the
Access
object you
want to
import.

5. **Select your target table or query and click OK.**

The Import Data dialog box shown in Figure 13-6 opens. Here you define where and how to import the table. You have the option of importing the data into a Table, a PivotTable Report, a PivotChart, or a Power View Report. You also have the option of creating only the connection, making the connection available for later use.

Note that if you choose PivotChart or PivotTable Report, the data is saved to a pivot cache without writing the actual data to the worksheet. Thus your pivot table can function as normal without you having to import potentially hundreds of thousands of data rows twice (once for the pivot cache and once for the spreadsheet).

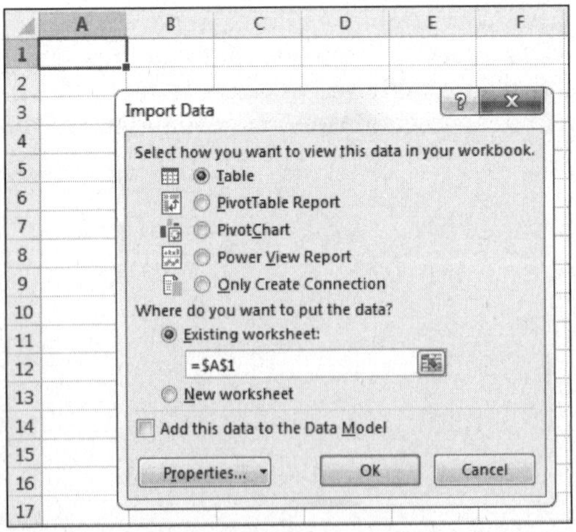

Figure 13-6:
Choosing
how and
where to
view your
Access
data.

6. **Select Table as the output view and define cell A1 as the output location, as shown in Figure 13-6.**

7. **Click OK.**

   Your reward for all your work is a table similar to the one shown in Figure 13-7, which contains the imported data from your Access database.

	A	B	C	D	
1	Region ▼	Market ▼	Branch_Number ▼	Employee_Number ▼	La
2	MIDWEST	TULSA	401612	1336	RA
3	MIDWEST	TULSA	401612	1336	RA
4	MIDWEST	TULSA	401612	60224	HE
5	MIDWEST	TULSA	401612	60224	HE
6	MIDWEST	TULSA	401612	55662	W
7	MIDWEST	TULSA	401612	60224	HE
8	MIDWEST	TULSA	401612	1336	RA
9	MIDWEST	TULSA	401612	55662	W
10	MIDWEST	TULSA	401612	55662	W
11	MIDWEST	TULSA	401612	1336	RA
12	MIDWEST	TULSA	401612	55662	W
13	MIDWEST	TULSA	401612	55662	W

Figure 13-7: Your imported Access data.

The incredibly powerful thing about importing data this way is that it's refreshable. That's right. If you import data from Access using this technique, Excel creates a table that you can update by right-clicking it and selecting Refresh from the pop-up menu, as shown in Figure 13-8. When you update your imported data, Excel reconnects to your Access database and imports the data again. As long as a connection to your database is available, you can refresh with a mere click of the mouse.

	Region ▼	Ma...		...umber ▼	Employee_Number ▼	Last
1			✂ Cut			
2	MIDWEST	TUI			1336	RAC
3	MIDWEST	TUI	▤ Copy		1336	RAC
4	MIDWEST	TUI	📋 Paste Options:		60224	HER
5	MIDWEST	TUI	📋 📋		60224	HER
6	MIDWEST	TUI			55662	WH/
7	MIDWEST	TUI	Paste Special...		60224	HER
8	MIDWEST	TUI	🔄 Refresh		1336	RAC
9	MIDWEST	TUI	Insert ▶		55662	WH/
10	MIDWEST	TUI	Delete ▶		55662	WH/

Figure 13-8: As long as a connection to your database is available, you can update your table with the latest data.

Again, a major advantage to using the Get External Data group is that you can establish a refreshable data connection between Excel and Access. In most cases, you can set up the connection one time and then just update the data connection when needed. You can even record an Excel macro to update the data on some trigger or event, which is ideal for automating the transfer of data from Access.

Managing external data properties

When you import external data into a table, you can control a few adjustable properties via the Properties dialog box. You can get to the properties of a particular external data table by clicking the target table and clicking the Properties icon under the Data tab.

This activates the External Data Properties dialog box. The properties found in this dialog box allow you to further customize your query tables to suit your needs. Take a moment to familiarize yourself with some of the useful options in this dialog box.

- ✔ **Include Row Numbers:** This property is deselected by default. Selecting this property creates a dummy column that contains row numbers. The first column of your dataset will be this row number column upon refresh.

- ✔ **Adjust Column Width:** This property is selected by default, telling Excel to adjust the column widths each time the data is refreshed. Deselecting this option will cause the column widths to remain the same.

- ✔ **Preserve Column/Sort/Filter/Layout:** If this property is selected, the order of the columns and rows of the Excel range

remains unchanged. This way, you can rearrange and sort the columns and rows of the external data in your worksheet without worrying about blowing away your formatting each time you refresh. Deselecting this property will make the Excel range look like the query.

- ✔ **Preserve Cell Formatting:** This property is selected by default, telling Excel to keep the applied cell formatting when you refresh.

- ✔ **Insert Cells for New Data, Delete Unused Cells:** This is the default setting for data range changes. This option will insert cells (not rows) when the imported table grows and delete cells (not rows) when it shrinks.

- ✔ **Insert Entire Rows for New Data, Clear Unused Cells:** This option will insert whole rows when the imported table grows and clear cells (not delete rows) when it shrinks.

- ✔ **Overwrite Cells for New Data, Clear Unused Cells:** This option will overwrite cells when the imported table grows clear cells (not delete rows) when it shrinks.

Importing Data from SQL Server

In the spirit of collaboration, Excel 2013 vastly improves your ability to connect to transactional databases such as SQL Server. With the connection functionality found in Excel, creating a connected table or pivot table from SQL Server data is as easy as ever.

Start on the Data tab and follow these steps:

1. **Click the From Other Sources icon to see the drop-down menu shown Figure 13-9; then select From SQL Server.**

    Selecting this option activates the Data Connection Wizard, as shown in Figure 13-10. Here, you configure your connection settings so Excel can establish a link to the server.

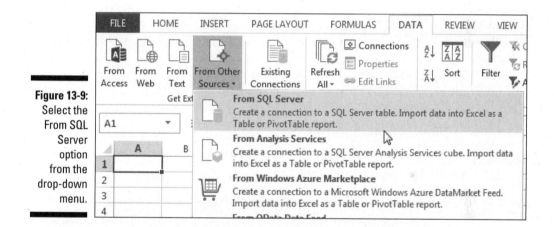

Figure 13-9: Select the From SQL Server option from the drop-down menu.

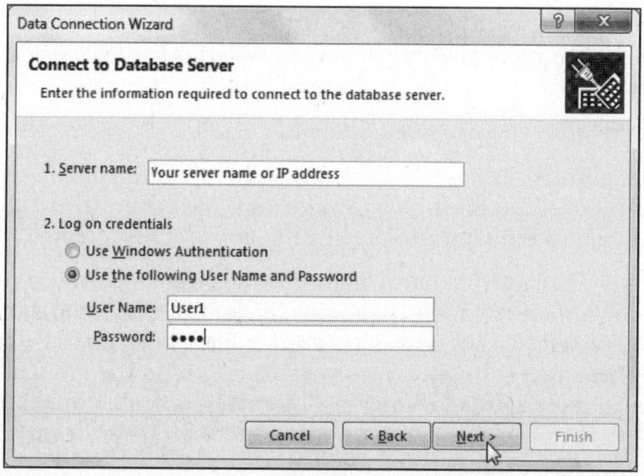

Figure 13-10: Enter your authentication information and click Next.

2. **Provide Excel with some authentication information.**

   Enter the name of your server as well as your username and password; see Figure 13-10. If you're typically authenticated via Windows authentication however, simply select the Use Windows Authentication option.

3. **Select the database with which you're working from a drop-down menu containing all available databases on the specified server.**

   As you can see in Figure 13-11, a database called `AdventureWorks2012` is selected in the drop-down box. All the tables and views in this database are shown in the list of objects below the drop-down menu.

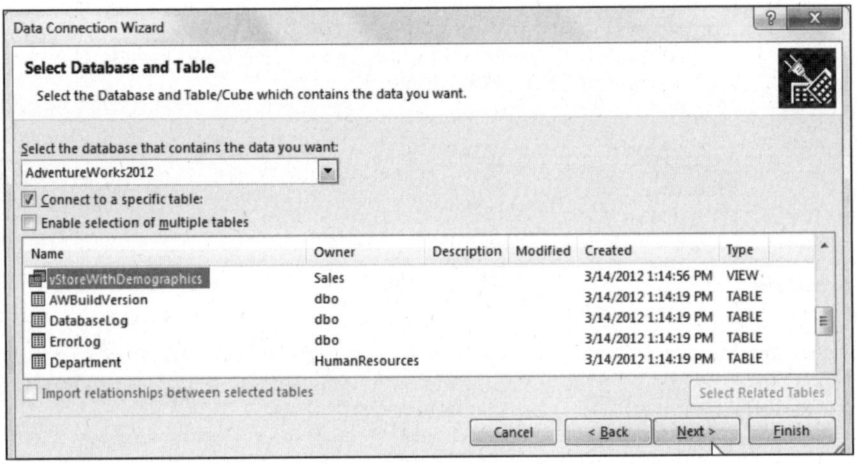

Figure 13-11: Specify your database and then choose the table or view you want to analyze.

4. **Choose the table or view you want to analyze and then click Next.**

5. **In the screen that appears in the wizard, enter descriptive information about the connection you've just created. See Figure 13-12 for an example.**

   This information is optional. If you bypass this screen without editing anything, your connection will work fine.

   The fields that you use most often are

   - *File Name:* In the File Name input box, you can change the filename of the ODC (Office Data Connection) file generated to store the configuration information for the link you just created.

   - *Save Password in File:* Under the File Name input box, you have the option of saving the password for your external data in the file itself (via the Save Password in File check box). Selecting this check box actually enters your password in the file. This password is not encrypted, so anyone interested enough could potentially get the password for your data source by simply viewing your file with a text editor.

- *Description:* In the Description field, you can enter a plain description of what this particular data connection does.

- *Friendly Name:* The Friendly Name field allows you to specify your own name for the external source. You typically enter a name that is descriptive and easy to read.

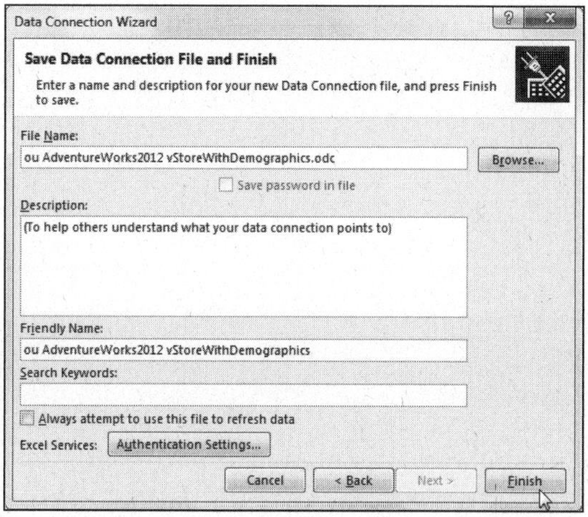

Figure 13-12:
Enter descriptive information for your connection.

6. **When you are satisfied with your descriptive edits, click Finish to finalize your connection settings.**

   You immediately see the Import Data dialog box where you can choose how to import your data. As you can see Figure 13-13, this data will be shown in a pivot table.

   When the connection is finalized, you can start building your pivot table.

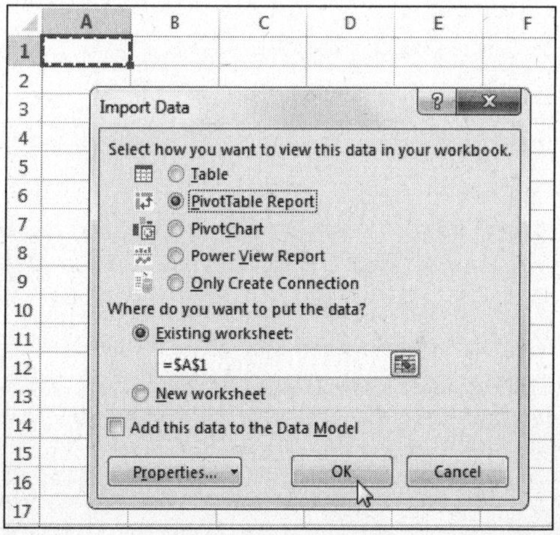

Figure 13-13:
Choosing how and where to view your SQL Server data.

Chapter 14

Sharing Your Workbook with the Outside World

· ·

In This Chapter

▶ Controlling access to your dashboards and reports

▶ Displaying your Excel dashboards in PowerPoint

▶ Saving your dashboards and reports to a PDF file

▶ Publishing your dashboards to the web

· ·

*L*et's face it; you're not making these dashboards and reports for your health. At some point, you'll want to share your handiwork with others. The focus of this chapter is on preparing your dashboards for life outside your PC. Here, you explore the various methods of protecting your work from accidental and intentional meddling, and discover how you can distribute your dashboards via PowerPoint, PDF, and the web.

Protecting Your Dashboards and Reports

You've put in a ton of hours getting your dashboard and reports to work the way you want them to. The last thing you need is to have a clumsy client or an overzealous power-user botching up your Excel file.

Before distributing any Excel-based work, you should always consider protecting your file using the protection capabilities native to Excel. Although none of Excel's protection methods are hacker-proof, they do serve to avoid accidental corruption and to protect sensitive information from unauthorized users.

Securing access to the entire workbook

Perhaps the best way to protect your Excel file is to use Excel's protection options for file sharing. These options enable you to apply security at the workbook level, requiring a password to view or make changes to the file.

This method is by far the easiest to apply and manage because there's no need to protect each worksheet one at a time. You can apply a blanket protection to guard against unauthorized access and edits. Take a moment to review the file-sharing options, which are as follows:

✔ Setting read-only access to a file until a password is given

✔ Requiring a password to open an Excel file

✔ Removing workbook-level protection

The next few sections discuss these options in detail.

Permitting read-only access unless a password is given

You can set your workbook to read-only mode until the user types the password. This way, you can keep your file safe from unauthorized changes, yet still allow authorized users to edit the file.

Here are the steps to force read-only mode:

1. **With your file open, click the File button.**

2. **To open the Save As dialog box, click Save As and then double-click the Computer icon.**

3. **In the Save As dialog box, click the Tools button and select General Options, as shown in Figure 14-1.**

   The General Options dialog box appears.

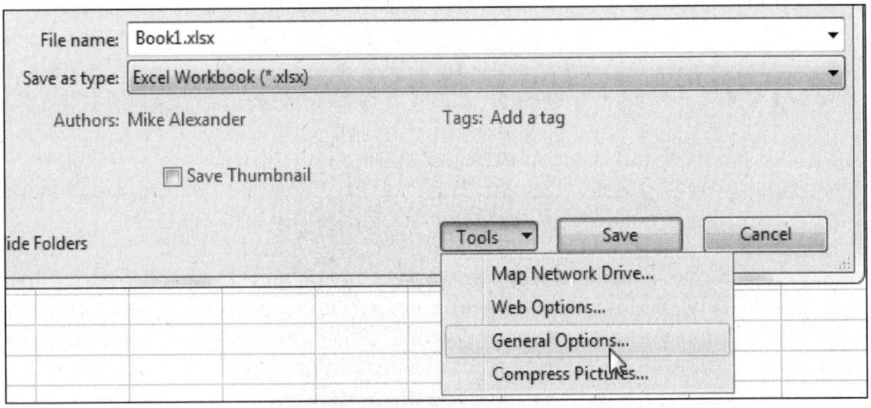

Figure 14-1:
The file-sharing options are hidden away in the Save As dialog box under General Options.

4. **Type an appropriate password in the Password to Modify input box shown in Figure 14-2, and click OK.**

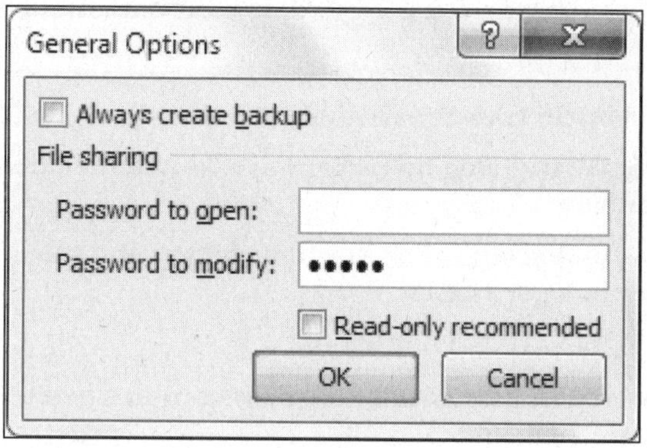

General Options

☐ Always create backup

File sharing

Password to open: [   ]

Password to modify: [●●●●●   ]

☐ Read-only recommended

[OK] [Cancel]

Figure 14-2:
Type the password needed to modify the file.

5. **Excel asks you to reenter your password, so reenter your chosen password.**

6. **Save your file to a new name.**

At this point, your file is password-protected from unauthorized changes. If you were to open your file, you'd see something similar to Figure 14-3. Failing to type the correct password causes the file to go into read-only mode.

Note that Excel passwords are case-sensitive, so make sure Caps Lock on your keyboard is turned off when entering your password.

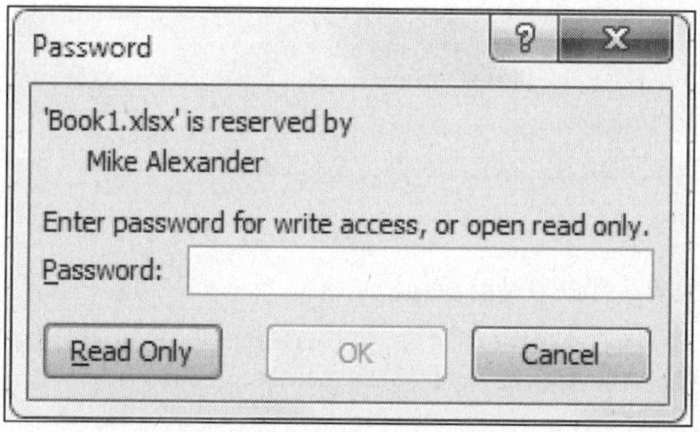

Password

'Book1.xlsx' is reserved by
    Mike Alexander

Enter password for write access, or open read only.

Password: [   ]

[Read Only] [OK] [Cancel]

Figure 14-3:
A password is now needed to make changes to the file.

Requiring a password to open an Excel file

You may have instances in which your Excel dashboards are so sensitive that only certain users are authorized to see them. In these cases, you can require users to enter a password to open the workbook. Here are the steps to set up a password for the file:

1. **With your file open, click the File button.**

2. **To open the Save As dialog box, click Save As and then double-click the Computer icon.**

3. **In the Save As dialog box, click the Tools button and select General Options (refer to Figure 14-1).**

   The General Options dialog box opens.

4. **Type an appropriate password in the Password to Open text box, as shown in Figure 14-4, and click OK.**

5. **Excel asks you to reenter your password.**

6. **Save your file to a new name.**

   At this point, your file is password-protected from unauthorized viewing.

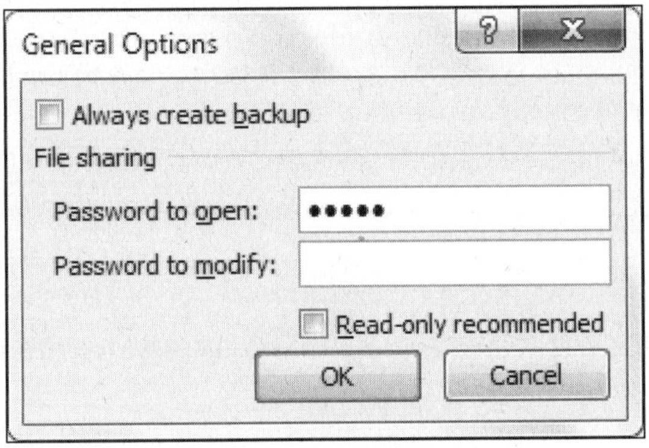

Figure 14-4:
Type the
password
needed to
modify the
file.

Removing workbook-level protection

Removing workbook-level protection is as easy as clearing the passwords from the General Options dialog box. Here's how you do it:

1. **With your file open, click the File button.**

2. **To open the Save As dialog box, click Save As.**

3. **In the Save As dialog box, click the Tools button and select General Options (refer to Figure 14-1).**

   The General Options dialog box opens.

4. **Clear the Password to Open input box as well as the Password to Modify input box and then click OK.**

5. **Save your file.**

When you select the Read-Only Recommended check box in the General Options dialog box (refer to Figure 14-4), you get a cute but useless message recommending read-only access upon opening the file. This message is only a recommendation and doesn't prevent anyone from opening the file as read/write.

Limiting access to specific worksheet ranges

You may find that you need to lock specific worksheet ranges, preventing users from taking certain actions. For example, you may not want users to break your data model by inserting or deleting columns and rows. You can prevent this by locking those columns and rows.

Unlocking editable ranges

By default, all cells in a worksheet are set to be locked when you apply worksheet-level protection. The cells on that worksheet can't be altered in any way. That being said, you may find you need certain cells or ranges to be editable even in a locked state, like the example shown in Figure 14-5.

Figure 14-5: Though this sheet is protected, users can enter 2006 data into the input cells provided.

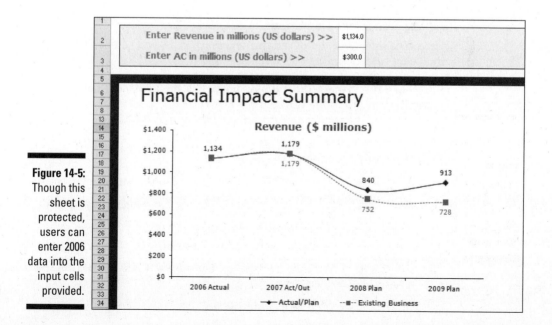

Before you protect your worksheet, you can unlock the cell or range of cells that you want users to be able to edit. (The next section shows you how to protect your entire worksheet.) Here's how to do it:

1. **Select the cells you need to unlock.**

2. **Right-click and select Format Cells.**

3. **On the Protection tab, as shown in Figure 14-6, deselect the Locked check box.**

4. **Click OK to apply the change.**

Figure 14-6:
To ensure
that a cell
remains
unlocked
when the
worksheet
is protected,
deselect
the Locked
check box.

Format Cells	? X

Number	Alignment	Font	Border	Fill	Protection

☐ Locked
☐ Hidden

Locking cells or hiding formulas has no effect until you protect the worksheet (Review tab, Changes group, Protect Sheet button).

OK   Cancel

Applying worksheet protection

After you've selectively unlocked the necessary cells, you can begin to apply worksheet protection. Just follow these steps:

1. **To open the Protect Sheet dialog box, click the Protect Sheet icon on the Review tab of the Ribbon; see Figure 14-7.**

Figure 14-7:
Click
Protect
Sheet in the
Review tab.

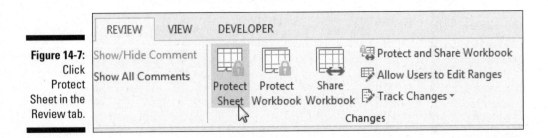

REVIEW   VIEW   DEVELOPER

Show/Hide Comment
Show All Comments

Protect Sheet   Protect Workbook   Share Workbook

Protect and Share Workbook
Allow Users to Edit Ranges
Track Changes

Changes

2. **Type a password in the text box shown in Figure 14-8, and then click OK.**

   This is the password that removes worksheet protection. Note that because you can apply and remove worksheet protection without a password, specifying one is optional.

3. **In the list box shown in Figure 14-8, select which elements users can change after you protect the worksheet.**

   When a check box is cleared for a particular action, Excel prevents users from taking that action.

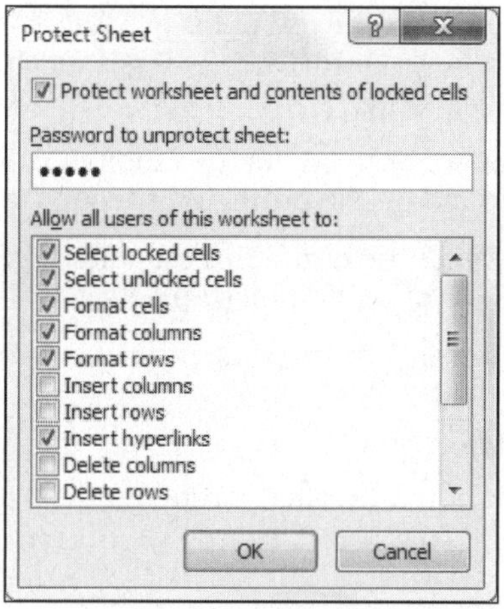

Figure 14-8:
Specify
a pass-
word that
removes
worksheet
protection.

4. **If you provided a password, reenter the password.**

5. **Click OK to apply the worksheet protection.**

Protect sheet elements and actions

Take a moment to familiarize yourself with some of the other actions you can limit when protecting a worksheet (refer to Figure 14-8). They are as follows:

- **Select Locked Cells:** Allows or prevents the selection of locked cells.

- **Select Unlocked Cells:** Allows or prevents the selection of unlocked cells.

- **Format Cells:** Allows or prevents the formatting of cells.

- **Format Columns:** Allows or prevents the use of column formatting commands, including changing column width or hiding columns.

- **Format Rows:** Allows or prevents the use of row formatting commands, including changing row height or hiding rows.

- **Insert Columns:** Allows or prevents the inserting of columns.

- **Insert Rows:** Allows or prevents the inserting of rows.

✔ **Insert Hyperlinks:** Allows or prevents the inserting of hyperlinks.

✔ **Delete Columns:** Allows or prevents the deleting of columns. Note that if Delete Columns is protected and Insert Columns is not protected, you can technically insert columns you can't delete.

✔ **Delete Rows:** Allows or prevents the deleting of rows. Note that if Delete Rows is protected and Insert Rows is not protected, you can technically insert rows you can't delete.

✔ **Sort:** Allows or prevents the use of Sort commands. Note that this doesn't apply to locked ranges. Users can't sort ranges that contain locked cells on a protected worksheet, regardless of this setting.

✔ **Use AutoFilter:** Allows or prevents the use of Excel's AutoFilter functionality. Users can't create or remove AutoFiltered ranges on a protected worksheet, regardless of this setting.

✔ **Use PivotTable Reports:** Allows or prevents the modifying, refreshing, or formatting pivot tables found on the protected sheet.

✔ **Edit Objects:** Allows or prevents the formatting and altering of shapes, charts, text boxes, controls, or other graphics objects.

✔ **Edit Scenarios:** Allows or prevents the viewing of scenarios.

Removing worksheet protection

Just follow these steps to remove any worksheet protection you may have applied:

1. **Click the Unprotect Sheet icon on the Review tab.**

2. **If you specified a password while protecting the worksheet, Excel asks you for that password; see Figure 14-9. Type the password and click OK to immediately remove protection.**

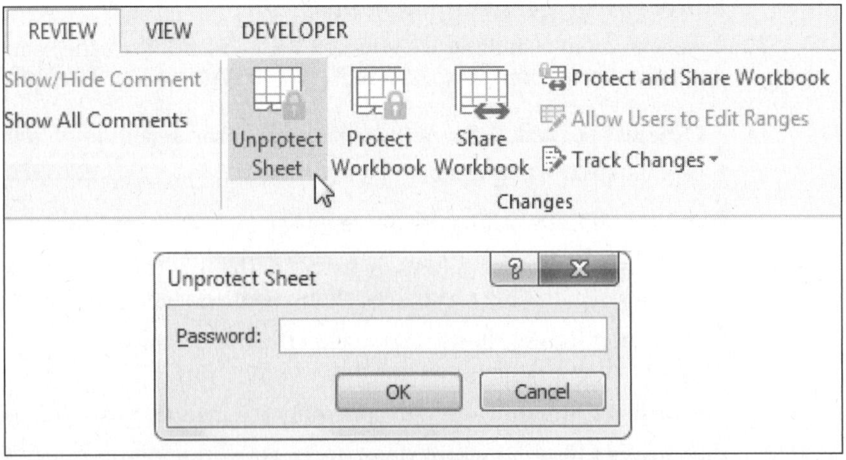

Figure 14-9: The Unprotect Sheet icon removes worksheet protection.

Protecting the workbook structure

If you look under the Review tab on the Ribbon, you see the Protect Workbook icon next to the Protect Sheet icon. Protecting the workbook enables you to prevent users from taking any action that affects the structure of your workbook, such as adding/deleting worksheets, hiding/unhiding worksheets, and naming or moving worksheets. Just follow these steps to protect a workbook:

1. **To open the Protect Structure and Windows dialog box shown in Figure 14-10, click the Protect Workbook icon on the Review tab of the Ribbon.**

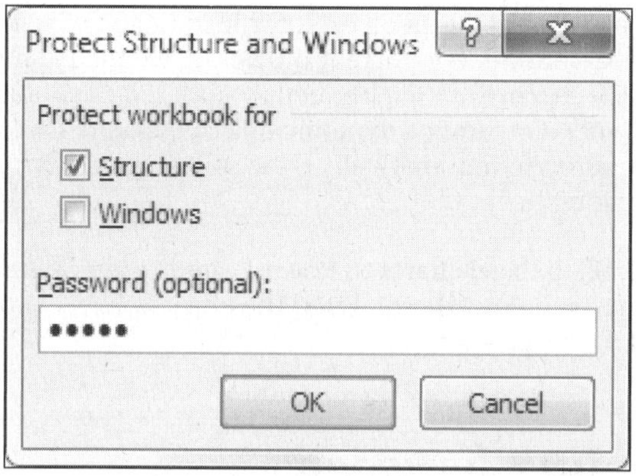

Figure 14-10:
The Protect
Structure
and
Windows
dialog box.

2. **Choose which elements you want to protect: workbook structure, windows, or both. When a check box is cleared for a particular action, Excel prevents users from taking that action.**

Selecting Structure prevents users from doing the following:

- Viewing worksheets that you've hidden

- Moving, deleting, hiding, or changing the names of worksheets

- Inserting new worksheets or chart sheets

- Moving or copying worksheets to another workbook

- Displaying the source data for a cell in a pivot table Values area or displaying pivot table Filter pages on separate worksheets

- Creating a scenario summary report

- Using an Analysis ToolPak utility that requires results to be placed on a new worksheet

- Recording new macros

Choosing Windows prevents users from changing, moving, or sizing the workbook windows while the workbook is open.

3. **If you provided a password, reenter the password.**

4. **Click OK to apply the worksheet protection.**

Linking Your Excel Dashboards to PowerPoint

You may find that your organization heavily favors PowerPoint presentations for periodic updates. Several methods exist for linking your Excel dashboards to a PowerPoint presentation. For current purposes, we focus on the method that is most conducive to presenting frequently updated dashboards and reports in PowerPoint — creating a dynamic link. A *dynamic link* allows your PowerPoint presentation to automatically pick up changes that you make to data in your Excel worksheet.

This technique of linking Excel charts to PowerPoint is ideal if you aren't proficient at building charts in PowerPoint. Build the chart in Excel and then create a link for the chart in PowerPoint.

Creating a link between Excel and PowerPoint

When you create a link to a range in Excel, PowerPoint stores the location information to your source field and then displays a representation of the linked data. The net effect is that when the data in your source file changes, PowerPoint updates its representation of the data to reflect the changes.

You can find the example `Chapter 14 Samples.xlsx` file for this chapter on this book's companion website.

To test this concept of linking to an Excel range, follow these steps:

1. **Open the `Chapter 14 Samples.xlsx` file.**

2. **Click the chart to select it and press Ctrl+C on your keyboard to copy the chart.**

3. **Open a new PowerPoint presentation and place your cursor at the location that you want to display the linked table.**

4. **On the Home tab in PowerPoint, choose Paste➪Paste Special, as shown in Figure 14-11.**

   The Paste Special dialog box appears, illustrated in Figure 14-12.

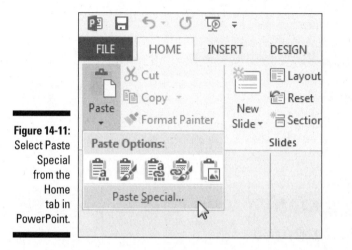

Figure 14-11:
Select Paste
Special
from the
Home
tab in
PowerPoint.

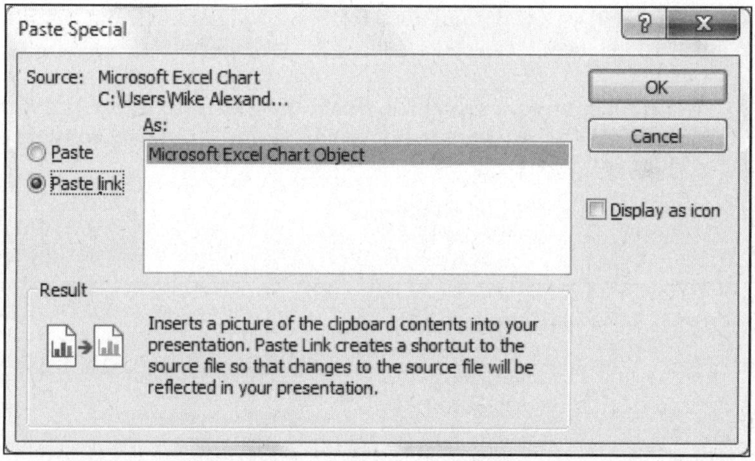

Figure 14-12:
Be sure
to select
Paste Link
and set
the link as
an Excel
Chart Object.

5. **Select the Paste Link radio button and choose Microsoft Excel Chart Object from the list of document types.**

6. **Click OK to apply the link.**

   Your chart on your PowerPoint presentation now links back to your Excel worksheet. See Figure 14-13 for an example.

   If you're copying multiple charts, select the range of cells that contains the charts and press Ctrl+C to copy. This way, you're copying everything in that range of cells — charts and all.

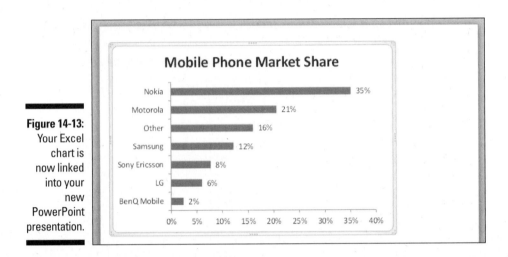

Figure 14-13:
Your Excel
chart is
now linked
into your
new
PowerPoint
presentation.

Manually updating links to capture updates

The nifty thing about dynamic links is that they can be updated, enabling you to capture any new data in your Excel worksheets without re-creating the links. To see how this works, follow these steps:

1. **Go back to your Excel file (from the example in the previous section) and change the values for Samsung and Nokia, as shown in Figure 14-14.**

   Note the chart has changed.

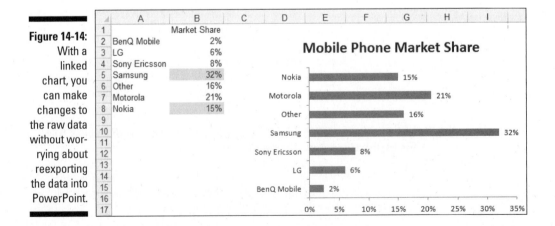

Figure 14-14:
With a
linked
chart, you
can make
changes to
the raw data
without wor-
rying about
reexporting
the data into
PowerPoint.

2. **Return to PowerPoint, right-click the chart link in your presentation, and choose Update Link, as demonstrated in Figure 14-15.**

   You see that your linked chart automatically captures the changes.

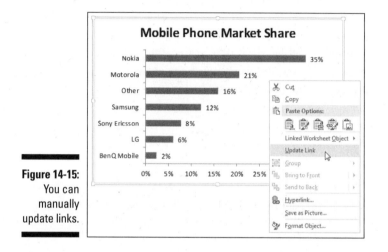

Figure 14-15:
You can
manually
update links.

3. **Save and close both your Excel file and your PowerPoint presentation and then open only your newly created PowerPoint presentation.**

   Now you see the message shown in Figure 14-16. Clicking the Update Links button updates all links in the PowerPoint presentation. Each time you open any PowerPoint presentation with links, it asks you whether you want to update the links.

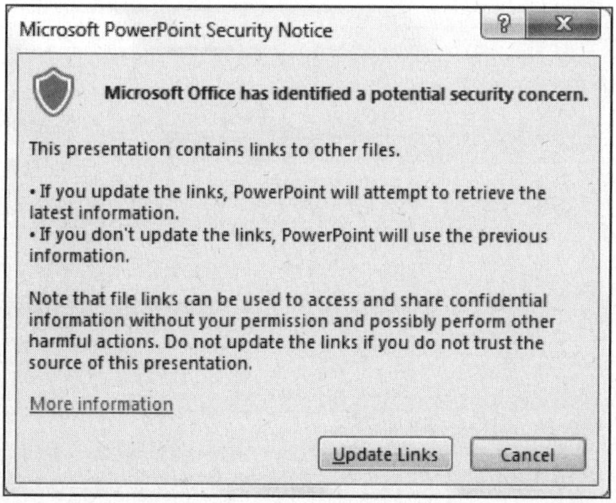

Figure 14-16:
PowerPoint,
by default,
asks if
you want to
update all
links in the
presentation.

Automatically updating links

Having PowerPoint ask you whether you want to update the links each and every time you open your presentation quickly gets annoying. You can avoid this message by telling PowerPoint to automatically update your dynamic links upon opening the presentation file. Here's how:

1. **In PowerPoint, click the File button to get to the Backstage View.**

2. **In the Info Pane, go to the lower-right corner of the screen and select Edit Links to Files, as shown in Figure 14-17.**

   The Links dialog box opens, as shown in Figure 14-18.

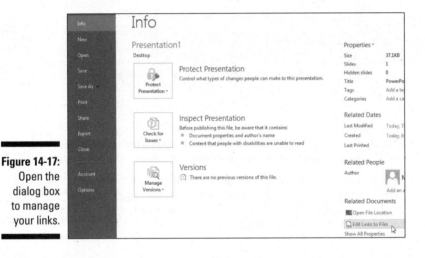

Figure 14-17:
Open the dialog box to manage your links.

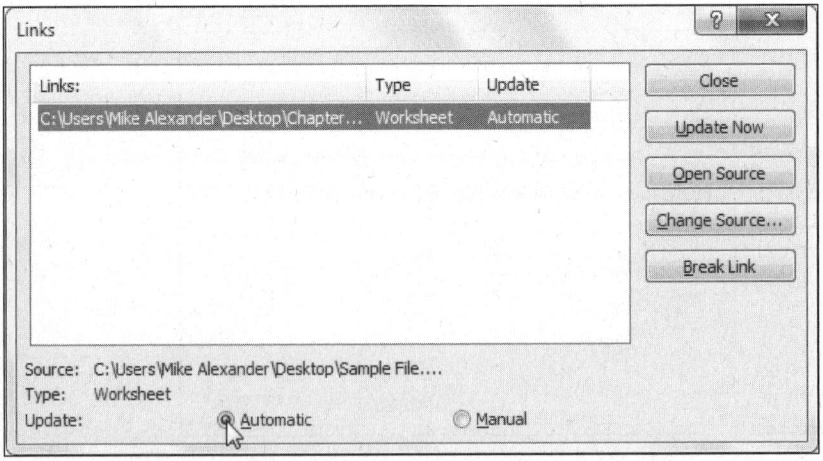

Figure 14-18:
Setting the selected links to update automatically.

3. Click each of your links and select the Automatic radio button.

When your links are set to update automatically, PowerPoint automatically synchronizes with your Excel worksheet file and ensures that all your updates are displayed.

To select multiple links in the Links dialog box, press the Ctrl key on your keyboard while you select your links.

Distributing Your Dashboards via a PDF

Starting with Excel 2010, Microsoft has made it possible to convert your Excel worksheets to a PDF (portable document format). A PDF is the standard document-sharing format developed by Adobe.

Although it may not seem intuitive to distribute your dashboards with PDF files, some distinct advantages make PDF an attractive distribution tool:

- ✔ Distributing your reports and dashboards as a PDF file allows you to share your final product without sharing all the formulas and back-end plumbing that comes with the workbook.

- ✔ Dashboards appear in PDF files with full fidelity, meaning they appear consistently on any computer and screen resolution.

- ✔ PDF files can be used to produce high-quality prints.

- ✔ Anyone using the free Adobe Reader can post comments and sticky notes on the distributed PDF files.

- ✔ Unlike Excel's security, the security in a PDF is generally better, allowing for multiple levels of security, including public-key encryption and certificates.

To convert your workbook to a PDF, follow these simple steps:

1. Click the File button and then choose the Export command.

2. In the Export pane, select Create PDF/XPS Document, and then click the Create PDF/XPS button see Figure 14-19.

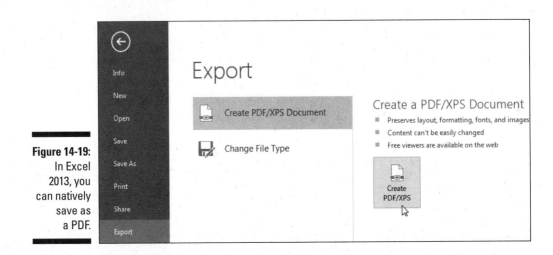

Figure 14-19:
In Excel
2013, you
can natively
save as
a PDF.

3. **The Publish as PDF or XPS dialog box opens. Click the Options button as demonstrated in Figure 14-20.**

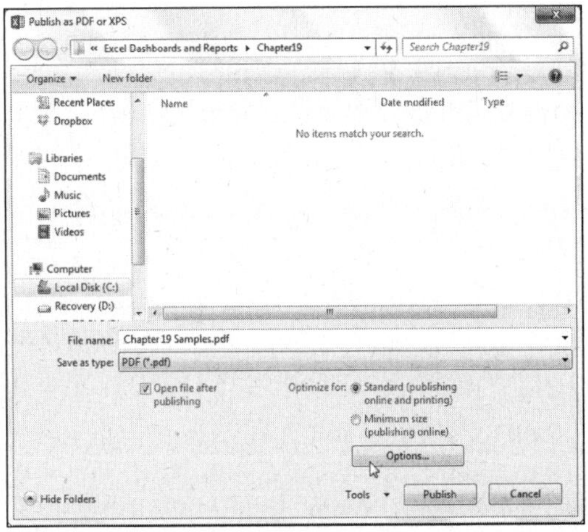

Figure 14-20:
Select a
location for
your PDF;
then click
the Options
button.

4. **In the Options dialog box illustrated in Figure 14-21, you can specify what you want to publish. You have the option of publishing the entire workbook, specific pages, or a range that you've selected.**

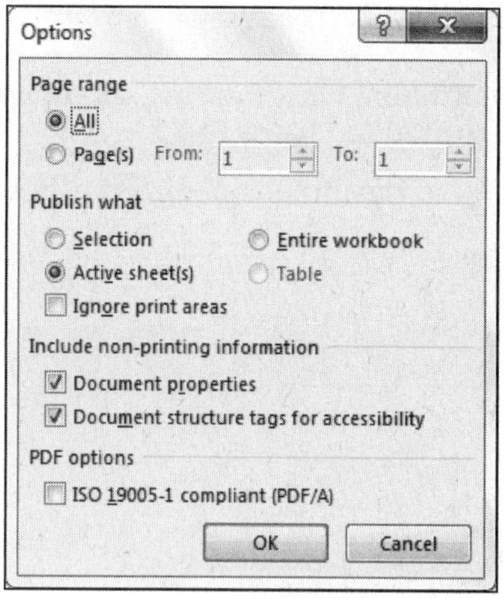

Figure 14-21:
Excel
allows you
to define
what gets
sent to PDF.

5. **Click OK to confirm your selections.**

6. **Click Publish.**

Distributing Your Dashboards to SkyDrive

SkyDrive is Microsoft's answer to Google Docs. You can think of it as a Microsoft Office platform in the cloud, allowing you to save, view, and edit your Office documents on the web.

When you publish your Excel dashboards or reports to SkyDrive, you can

✓ View and edit your workbooks from any browser, even if the computer you're using doesn't have Excel installed.

✓ Provide a platform where two or more people can collaborate on and edit the same Excel file at the same time.

✓ Share only specific sheets from your workbook by hiding sheets you don't want the public to see. When a sheet in a published workbook is hidden, the browser doesn't even recognize its existence, so there is no way for the sheet to be unhidden or hacked into.

✓ Offer up web-based interactive reports and dashboards that can be sorted and filtered.

To publish a workbook to SkyDrive, follow these steps:

1. **Click the File button on the Ribbon, click the Save As command, and choose SkyDrive as demonstrated in Figure 14-22.**

   The SkyDrive pane allows you to sign in to your SkyDrive account.

   If you don't have a SkyDrive account, you can sign up for one using the Sign Up link.

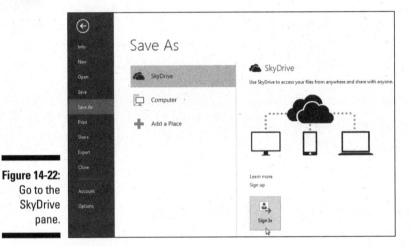

Figure 14-22: Go to the SkyDrive pane.

2. **Sign in to your SkyDrive account.**

   After signing in, the Save As dialog box in Figure 14-23 appears.

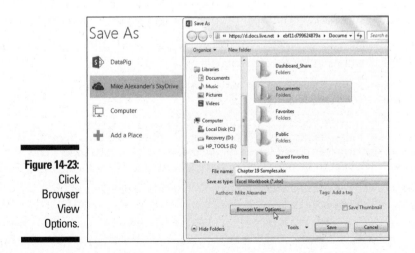

Figure 14-23: Click Browser View Options.

3. **Click Browser View Options to select which components of your workbook will be viewable to the public.**

   The Browser View Options dialog box allows you to control what the public is able to see and manipulate in your workbook.

4. **Click the Show tab illustrated in Figure 14-24.**

   Here, you can select and deselect sheets and other Excel objects. Removing the check next to any sheet or object prevents it from being viewable through the browser. Again, this is a fantastic way to share your dashboard interfaces without exposing the back-end calculations and data models.

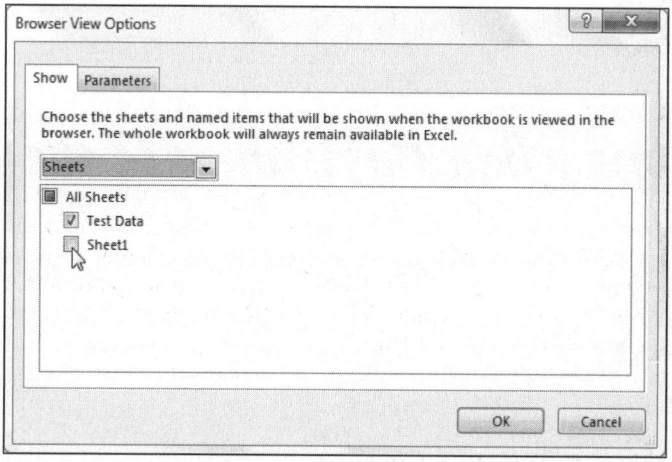

Figure 14-24: You have full control over which sheets and objects are available to the public when publishing to the web.

5. **After you confirm your browser view options, save the file into your Documents folder.**

   At this point, you can sign in to Live.com and navigate to your SkyDrive documents to see your newly published file.

There are several ways to share your newly published workbook:

- ✔ Copy the web link from the browser address bar and e-mail that to your cohorts.

- ✔ Click the File button in the web version of your file, choose Share, as shown in Figure 14-25, and then click the Share with People command to send an e-mail to anyone you specify.

- ✔ Use the Embed command on the same Share pane to generate HTML code to embed your workbook into a web page or blog.

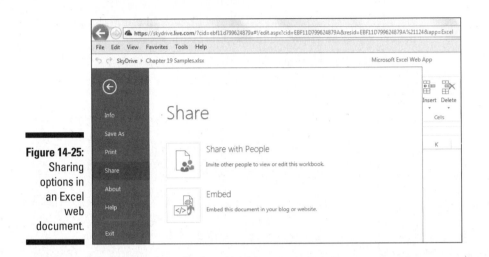

Figure 14-25:
Sharing
options in
an Excel
web
document.

Limitations when Publishing to the Web

It's important to understand that workbooks that run on the web are running in an Excel Web App that is quite different from the Excel client application you have on your PC. The Excel Web App has limitations on the features it can render in the web browser. Some limitations exist because of security issues, whereas others exist simply because Microsoft hasn't had time to evolve the Excel Web App to include the broad set of features that come with standard Excel.

In any case, the Excel Web App has some limitations:

- ✔ **Data Validation doesn't work on the web.** This feature is simply ignored when you publish your workbook to the web.

- ✔ **No form of VBA, including macros, will run in the Excel Web App.** Your VBA procedures simply will not transfer with the workbook.

- ✔ **Worksheet protection will not work on the web.** Instead, you need to plan for and use the browser view options demonstrated earlier in Figure 14-23 and 14-24.

- ✔ **Links to external workbooks will no longer work after publishing to the web.**

- ✔ **You can use any pivot tables with full fidelity on the web, but you cannot create any new pivot tables while your workbook is on the web.** You need to create pivot tables in the Excel client on your PC before publishing to the web.

Part VI
The Part of Tens

Get some advice on how to choose the most appropriate chart type for your data in the article found at www.dummies.com/extras/exceldashboardsandreports.

In this part . . .

✔ Take a look at a few chart-building best practices that help you design more effective charts.

✔ Discover how to avoid common charting mistakes.

✔ See what questions you should ask yourself before sharing your Excel dashboards and reports.

✔ Gain insight to the actions you can take to ensure the success of your dashboards and reports.

Chapter 15

Ten Chart Design Principles

· ·

I'm the first to admit, I've created my share of poorly designed charts — bar charts with every color known to man, line charts with ten or more lines slapped on top of each other, and pie charts with slices so thin they melded into a blob of black ink. When I look at these early disasters, I feel the shame of a baby boomer looking at pictures of himself in white bell-bottom jeans.

Excel makes charting so simple that it's often tempting to accept the charts it creates no matter how bad the default colors or settings are. But I'm here to implore you to turn away from the glitzy lure of the default settings. You can easily avoid charting fiascos by following a few basic design principles.

In this chapter, I share a few of these principles and help you avoid some of the mistakes I've made in the past. (No thanks needed.)

Avoid Fancy Formatting

Excel makes it easy to apply effects that make everything look shiny, glittery, and oh-so-pretty. Now don't get me wrong, these new graphics are more than okay for charts created for sales and marketing presentations. However, when it comes to dashboards, you definitely want to stay away from them.

Remember that a *dashboard* is a platform to present your case with data. Why dress up your data with superfluous formatting when the data itself is the thing you want to get across? It's like making a speech in a Roman general's uniform. How well will you get your point across when your audience is thinking, "What's the deal with Tiberius?"

Take Figure 15-1, for instance. I created this chart (formatting and all) with just a few clicks. Excel makes it super easy to achieve these types of effects with its Layout and Style features. The problem is that these effects subdue the very data you're trying to present. Furthermore, if you include this chart on a page with five to ten other charts with the same formatting, you get a blinding mess that's difficult to look at, much less read.

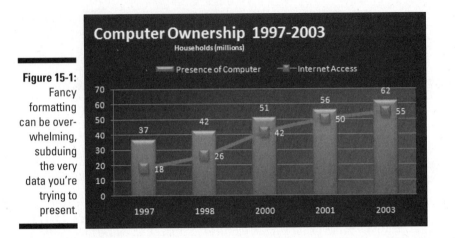

Figure 15-1:
Fancy
formatting
can be over-
whelming,
subduing
the very
data you're
trying to
present.

The key to communicating effectively with your charts is to present your data as simply as possible. I promise you, your data is interesting on its own. There's no need to wrap it in eye candy to make it more interesting.

Figure 15-2 shows the same data without the fancy formatting. I think you'll find that the chart is not only easier to read, but you can also process the data more effectively.

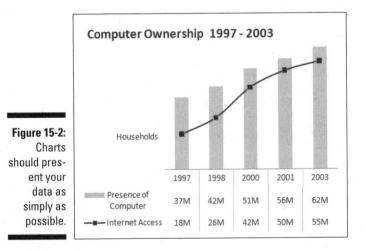

Figure 15-2:
Charts
should pres-
ent your
data as
simply as
possible.

Here are some simple tips to keep from overdoing the fancy factor:

✔ **Don't apply background colors to the Chart or Plot area.** Colors in general should be reserved for key data points in your chart.

✔ **Don't use 3D charts or 3D effects.** No one's going to give you an Oscar for special effects. Anything 3D doesn't belong on a dashboard.

✔ **Avoid applying fancy effects such as gradients, pattern fills, shadows, glow, soft edges, and other formatting.** Again, the word of the day is *focus,* as in "focus on the data and not the shiny happy graphics."

✔ **Don't try to enhance your charts with clip art or pictures.** They do nothing to further data presentation and they often just look tacky.

Skip the Unnecessary Chart Junk

Data visualization pioneer Edward Tufte introduced the notion of *data to ink ratio.* Tufte's basic idea is that a large percentage of the ink on your chart or dashboard should be dedicated to data. Very little ink should be used to present what he calls *chart junk:* borders, gridlines, trend lines, labels, backgrounds, and so on.

Figure 15-3 illustrates the impact chart junk can have on your ability to communicate your data. At first glance, the top chart in Figure 15-3 may look exaggerated in its ambition to show many chart elements at one time, but believe me, there are charts out there that look like this. Notice how convoluted and cramped the data looks.

Figure 15-3: Charts with too many chart elements can become convoluted and hard to read. Removing the unnecessary elements clarifies the message.

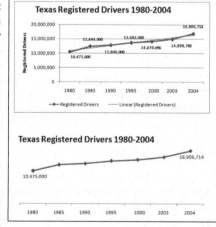

The bottom chart presents the same information as the top chart. However, the bottom chart more effectively presents the core message that driver registrations in Texas rose from more than 10 million to almost 17 million (a message that was diluted in the top chart). You can see from this simple example how a chart can be dramatically improved by simply removing the elements that don't directly contribute to the core message of the chart.

Here are a few ways to avoid chart junk and ensure your charts clearly present your data:

- ✔ **Remove gridlines:** Gridlines (both vertical and horizontal) are almost always unnecessary. The implied reason for gridlines is that they help to visually gauge the value represented by each data point. The truth is, however, you typically gauge the value of a data point by comparing its position to the other data points in the chart. So gridlines become secondary reference points that simply take up ink.

- ✔ **Remove borders:** You'll find that eliminating borders and frames gives your charts a cleaner look and helps avoid the dizzying lines you get when placing many charts with borders on a single dashboard. Instead of borders, use the white space between the charts as implied borders.

- ✔ **Skip the trend lines:** Seldom does a trend line provide insight that can't be gained with the already plotted data or a simple label. In fact, trend lines often state the obvious and sometimes confuse readers into thinking they're another data series. Why place a trend line on a line chart when the line chart is itself a trend line of sorts? Why place a trend line on a bar chart when it's just as easy to look at the top of the bars? In lieu of trend lines, add a simple label that states what you're trying to say about the overall trend of the data.

- ✔ **Avoid data label overload:** Nothing says you need to show the data label for every value on your chart. It's okay to plot a data point and not display its value. You'll find that your charts have more impact when you show only numbers relevant to your message. For example, Figure 15-3 shows a trend that includes seven years of data. Although all the years are plotted to show the trend, only values of the first and last plotted years are shown. The first and last plotted years' data is enough to fulfill the purpose of this chart, which is to show the trend and ultimate growth of driver registrations.

- ✔ **Don't show a legend if you don't have to:** When you're plotting one data series, there's no need to display a space-taking chart legend. If you allow your chart title to identify the one data series in your chart, you can simply delete the legend.

- ✔ **Remove any axis that doesn't provide value:** The purpose of the x- and y-axes are to help a user visually gauge and position the values represented by each data point. However, if the nature and utility of the chart doesn't require a particular axis, you should remove it. In Figure 15-3, there's no real need for the y-axis because the two data points I'm trying to draw attention to are labeled already. Again, the goal here isn't to hack away at your chart. The goal is to include only those chart elements that directly contribute to the core message of your chart.

Format Large Numbers Where Possible

It's never fun to count the zeros in a large number, especially when you're staring at 8-point font. When plotting very large numbers on a chart, consider formatting the values so that they're truncated for easy reading.

For instance, in Figure 15-4, I've formatted the values to appear as 10M and 17M instead of the hard-to-read 10,475,000 and 16,906,714.

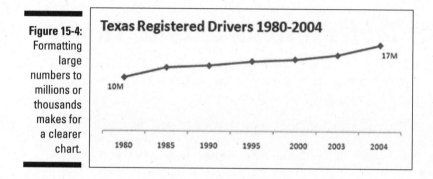

Figure 15-4:
Formatting
large
numbers to
millions or
thousands
makes for
a clearer
chart.

You can easily format large numbers in Excel by using the Format Cells dialog box. Here you can specify a custom number format by selecting Custom in the Category list and entering the desired number format code in the Type input box. In Figure 15-5, the code 0,, "M" ensures the numbers are formatted to millions with an M appendage.

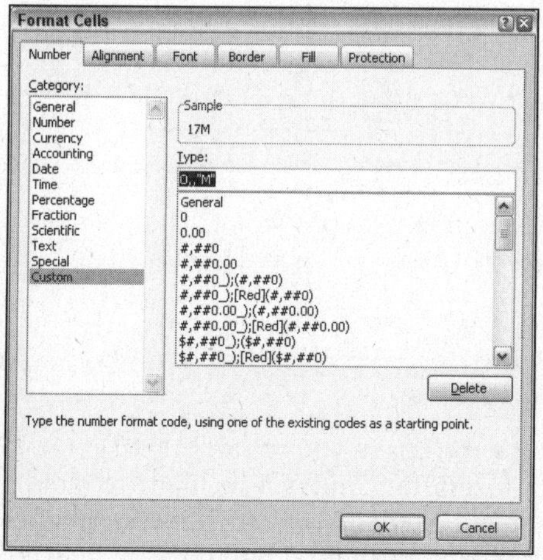

Figure 15-5:
Select
Custom
in the
Category list
and enter
a number
format code
in the Type
input box.

To get to the Format Cells dialog box, highlight the numbers you're formatting, right-click, and then choose Format Cells.

It's generally good practice to format the source data that feeds your chart as opposed to the data labels on your chart. This way, your formatting persists even as you add and remove data labels.

In Chapter 3, you find a table that lists some common format codes and how they can affect your numbers.

Use Data Tables instead of Data Labels

There may be situations in which it's valuable to show all the data values along with the plotted data points. However, you've already seen how data labels can inundate your users with chart junk.

Instead of using data labels, you can attach a data table to your Excel chart. A *data table* allows you to see the data values for each plotted data point, beneath the chart. Figure 15-6 illustrates a data table, showing the data values for two series. As you can see, a lot of information is shown here without overcrowding the chart itself.

Figure 15-6:
Data tables enable you to show data values without overloading your chart with data labels.

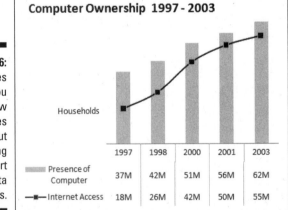

Although data tables increase the space your charts take up on your dashboard, they respond well to formatting and can be made to meld nicely into your charts. Data tables come in particularly handy if your clients are constantly asking to see the detailed information behind your charts.

Here are the steps you take to add a data table to your chart:

1. **Click your chart and select the Layout tab.**

2. **Click the Data Table icon and select Show Data Table with Legend Keys, as demonstrated in Figure 15-7.**

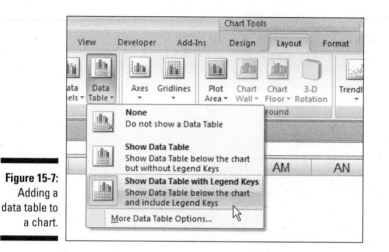

Figure 15-7:
Adding a data table to a chart.

3. **Right-click your newly added data table and choose Format Data Table.**

   The Format Data Table dialog box appears, as shown in Figure 15-8.

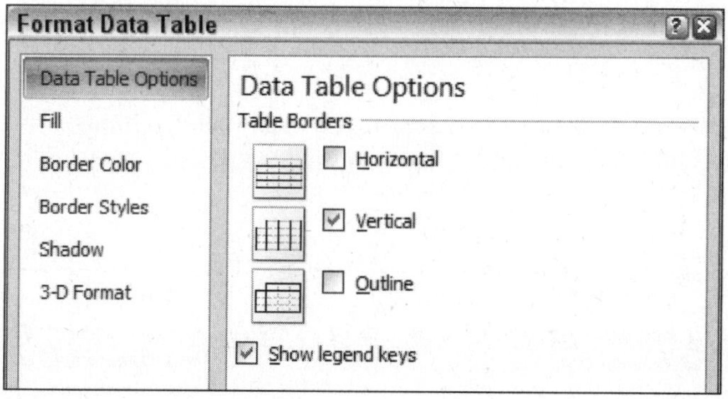

Figure 15-8:
The Format Data Table dialog box.

4. **Apply any additional formatting to your data table.**

Make Effective Use of Chart Titles

Chart titles don't have to be limited to simple labeling and naming duties. You can use chart titles to add an extra layer of information, presenting analysis derived from the data presented in the chart. Figure 15-9 demonstrates this.

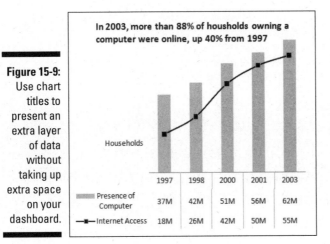

Figure 15-9: Use chart titles to present an extra layer of data without taking up extra space on your dashboard.

Sort Your Data before Charting

Unless there's an obvious natural order, such as age or time, it's generally good practice to sort your data when charting. By *sorting,* I mean sort the source data that feeds your chart in ascending or descending order by data value.

As you can see in Figure 15-10, building a chart using a dataset sorted by values enhances its readability and somehow gives the chart a professional look and feel.

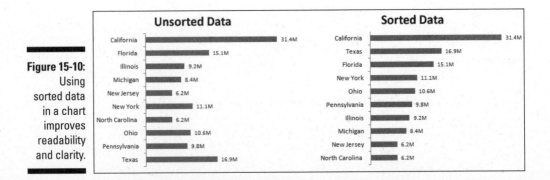

Figure 15-10: Using sorted data in a chart improves readability and clarity.

Limit the Use of Pie Charts

Although pie charts have long been considered a viable charting option for business reporting, they often aren't well suited for dashboard reporting. There are several reasons for this.

First, they typically take up more space than their cousins, the line and bar charts. Sure, you can make them small, but pixel for pixel, you get a lot less bang for your data-visualization buck with a pie chart.

Second, pie charts can't clearly represent more than two or three data categories. Figure 15-11 demonstrates this fact.

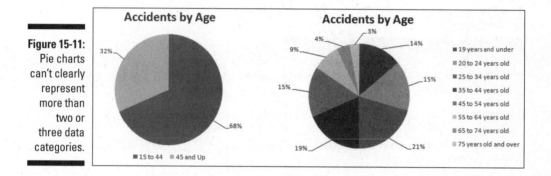

Figure 15-11: Pie charts can't clearly represent more than two or three data categories.

The pie chart on the left does a good job visually representing two data categories. You can easily distinguish the two categories and clearly get a sense of distribution for each category. The pie chart on the right is a different story. As you can see, when you go past two or three categories, a pie chart isn't as effective in relaying the proper sense of percent distribution. The slices are too similar in size and shape to visually compare the categories. Plus, the legend and data categories are disconnected, causing your eyes to jump back and forth from pie to legend (even in color the legend doesn't help). Sure, you could add category labels, but that would cause the chart to take up more real estate without adding much value.

So what's the alternative? Instead of a pie chart, consider using a bar chart. With a bar chart, you can clearly represent the distribution percentages for many categories without taking up extra real estate. In Figure 15-12, you can see the dramatic improvement in clarity you can achieve by using bar charts.

Figure 15-12:
Bar charts
are an
alternative
to pie charts
when you
have more
than two or
three data
categories.

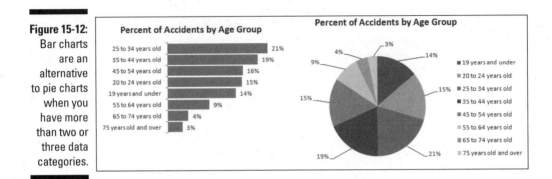

Figure 15-12:
Bar charts
are an
alternative
to pie charts
when you
have more
than two or
three data
categories.

Don't Be Afraid to Parse Data into Separate Charts

Be aware that a single chart can lose its effectiveness if you try to plot too much data into it. Take Figure 15-13, for example.

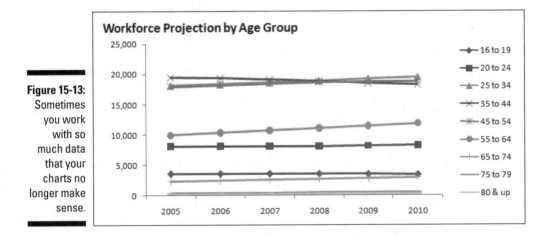

Figure 15-13:
Sometimes
you work
with so
much data
that your
charts no
longer make
sense.

This chart has a couple of problems. First, the data is split into nine age groups, which forces you to use nine lines. When you start plotting more than three lines on a line chart, your chart begins to look jumbled. Second, the age groups have a wide range of data values. This causes the chart's y-axis scale to be so spread out that each line essentially looks like a straight line.

In situations like this, step back and try to boil down what exactly the chart needs to do. What is the ultimate purpose of the chart? In this case, the ultimate purpose of this chart is to show the growth or decline of the workforce numbers for each age group. Now, you obviously can't show every data point on the same chart, so you have to show each age group in its own chart. So you want to make sure that you can see each age group alongside the other for comparison purposes.

Figure 15-14 shows just one of many solutions for this particular example.

Figure 15-14:
Creating
separate,
individual
charts is
often better
than one
convoluted
chart.

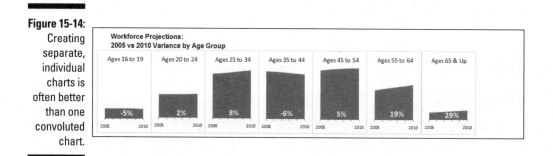

Here, I've created a separate area chart for each age group and then lined them up side by side. Each chart individually shows a general trend from 2005 to 2010. Because they're placed together, you can get an idea of the magnitude of each age group. Also, notice that I merged the last three age groups into one category called 65 & Up. This groups the three smallest categories into one that's worthy of plotting. Finally, I used data labels to quickly show the growth or decline percentage from 2005 to 2010 for each group.

Again, this isn't the only solution to this problem, but it does do the job of displaying the analysis I chose to present.

It's not always easy to know exactly how to display your data in a chart — especially when the data is multilayered and complex. Instead of jamming the world into one chart, step back and think about how to show the data separately, but together.

Maintain Appropriate Aspect Ratios

In terms of charts, *aspect ratio* refers to the ratio of height to width. That is to say, charts should maintain an appropriate height-to-width ratio in order for the integrity of the chart to remain intact. Take a look at Figure 15-15 to see what I mean.

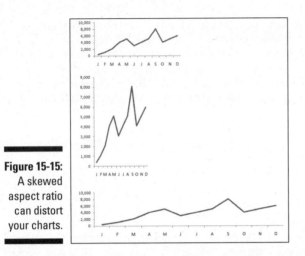

The chart at the top of Figure 15-15 is at an appropriate aspect ratio that correctly renders the chart. The bottom two charts display the same data, but the aspect ratios of these charts are skewed. The middle chart is too tall and the bottom chart is too wide. This essentially distorts the visual representation, exaggerating the trend in the chart that's too tall, and flattening the trend in the chart that's too wide.

I've seen lots of people contort their charts just to fit them into the empty space on their dashboards. If you want to avoid distorting your charts, you must keep them at an appropriate aspect ratio. What is that ratio?

Generally, the most appropriate aspect ratio for a chart is one in which the width of the chart is about twice as long as the height. For example, 1" tall by 2" wide is an appropriate ratio. 1.5" tall by 3" wide is also appropriate. The actual height and width isn't important. You can make your charts as small or as big as they need to be. What is important is the ratio of height to width.

Don't Be Afraid to Use Something Other Than a Chart

Ask yourself if a simple table will present the data just fine. If the data you're reporting can be more effectively shared in a table, then that's how it should be presented. Remember, the goal of a dashboard is not to present everything in a chart. The goal of a dashboard is to present key data in the most effective way possible.

Chapter 16

Ten Questions to Ask Before Distributing Your Dashboard

• •

You started this book with two chapters that discuss the design and data modeling principles that make up what could be considered dashboarding's best practices. Before you send out your finished product, it's valuable to check your reporting mechanism against some of these principles. Use the ten questions in this chapter as a checklist to ensure your dashboard follows the best practices covered in this book.

Does My Dashboard Present the Right Information?

Look at the information you're presenting and determine if it meets the purpose of the dashboard you identified during the requirements-gathering stage. Don't be timid about clarifying the purpose of the dashboard with the core users. Avoid building the dashboard in a vacuum. Allow a few test users to see iterations as you develop. This way, communication stays open, and you won't go too far in the wrong direction.

Does Everything on My Dashboard Have a Purpose?

Take an honest look at how much of the information on your dashboard doesn't support its main purpose. Keep your dashboard as valuable as possible; you don't want to dilute it with nice-to-know data that's interesting, but not actionable. Remember, if the data doesn't support the core purpose of the dashboard, leave it out. Nothing says you have to fill every bit of white space on the page.

Does My Dashboard Prominently Display the Key Message?

Every dashboard has one or more key messages. You want to ensure that these messages are prominently displayed. To test if the key messages in a dashboard are prominent, stand back and squint your eyes while you look at the dashboard. Look away and then look back at the dashboard several times. What jumps out at you first? If it's not the key components you want displayed, you have to change something. Here are a few actions you can take to ensure your key components have prominence:

- ✔ **Place the key components of your dashboard in the upper-left or middle-left portion of the page.** Studies have shown that these areas attract the most attention for longer periods of time.

- ✔ **De-emphasize borders, backgrounds, and other elements that define dashboard areas.** Try to use the natural white space between your components to partition your dashboard. If borders are necessary, format them to a hue lighter than the one you've used for your data.

- ✔ **Format labels and other text to hues lighter than the ones you've used for your data.** Lightly colored labels give your users the information they need without distracting them from the information displayed.

Can I Maintain This Dashboard?

There's a big difference between refreshing a dashboard and rebuilding a dashboard. Before you excitedly send out the sweet-looking dashboard you just built, take a moment to think about the maintenance of such a dashboard. You want to think about the frequency of updates, how often data needs to be refreshed, and what processes you need to go through each time you refresh the data. If it's a one-time reporting event, set that expectation with your users. If you know it'll become a recurring report, you want to really negotiate development time, refresh intervals, and phasing before agreeing to any time table.

Does My Dashboard Clearly Display Its Scope and Shelf Life?

A dashboard should clearly specify its scope and shelf life. That is to say, anyone should be able to look at your dashboard and know the relevant time period and the scope of the information on the dashboard. This comes down to a few simple things you can do to effectively label your dashboards and reports:

- ✔ **Always include a timestamp on your reporting mechanisms.** This minimizes confusion when distributing the same dashboard or report at regular intervals.

- ✔ **Always include some text indicating when the data for the measures was retrieved.** In many cases, timing of data is a critical piece of information when analyzing a measure.

- ✔ **Use descriptive titles for each component on your dashboard.** Be sure to avoid cryptic titles with lots of acronyms and symbols.

Is My Dashboard Well Documented?

It's important to document your dashboard and the data model behind it. Anyone who has ever inherited an Excel spreadsheet knows how difficult it can be to translate the various analytical gyrations that go into a report. If you're lucky, the data model will be small enough to piece together in a week or so. If you're not so lucky, you'll have to ditch the entire model and start from scratch.

By the way, the Excel model doesn't even have to be someone else's to be difficult to read. I've actually gone back to a model that I built, and after six or so months, I'd forgotten what I had done. Without documentation, it took me a few days to remember and decipher my own work.

The documentation doesn't even have to be highfalutin' fancy stuff. A few simple things can help in documenting your dashboard:

- ✔ **Add a *model map tab* to your data model.** The model map tab is a separate sheet you can use to summarize the key ranges in the data model, and how each range interacts with the reporting components in the final presentation layer.

- ✔ **Use comments and labels liberally.** It's amazing how a few explanatory comments and labels can help clarify your model even after you've been away from your data model for a long time.

✔ **Consider using colors to identify the ranges in your data model.** Using colors in your data model enables you to quickly look at a range of cells and get a basic indication of what that range does. Each color can represent a range type. For example, yellow could represent staging tables, gray could represent formulas, and purple could represent reference tables.

Is My Dashboard Overwhelmed with Formatting and Graphics?

When it comes to formatting dashboards and reports, less is more. Eye candy doesn't make your data more interesting. If you're not convinced, try creating a version of your dashboard without the fancy formatting:

✔ **Remove distracting colors and background fills.** If you must have colors in charts, use colors commonly found in nature: soft grays, browns, blues, and greens.

✔ **De-emphasize borders by formatting them to hues lighter than the ones you've used for your data.** Light grays are typically ideal for borders. The idea is to indicate sections without distracting from the information displayed.

✔ **Remove all fancy graphical effects such as gradients, pattern fills, shadows, glows, soft edges, and other formatting.**

✔ **Remove the clip art and other pictures.**

I think that when you compare the two versions, you'll find that the toned-down version does a better job of highlighting the actual data.

Does My Dashboard Overuse Charts When Tables Will Do?

Just because you're building a dashboard doesn't mean everything on it has to be a chart. In some analyses, a simple table will present the data just fine. You typically use a chart when there's some benefit to visually seeing trends, relationships, or comparisons. Ask yourself if there's a benefit to seeing your data in chart form. If the data is relayed better in a table, that's how it should be presented.

Figure 16-1 illustrates a simple example. The chart on the left and the table on the right show the exact same data. The table does a fine job at presenting the key message of the analysis — revenue is at 95 percent of plan. Why use the chart that requires more real estate, not to mention more work and maintenance?

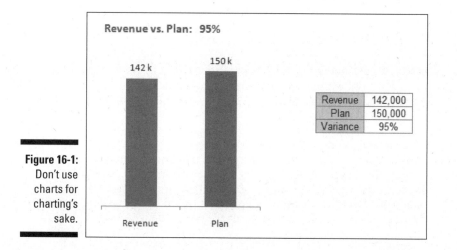

Figure 16-1:
Don't use charts for charting's sake.

Is My Dashboard User-Friendly?

Before you distribute your reporting mechanism, you want to ensure that it's user-friendly. It's not difficult to guess what user-friendly means. Usually a user-friendly mechanism has the following characteristics:

✔ **Intuitive:** Your reporting mechanism should be intuitive to someone who has never seen it before. Test your dashboard on someone and ask her if it makes sense. If you have to start explaining what the dashboard says, something is wrong. Does the dashboard need more labels, fewer complicated charts, a better layout, or more data? It's a good idea to get feedback from several users.

✔ **Easy to navigate:** If your dashboard is dynamic, allowing for interactivity with macros or pivot tables, you should make sure the navigation works well. Does the user have to click several places to get to her data? Is the number of drill-downs appropriate? Does it take too long to switch from one view to another? Again, you want to test your dashboard on several users. Be sure to test any interactive dashboard on several computers other than yours.

✔ **Prints properly:** Nothing is more annoying than printing a report only to find that the person who created the report didn't take the time to ensure it prints correctly. Be sure you set the print options on your Excel files so that your dashboards print properly.

Is My Dashboard Accurate?

Nothing kills a dashboard or report faster than the perception that its data is inaccurate. It's not within my abilities to tell you how to determine if your data is accurate. I can, however, highlight three factors that establish the perception of an accurate dashboard:

✔ **Consistency with authoritative sources:** It's obvious that if your data doesn't match other reporting sources, you have a data credibility issue, especially if those other sources are deemed to be the authoritative sources. Be sure you're aware of the data sources considered to be gospel in your organization. If your dashboard contains data associated with an authoritative source, compare your data with that source to ensure consistency.

✔ **Internal consistency:** It's never fun to explain why one part of your dashboard doesn't jive with other parts of the same dashboard. You should ensure some level of internal consistency within your dashboard. Be sure comparable components in different areas of your dashboard are consistent with each other. If there's a reason for inconsistency, be sure to clearly notate those reasons. It's amazing how well a simple notation can clear up questions about the data.

✔ **Personal experience:** Have you ever seen someone look at a report and say, "That doesn't look right?" She's using what some people call "gut feel" to evaluate the soundness of the data. None of us looks at numbers in a vacuum. When you look at any analysis, you bring with you years of personal knowledge, interaction, and experience. You subconsciously use these experiences in your evaluation of information. When determining the accuracy of your dashboard, take into consideration organizational *anecdotal knowledge.* If possible, show your dashboard to a few subject-matter experts in your company.

Index

About the Author

Michael Alexander is a Microsoft Certified Application Developer (MCAD) with over 15 years' experience consulting and developing office solutions. He is the author of over a dozen books on business analysis using Microsoft Excel and Access. He has been named Microsoft Excel MVP for his contributions to the Excel community. Visit Michael at DataPigTechnologies.com where he offers free Excel and Access training.

Dedication

To my twelve fans at DataPigTechnologies.com.

Author's Acknowledgments

My deepest thanks to everyone who helped bring this book to fruition. And a special thank you to Mary, who will open this book just long enough to read the dedication and acknowledgments.

Publisher's Acknowledgments

Acquisitions Editor: Katie Mohr

Sr. Project Editor: Christopher Morris

Copy Editor: Amanda Graham

Technical Editors: Mike Talley

Editorial Assistant: Annie Sullivan

Sr. Editorial Assistant: Cherie Case

Project Coordinator: Erin Zeltner

Project Manager: Laura Moss-Hollister

Cover Image: ©iStockphoto.com/Warchi